CATHOLICS IN CONVERSATION

CATHOLICS

IN

CONVERSATION

Seventeen Interviews
with Leading American Catholics

BY

DONALD McDONALD

J. B. LIPPINCOTT COMPANY

PHILADELPHIA AND NEW YORK

CONTENTS

Introduction   7

I. Perspective
    BISHOP JOHN J. WRIGHT   13
    REV. JOSEPH FICHTER, S.J.   32

II. Encounter
    REV. GUSTAVE WEIGEL, S.J.   53
    JOHN COGLEY   71

III. Forum
    SENATOR EUGENE J. MC CARTHY   87
    DOROTHY DAY   100
    MONSIGNOR GEORGE G. HIGGINS   121

IV. Worship
    REV. GODFREY DIEKMANN, O.S.B.   137
    REV. ALFRED LONGLEY   154

V. Writing

WALTER KERR   173

J. F. POWERS   187

PHYLLIS MC GINLEY   202

J. L. O'SULLIVAN   216

JAMES O'GARA   228

VI. Learning

MONSIGNOR JOHN TRACY ELLIS   247

REV. ROBERT J. HENLE, S.J.   257

SISTER MARY EMIL, I.H.M.   274

INTRODUCTION

In 1958 and 1959, when I was editing *The Catholic Messenger*, the Davenport, Iowa, diocesan weekly newspaper, we published the texts of two tape-recorded conversations I had had with Bishop John J. Wright of Pittsburgh and Senator Eugene J. McCarthy of Minnesota.

Publication of these conversations in dialogue form was an experiment. It seemed to me that, for one thing, readers would find conversation itself, rather than a report of a conversation, much more interesting to read. I knew from my own experience that I had enjoyed reading several dialogues—conversations with Casals, with Stravinsky; the *Paris Review* interviews.

Secondly, it seemed to me that frequently the way in which a person speaks, the way in which he responds to questions and presents his point of view, reveal almost as much as what is actually said. The hesitations, the repetitions, the parallelisms, the turns of mind and phrase, the selection of illustrations —all these, it seemed to me, play an important part in conversational communication. They also, of course, reveal something of the personality of the speaker.

Finally, the dialogue, it seemed to me, would reduce to an absolute minimum the chance for error. Letting a person speak for himself would eliminate even the minor and unintentional errors that tend to creep into related reports of what a person

7

has said. Although I have for years used shorthand in my reporting of events and interviews, I would not maintain that such reports, even with that advantage, were absolutely accurate.

Well, the response of the readers to our two published dialogues with Bishop Wright and Senator McCarthy was gratifying. They had found the conversations immensely interesting to read. And they had absorbed, apparently, a great amount of the substance of what both the Bishop and the Senator had said in their conversations. Our letters-to-the-editor column and word-of-mouth discussion reflected wide interest. Indeed, I am still hearing some of the views of these two men, as reported in *The Catholic Messenger*, discussed and debated in occasional conversations wherever I go today.

Why not, then, a volume of such tape-recorded interviews with fifteen or twenty American Catholics, each a leader and an expert in his or her field of work? The question was put to my publishers, J. B. Lippincott Company. They thought it was a capital idea, or at least that it was an idea with capital possibilities. I went to work.

The result is now at hand—*Catholics in Conversation*, seventeen interviews with as many American Catholics on a number of subjects: poetry, theater criticism, Catholic-Protestant-Jewish relations, sociology, social action, the Catholic Worker movement, parish life, the liturgy, Catholic higher education, the formation of Sisters, journalism, politics, the short story and Catholicity in general.

Let me say, at the start, that the people whom I interviewed for this book were not picked at random. Singly and together they represent what I am convinced is the authentic tradition of the Catholic Church—a tradition of progressiveness, openness, apostolic zeal and professional competence, intolerance of the mediocre and the narrow, enthusiasm for excellence no matter where and in whom it is to be found: in the spiritual and secular order, among non-Catholics and Catholics alike.

As I gathered these interviews, it became apparent that virtually all of the people wished to speak not only about their own specialized fields of interest but also about the general condition of Catholicity in the United States. They spoke candidly and freely and the results amount, I think, to a valuable con-sensus—valuable because of the obvious maturity, experience and insight of each man and woman interviewed in this book.

Inevitably there is a certain amount of repetition, since those interviewed did not, of course, know the remarks that had been made or would be made by the others. But the repetition is not one of expression. It is rather a repetition of what are considered to be the major problems confronting the Catholic Church in the United States today. And in significant instances (education, for example), there is some fundamental agreement concerning basic approaches to the solutions of those problems.

I must emphasize, however, that this book has not intended, and does not pretend, to solve any problems. It is intended to reveal the thoughts and the views of a group of truly brilliant American Catholics.

Some readers, I know, will think of questions I should have asked this or that person in the book. I myself have thought of many questions I would have liked, upon later reflection, to have asked a number of the persons interviewed. It seems to me, however, that post-conversational questions and answers, obtained by correspondence, would violate the dialogue nature of this work. I am not a primitivist, but I do think that conversations are in fact often full of gaps and that, to some extent, they should be left that way even when they are presented in printed form. One comes away from a conversation, even a most stimulating and interesting conversation, with the feeling that there were a number of loose ends, incompletely developed points, unasked questions. It is natural that some of that feeling should exist here. However, these conversations are edited conversations. An attempt has been made to reduce the loose-end material to a minimum, without losing the conversational tone and flavor of the interviews.

The Bishop Wright and Senator McCarthy conversations are reprinted, in part, from *The Catholic Messenger*. Permission was also granted to other Catholic magazines to publish brief extracts from a few of the interviews before the appearance of the book.

I wish to express here my gratitude to Marquette University

for permitting me to complete the book; to the people who appear in it for the generosity with which they gave of their time and thoughts; to Bea Hector for much of the typing of the manuscript; to George Stevens of Lippincott for his wisdom and patience; and to my wife, Virginia, and children for accommodating themselves to the domestic dislocation which invariably attends the making of a book by an author who is also a husband and a father.

DONALD MCDONALD

Milwaukee, Wisconsin
June, 1960

I

---◆---

Perspective

BISHOP JOHN J. WRIGHT

BISHOP JOHN J. WRIGHT was born in Boston on July 18, 1909. He attended Boston Latin School, Boston College and St. John's Seminary. After one year at St. John's, he entered the North American College, Rome, and was ordained there in 1935.

He completed his graduate work in Rome in 1939 and was asked by the new Pope Piux XII to defend his thesis before the usual jury of theologians, augmented on this occasion by a battery of motion-picture cameramen. The thesis was particularly significant in the light of national and international developments that were to issue in general war two months later. Against a background of Nazism, Fascism and Communism, each claiming total allegiance from the people, Father Wright delivered and defended this thesis which was later published under the title: *National Patriotism in Papal Teaching.*

Bishop Wright, after serving successively as a professor at St. John's Seminary and secretary to Cardinals O'Connell and Cushing of Boston, was made bishop of the new See of Worcester, Massachusetts, in 1947. In 1959 he was made bishop of the Pittsburgh diocese.

Witty, profound, scholarly, Bishop Wright is acknowledged as one of the most brilliant members of the Church's hierarchy in this or any other country. Though his interests range widely, he has spoken out and written most frequently on two subjects: the condition of intellectual life among Catholics and the problem of international peace and world order.

The interview with Bishop Wright took place in the library of *The Catholic Messenger*, diocesan newspaper in Davenport, Iowa.

McDONALD: Bishop Wright, a couple of years ago, at the St. Louis University Founders Day celebration, you said that the term "intellectual" seems to have become a term of reproach and that this need not be and should not be, especially in Catholic circles. Would you say that that anti-intellectualism, which seemed to be so much in the air then, is now abating?

WRIGHT: I think the air has cleared around that argument, rather more rapidly than many people thought it would. I'd like to insist, by the way, that I never shared the contention that our Catholic colleges and universities, or our schools on any level, had proved notably deficient in turning out people appreciative of the intellectual life. I never went along with the thesis of some who seemed to feel that our schools had "let us down" by a failure to produce competent intellectuals. Nonetheless, I thought that whole argument very important because it speeded the end of an anti-intellectualism that was indubitably abroad in the land; it still is, but it has already gone underground precisely because of the attention focused on it by the debate stirred up two and three years ago by Monsignor [John Tracy] Ellis and others.

I think there was an unfortunate equivocation in the discussion with respect to what, exactly, we mean by an "intellectual." Our schools and colleges and universities, by and large, probably do not turn out as many professional intellectuals as other institutions of a more specialized kind do. But I am not at all sure that this is lamentable. I believe that our colleges, and in perhaps proportionate degree our universities, are turning out people who, whatever their work may be, have authentic intellectual interests; they love music and like to read; they enjoy the conversations and ideas which I take to be the joy of the intellectual, as opposed to the formulae and skills which I suppose are the delight of the craftsman.

I derive satisfaction, not regret, from the thought that my own college back in Boston has turned out a large number of men who are quite content to work as insurance men, furniture sales-men or at other useful occupations to earn their living, but who never make the mistake of supposing that's why they came into the world. They go home at night to good books, good conversa-tion, good intellectual company, but they are not professional intellectuals, nor would they wish to be.

McDONALD: Your distinction, then, is between specialists and intellectuals in general?

WRIGHT: I am distinguishing between people who live by their intellectual pursuits and those who are nourished by them and live by something else. And I think our schools have turned out and do turn out a very notable number of the latter group, and that these are the best intellectual leaven of the good society.

McDONALD: Do you think we should be turning out more of the others, the professional intellectuals?

WRIGHT: I'm not at all certain, and one reason I'm not cer-tain is because I'm not sure but what society may have too many of the others, the mere professional intellectuals. I'm not sure but what they have given intellectuality a bad name. For ex-ample, when Frenchmen were talking about the "treason of the intellectuals," they were talking precisely about professional intel-lectuals who became divorced from the everyday business of having babies, buying homes, planning communities, living in parishes and meeting people . . .

McDONALD: Meeting their political responsibilities . . .

WRIGHT: . . . and taking part in the general life of the com-munity. The debate over the *"trahison des clercs"* in France was along that line exactly. Whereas, I think the Catholic com-munity is producing people who properly subordinate their intel-lectual life to their total personal life, as they subordinate their economic life, sometimes in a manner which seems heroic, to their total personal life, and as they subordinate, or try to, every-thing to the total business of personal perfection and of serving God in this world that they may be happy with Him in the next. In other words, I think the emphasis on the need for specialists who have the kudos attached to professional intellectualism may be a passing thing. When one meets some such specialists he hopes it is (a passing thing), because it is hard to imagine a good society made up of these Magi. I can't imagine its being humane, that's my point.

McDONALD: Bishop Wright, there is a good deal of discussion nowadays about the future shape of the parish. Now I realize there is a trend to "suburbia" and that there is, in fact, a good deal of vitality in the new suburban parishes, such as Father Longley's parish in Minneapolis and Monsignor Josiah Chatham's parish down in Jackson, Mississippi.

On the other hand, we have testimony from some of the religious sociologists who emphasize the new mobility of the people, the breakdown of former ethnological bonds that used to be a cohesive in so many of our parishes, and the question is raised: Is the present parish structure outmoded? Can the parish serve as more than just the place where people go to Mass and receive the Sacraments—the "service-station" idea? What can the parish do with people so spread out and so very mobile?

WRIGHT: I don't think it's possible yet to answer the question: What's becoming of the parish? The "revolution" in the concept of the parish has, in point of fact, hardly started among us. . . .

All this introduces immediately a problem, namely, whether the parish is something with which one is individually affiliated because of his individual interests, vocation, profession or perhaps social class, or whether the parish is a "family of families," whether it's a family thing. Along with the trend toward the former idea, the emphasis on family Communion and family activity seems to constitute a contrary trend. I know many small parishes where it is popular for whole families to go to Mass together all the time on the principle that the family that prays together should pray together, above all, in church where prayer is or should be at its best.

So I think that the "revolution" in parish structure has a long way to go before the general lines of it will be clear. I think, too, that it will be very different in different parts of our own country, as well as in different parts of the world. I would be extremely suspicious of any generalization about the breakdown of the parish and its reorganization, because even within a single diocese the patterns of parish life are so very, very different.

McDONALD: Is size a factor? I know some scholars say that the smaller the parish obviously the closer . . .

WRIGHT: More cohesive . . .

McDONALD: . . . yes, and the closer the priest to the people.

WRIGHT: Yes, we try to break down our parishes to achieve just that, our territorial parishes. But before it will be possible to generalize about any "revolution" in the concept of the parish, and before any sociological or other processes will act as catalytic agents in any transformation of the parish, we must face a further question: Are we going to think of the parish, as we have come traditionally to do, chiefly as an administrative unit or are we going to think of it as an educative unit?

Now, every parish is, of course, an administrative unit of the praying community and an educative unit of that same praying community. But whereas in the immigrant days of the Church in America, the parish perforce had to be primarily an administrative unit and to take its structure and emphasis from that fact, now the parish is more and more an educative unit. The administrative unit in most parts of the country is becoming more emphatically the diocese. People are much closer to the bishop than they used to be, sometimes as close as to the parish priest. Bishops now work directly all over the diocese and are available to people more than ever before. The telephone numbers of the bishop are listed now. They have office hours. They no longer receive in throne rooms; they see people across desks. The administrative aspect of the diocese is stronger. Diocesan programs of the NCWC, Diocesan Council of Catholic Men, Youth Council impinge their administrative apparatus on areas that used to be confined to the parish, the parish lyceum and the special administrative programs of the city or rural parish.

What, therefore, does the function of the parish tend to become? Perhaps the parish will be less and less the administrative unit and more and more the educative and, please God, above all, more and more the liturgical center of Catholic lives.

McDONALD: Do you think the Catholic laity in general then should draw their vitality and their educational material—some of it at any rate—from the parish and from under parish auspices?

WRIGHT: The parish altar remains the most effective center of worship, it seems to me. For the indefinite future the ideal pattern in worship will make the parish altar the center of our liturgical lives; the parish tabernacle, the parish baptismal font, the parish confessional the center of our Sacramental lives. I say this even though well aware of the tremendous part played in the spiritual lives of our people by the various non-parochial groups to which they belong, retreat leagues or specialized professional guilds. . . .

MCDONALD: To come back to size again for a moment. Some scholars note that sermons, for example, can't be over six or seven minutes long because you've got to "get the people out." And, since the sermon is frequently the only educative contact between priest and people, it should be of a reasonable length, allowing time for the priest to develop a point.

WRIGHT: I think certain requirements of our civilization are going to take care of that. If we're going to have a different economic, social and industrial set-up from what our forefathers had, we're going to have a different understanding of where instruction has to be done and of where it's best done. Back in the days when people worked six days a week and on the seventh day rested, on that day they heard an hour's sermon and heard it gladly.

They heard it gladly for a hundred reasons. First of all, it was almost the only instruction they ever had, in the absence of television, radio and widely diffused periodical and other literature. Secondly, it was so much better than the bang of the machine and the other things they heard all week that it was welcome. Third, they had no place else to go. Moreover, Sunday was the day they left aside for just that—the Mass, the sermon and Sunday school.

When I was a boy the afternoon Sunday school from two to three o'clock was jammed with hundreds of kids who came back in the afternoon after having been to Mass in the morning. You could never get attendance like that now for any purpose whatsoever, no matter what it might be, all the year round.

In other words, the whole civilization has changed and since this question of *when* you give instruction is a peripheral matter and the *instruction* is the substance of the thing, the influence of civilization need not be feared. I anticipate, then, that we may reach the blessed day where at Sunday Mass there'll be no sermon—perhaps a brief homily but, please God, no announcements. There'll be the reading of the Gospel and then a homily on that Gospel, not a developed instruction. It wasn't expected that the few minutes between the reading of the Gospel and the Creed would be the time when we would teach theology, inspire to the good life, reprove the sinner, encourage the saint and do all the things that have to be done by instruction.

I think the time will come when the Sunday Mass, in line with what we've been saying about the parish as the liturgical unit, will include a homily of a pastoral kind, and then, with the present forty-hour week, and now the four-day week under consideration in some circles, it may become possible to figure out a pattern whereby study clubs, parish instruction hours, schools of religion, something like the old lyceum program will come back into parish life. The Confraternity of Christian Doctrine could bring this to pass. I hope it does. People are going to get so sick of television and of all the present uses of leisure time that an alert clergy will have a golden opportunity to instruct them in CCD adult and specialized groups—if only we have the vision and vitality. . . .

McDONALD: You say homily is what the people want.

WRIGHT: Homily is the word. You see, the rebirth of the homily will bring with it a whetting of the appetite to study the Faith. We don't love things until we know them, but we're not likely to take the trouble to know them until we've fallen a bit in love with the beginnings of them. And it's the function of the homily to fire love of the Faith.

McDONALD: That brings up, it seems to me, the whole general problem of lay spirituality. Take a professional man, for example —a doctor, a professor, editor, lawyer—and if he is married, he has certain obligations—to his wife, to his children, to his work and, of course, to his own spiritual life. He has a problem, it seems to me, of keeping things in balance, and not just in balance, but so that these things nourish each other and so that his work is also spiritual and so that his family isn't slighted. And it comes down, sometimes, to something seemingly as simple as budgeting one's time, of which there never seems to be a sufficiency.

Now, is there any one pattern—whether it be Third Order,

secular institutes, specialized Catholic Action—which will help a layman who wants to ascend to God and also to meet all of his temporal obligations and do all the things he must do in the temporal order?

WRIGHT: Well, you've left out the thing that I would most wish to talk about. It's the lay retreat movement. I don't know anything more likely, properly utilized, to accomplish what I think you mean than is the lay retreat movement. Nor do I know, by the way, any more encouraging sign of the vitality and the spirituality of our laity than, again, the lay retreat movement. . . . But all have recognized the great necessity, precisely in order to meet one's essential obligations, of withdrawing periodically for that thinking in the heart without which the world grows desolate.

McDONALD: Well, that is once a year, or at most twice a year. Can the layman develop a pattern from that?

WRIGHT: Well, it's once a year like the income-tax return is once a year but it dominates one's budgeting for all the rest of the year.

McDONALD: Will that carry him through a year?

WRIGHT: I think it would if a man were able to pick the place and the company of his annual retreat. I think it would accomplish wonders for him in providing him a solid, three-day spiritual check-up on what he did during the year gone by and on what he intends to do during the coming year. It gives him an opportunity to meditate on the duties of one's state in life, which should be the first question we ask ourselves when we prepare for our weekly confession. If a retreat were properly made each year, it would gravitate around the man's vocation; it would highlight the duties of his state in life for the year to come. . . .

McDONALD: Not everyone can give a retreat; it takes experience.

WRIGHT: That's true, very true. A retreat, again, is not a series of lectures; it's not an instruction course. Nor should it be the same as a parish mission. It isn't to de-alcoholize drunks or to bring sinners to repentance. It is to take men who are leading completely normal, integrated Catholic lives and provide them with the annual opportunity to consider their greater perfection in their own state in life. That aspect of the retreat movement is growing and I mention it first as one of the signs of the vitality of modern lay spirituality. . . .

McDONALD: Certainly it's difficult to know in a particular instance whether spending more time on something connected with one's work is proper if it means a lessening of one's time with family or spiritual life. It is difficult to know, with any great degree of confidence, that a particular allocation of time is proper. . . . If you wanted to make a hierarchy, what would you do—put God, family and work in that order?

WRIGHT: Hierarchy of values?

McDONALD: Yes.

WRIGHT: Yes, except that, you see, the moment you begin to say "God, family and work," you imply that there are sharply distinct and isolated responsibilities involved, or levels cut off from one another like the cells of a honeycomb or like the floors of a steel-girdered building. There's something the matter with that concept of the spiritual life.

It seems to me that the member of a learned profession—in some degree every Christian, but certainly a member of a learned profession—has to have a rule of life, a spiritual philosophy and ascetical code which is humanistic and which, therefore, doesn't make that dichotomy of "God and family" or "God and my work" but rather makes him the servant of God in the law, a lover of God in his wife and family, and so on. I mean that an "incarnational" spirituality eliminates the necessity of thinking of God and family and work in such distinct and almost conflicting, even antagonistic terms.

McDONALD: It eliminates the tension between the obligations?

WRIGHT: The duty that the Catholic spouse owes his wife is also his duty to God in a real sense, and if he understands that sense he keeps both duties. One isn't likely to be forgotten in the other. The "thank you" he says to his wife is a "thank you" to God and his *Deo gratias* is a "thank you" for his wife. Our failure to realize the humanistic aspects of the Incarnation and its effect on spirituality accounts for this tension of which you

speak. You see, we've been haunted by the absence of a humanistic spirit, born of appreciation of the Incarnation, in Christian
spirituality.

McDONALD: Are you suggesting there is an anti-naturalistic
strain running through this thing?

WRIGHT: Well, it is anti-humanistic, certainly. It's the "two
loves have I" idea that, pressed far enough, is Manichean.
Claudel has a good handling of it; he protests that there are not
two loves, there is only one. With the same love by which my
heart of flesh embraces the created order, he asserts, my heart of
spirit loves its God. The human personality involves a psycho-
physical unity, and the God we love is immanent in creation as
well as transcendent to it.

Sometimes some of our disjunctions bedevil this question at
every turn. For example, the constant disjunction that we imply
in some of our spiritual direction—"seeing things in the light of
reason and seeing them in the light of Faith," "seeing things in
the light of eternity and seeing them in the light of time"—
almost suggests that these lights were lights beating against one
another, as if they admitted of no synchronizing.

McDONALD: I suppose St. Thomas would be the best example
of one who brought in both Faith and reason and produced
something new and unified.

WRIGHT: Yes, and that is why he gives such aid and comfort
to Christian humanism. He talked of "the Apostle" and "the
Philosopher," and capitalized both words. The Philosopher was
Aristotle and the Apostle was Paul. He continually starts off with
"the Philosopher says" and appeals to what "the Apostle says,"
bringing their testimony together without this hideous dichotomy
that has haunted even Catholics since Descartes pitted Faith and
Reason against one another and made the spiritual life somehow
schizoid. "Lest having Him we must have naught besides"—and
all this business.

We build up with spurious and disastrous romanticism the
spiritual choices involved in the vocations of our children, for
example. If our daughters elect to be nuns, we say "they have
rejected the world" or "died to the world," which can be vicious
talk, since you can't die to anything that God so loves that He

identified His only begotten Son with it, so that whosoever believeth in Him might not die, but have life everlasting.

This humanistic aspect of the Incarnation—the fact that Pilate did not need to send God to death (since he couldn't anyway) in order to be guilty of deicide, but only had to send unjustly to death the man before him, deserves immeasurably greater place in our preaching and meditation. It would unify and purify our concepts concerning spirituality. . . .

McDONALD: I wonder if we could go to the subject of Catholics and international life and international relations. One of the contributors to the book *"The Catholic Mind" Through Fifty Years, 1903-1953*, published a few years ago, commented that there is frequently a gap between what we Catholics believe and what we do, and he said that nowhere is that gap so large and formidable as in the area of international relations. And he pointed out that Catholicism of its very nature is international, or supra-national.

Now I know that you are interested and active in the Catholic Association for International Peace. Do you think this gap between Catholic belief and Catholic action is as wide today as apparently it was thirty or thirty-five years ago when that statement was made following the first World War? Or are we closing it?

And, relating to that, you spoke a few years ago at the National Liturgical Week about "The Mass and the International Order" and I believe you said then that Catholic universality is primarily moral and religious in its postulates and that the Catholic sees that, discerns it in the liturgy and in the Mass. Now do you think we can give political expression to this moral and religious solidarity and universality?

WRIGHT: First of all, on this suggestion that there is a seeming apathy among Catholics with respect to international interests and international movements, I am afraid there is no more irrefutable proof of that than the half-starved condition of our little Catholic Association for International Peace, by all odds the smallest organization in the whole set-up of the National Catholic Welfare Conference. That is perhaps a symbol of the situation that exists among us, I'm afraid.

If one goes to meetings where people get together to talk about the possible organization of the human community, he invariably discovers that if he's not the only Catholic present, the only other Catholic is probably someone who is believed to be on the eccentric side. On the other hand, he finds there, to his scandal from a Catholic point of view, all manner of Episcopalians, Quakers above all, a few Congregationalists, many Unitarians and, appropriately enough, practically all the Universalists there are. But any semantic reason which explains the presence of the Universalists should apply even more to us on account of the meaning of the word "Catholic." We know why the Universalists are there. We don't know why the Catholics aren't.

The more you think of it, and sometimes during the long keynote addresses at peace conferences you think quite a bit on it, one possible explanation occurs to you. One almost dislikes accepting the explanation because it doesn't seem fair to our dissident neighbors and, in a way, it doesn't seem fair to our own people either. But I think it's part of the explanation. I've often reflected that while Catholics are, in theological and religious matters, the most cosmopolitan and world-minded people on earth, somehow in political, social and economic matters they turn out to be ultra-nationalists. On the other hand, those who are so ultra-nationalist theologically that their very church names reflect the names of their nations—the Church of Scotland, the Church of England, the Boston Unitarians—are, as a matter of fact, usually among the most international-minded in what pertains to politics, problems of peace and war and like temporal problems of a cultural or social kind.

Isn't it a strange paradox which finds those who are worldwide in their religious loyalty so fiercely nationalist in their political sentiments? No one is more pro-Papal nor more completely British than a British Catholic, impatient, as my friend Douglas Woodruff tends to be, with the gross manifestations of American Catholicism; ultra-Papal, ultra-montane in the extreme, sometimes to the bewilderment of the Italians and even of the Spaniards, in religious matters, yet ultra-insular in economic, political and social matters. Whereas the Anglican, whose very name means that he has broken with world Catholicism, is in temporal matters more likely to have a world view.

McDONALD: Are these compensations, on both sides?

WRIGHT: Perhaps. But I think there is another explanation. Possibly it is unjust to the Protestants, but I think that the Messianic vision and the world impulse that belong in religion, and which some Protestants no longer find in religion, find their expression in a secularized form, in interest in belonging to peace movements and seeking a better world order on the political and social level.

Meanwhile, the Catholic has been put on the defensive in terms of his national loyalties precisely because of his ecumenicism and his world-wide religious unity. He has spent 300 years saying that one mustn't think he isn't a good American, a good Englishman or a good German simply because he doesn't go along with religious "Americanism" or "Anglicanism" or the *los von Rom Kulturkampf* as a result of his having a world loyalty in his relationship to the Pope and to the "one Lord, one Faith, one Baptism" essence of Catholicism, while at the same time, to make himself acceptable in the Protestant-dominated political and intellectual community, he has hammered away on what was Catholic in Thomas Jefferson's library and on how Catholic it is to be a good American.

As a result, the discerning Protestant politician was quite prepared to exploit that Catholic nationalism and he garnered, by the basketful, Irish Catholic votes on the grounds that he was opposed to the League of Nations! The sectarian Protestant, I regret to say, has until recently cared little about what became of world Christianity, but has taken keen interest in world social organization.

McDONALD: Will Herberg made the remark, in that Fund for the Republic seminar on religion in 1958, that he shocked a group of students at a Catholic university when he criticized Jack Kennedy for, as he said, "bending over backwards" to prove he is 400 per cent American. . . .

WRIGHT: He was quite right; it's a characteristic Catholic pattern.

McDONALD: And it seemed to Herberg that Kennedy seemed

to epitomize Catholics in general who are so anxious to show they are American that they are going to an unnecessary extreme.

WRIGHT: But you see the historical explanation of it. I shouldn't be at all surprised if we may some day see little colored children saying they had white ancestors, and yet being proud of their pretty color, perhaps saying, "You know, we get our particular blend of black from the fact that remotely we were white." Just as Catholics go around trying to show that Bellarmine was actually the author of whatever at the moment is considered truly American.

We're perpetually scandalized to discover that the Protestants apparently do not take these things as seriously as we do, and that they sometimes seem less interested in what is 100 per cent American than in a wider world community of which America is but a part. Catholic Americans are sometimes shocked by this wider interest, despite the fact that it is really part of *our* moral heritage, more than theirs!

McDONALD: My own feeling would be to blame some of my fellow editors for some of this ultra-nationalism, aside from the historical reasons here.

WRIGHT: But you must remember that your fellow editors are also readers and subject to all the pressures of the rest of the crowd. I think the responsibility of Catholic editors in this department is greater than in any other, as is that of a priest, or that of a bishop, as it is the Pope's.

The Popes seem to be meeting theirs admirably. They almost never say things that are specifically Italian. Each knows that he is an Italian and he may look like one or have the gestures of one. I am sure that he has something of a preferential charity for Italy. He should have. Nevertheless, one marvels at the manner with which they rise above their "Italianness" in their churchmanship and in their pastoral office. I think they should be our norm.

McDONALD: What do you mean when you say, "editors are also readers"?

WRIGHT: We sometimes think of the priest or the editor as being up on the mountain apart from the mob on the plain. The fact is that the editor is putting out a paper down on the

plain. The further fact is that he goes home every night to
the plain, back to his nationalistic relatives and friends. He goes
out to lunch with businessmen or the fellow in the shop next
door, and he is perpetually being influenced by them even as he
perpetually influences them. He doesn't, as a matter of fact, do
his thinking up on the mountain, even if he withdraws to an
ivory tower to do his writing. He is conditioned by all the things
that condition the rest of us lowly folk—even though he should
strive for greater detachment.

So the priest goes into the pulpit. It would be wonderful if
he came down every Sunday from Sinai and spoke to us of what
God had just said to him, but the fact is that he often goes into
the pulpit and talks of what *we* said to him at clubs or in conversations, of what we were saying all week in the office and of
what was said when he went home for a day off to his mother,
his brothers and his sisters. These colonies of thought are very
real.

Hence, the function of the retreat movement and of like means
to pull us up to Sinai for a few days every now and again, and
of the liturgy to give us the mind of the Church and of eternity,
thus offsetting the partisan and temporal influences all around us.

McDONALD: Do you think the priest should give more explicit
expression to this "moral and religious solidarity" that seems to
be a corollary of Catholic belief?

WRIGHT: I think he should, and I think he will if he really
goes up to Sinai and listens there for a while. The theological
and spiritual realities behind those corollaries are the things that
we pick up on Sinai.

But, remember, while Moses was up on the mountain, the
people were down on the plain doing business and worshiping
the golden calf. And so, when he came down, he seemed so
strange that he looked as if he had horns. Alas, often Moses
speedily talks their language, as the expression is, so that he won't
seem too strange and be repudiated or ignored. That's the fear of
the good priest. So he "talks their language," and there the
compromise and dilution set in.

But the more often the theological and spiritual realities picked
up on the mountain are brought down into the market place or

the more frequently the crowd is brought up into the mountain, as by the Mass liturgically celebrated, as in the retreat movement, as in the worthwhile study club, the more the jargon and the coin of the market place are subordinated and the influence of the mountaintop is felt. . . .

McDONALD: I hope there's still a place for the journalist here. . . .

WRIGHT: There is, of course—to record and encourage our progress and to point out the occasions when we fall away from our own ideal.

McDONALD: And I suppose to keep the Papal messages clear, to keep the lines of communication open . . .

WRIGHT: Surely. All this the journalist is called to do.

McDONALD: St. Thomas discussed at one point in his writings the common origin and common destiny of man and I suppose that is relevant in any discussion of the international community, but there again you find yourself on the mountaintop. . . .

WRIGHT: But it is to the mountaintop that we have to make periodic excursions lest we talk exclusively the jargon of the crowd, which is always the jargon of division. Thence, of course, comes the terrible temptation to the preacher or to the journalist. He thinks: "I must talk their language without saying the things that they say." Now *there's* a problem!

McDONALD: Here's another problem. Father Gustave Weigel recently wrote that it seemed to him the best way for religious leaders to approach statesmen faced with moral problems is not through religious tenets but through the natural law. On the other hand, Dr. Michaelsen, the Protestant director of the School of Religion at Iowa City, says that, outside of Catholics, there seems to be no basic agreement as to what is the natural law, or whether it is acceptable. Isn't this a problem, then, that goes deeper, that goes into theories of knowledge and criteria of truth and so on?

WRIGHT: I think we have a couple of problems in connection with this business of the natural law. First of all, I don't think that outside of the Catholic Church many people any longer believe in the natural law. I use the word "believe" because I think that's the word they would use, which shows right away that they don't even know what it is. The natural law is something that one recognizes; it is not an article of faith.

By what curious, collective astigmatism it has come to pass that men do not recognize the natural law that was so clear to Cicero, to Aristotle and to Aquinas and to the Founding Fathers of America, I don't know. But the fact is, men don't. I think the probable explanation is that the Founding Fathers, Aristotle, Thomas Aquinas and Cicero, whatever else they may have been, were not subjectivists, as our generation is.

There's been a rise of subjectivism not only in religion—for Protestantism historically has appealed to strongly subjective elements as opposed to what they would probably declare improperly objective or "extrinsic" elements—but you also have, of course, the rise of subjective schools of epistemology, ethics, psychology, ontology and comparative religion. Whatever is by its every emphasis non-subjective has hard acceptance in so subjectively conditioned a generation as ours. . . . I would think it likely that there isn't a single member of the Supreme Court as of this moment who is a natural-law legal philosopher.

McDonald: There is one Catholic on the Court.

Wright: I would be quite prepared to learn that he didn't have a "natural law" approach to cases. Surely Mr. Murphy didn't have. Probably the most brilliant mind on the Court is Frankfurter, and he would be quite candid in saying that he has no notion of "the natural law."

McDonald: Learned Hand said much the same thing when he bowed out from the New York judiciary several years ago; that "I don't know what you mean by 'natural law.' "

Wright: Chief Justice Holmes found the concept laughable. One of the few men on the Harvard Law School faculty in the last generation who was a natural-law legal philosopher was Dean Pound. . . .

What, therefore, to do in order to get a bridgehead with a generation which has repudiated the natural law as well as the ancient Faith, though continuing to call themselves Christians? How to reach them? What's the ground on which to stand? It's not the acceptance of the natural law that we have in common with these separated brethren. Nor is it the natural law that

Catholics can now think of as our bond with them. Ed Marciniak probably said the correct thing when he remarked that the bond we have with them is not the natural law, it's charity. . . .

Any great intellectual agreement is at the moment, in my opinion, illusory. We're using the same words to mean totally different things. We use the word "freedom" to say totally different things.

McDonald: Or "authority."

Wright: We certainly don't mean the same thing by "authority." We certainly don't mean the same thing by "Faith." We don't mean the same thing by "brotherhood of man." We don't mean the same thing by "fatherhood of God."

We assuredly don't mean the same thing by "children of God." We are not all God's "children." We are all God's "creatures" in a natural-law concept, but that is quite another matter. Some of those creatures have received the spirit of adoption by which they are enabled to say, "Abba, Pater," and therefore become His "children." Some of His creatures through no fault of their own, and some through fault of their own, are not children of God, but only creatures of God.

When we meet and we say we are all "children of the same God," we are in danger of defrauding one another, and we delay a showdown which, if it be in all charity, need not result in bitterness or non-co-operation, but might easily result in fruitful dialogue on the level of mutual sympathy and forbearance.

McDonald: Father Weigel raised this question at a recent Catholic Press Association convention. He said: "Why meet with one another at all, since the Catholic cannot hope to convert the Protestant, and the Protestant certainly cannot expect the Catholic to join with him in some higher form of unified Protestantism. . . ." Father Weigel then gave the answer in his talk: it's because we have to live together.

Wright: We have to use the same public buses, the same public library. Therefore, we have to reach a practical formula under which we can use those things which are in common while having few ideas in common.

I think it's dangerous to focus on such things as the birth-control argument, or on any aspect of sex, because there are highly charged overtones there, of tension, passion, even guilt, and therefore both sides get worked up more rapidly and the dialogue breaks down, whether it's on birth control or companionate marriage . . . or "feelthy" pictures. It seems to me that the general problem has to be faced in a more calm and quite literally cold area so that we can there discern the principles which can then be transferred to the more heated moral arguments.

It's in another area that we shall best face our differences and where they may be more fruitfully approached. Suppose we could agree for a generation, or a century, to direct our attention away from these differences except where they involve police action. We might say, in effect, to our neighbors: "If you find us actually hard at work nullifying the actions of the Congress, or rulings of the courts, as your relatives do in the South, arrest us by all means in the name of precisely what you find us doing. And if we find you handing corrupting stuff to our people, we shall arrest you, certainly. But in the meantime, for purposes of this Catholic-Protestant dialogue which is needed in order to restore something like Christian order to the world, suppose we leave off mutual suspicion and recrimination long enough to face the basic questions in the dialogue—What is God? What think ye of Christ?—before we come to grips with questions of a peripheral kind."

If we could only agree, as the Christians we profess to be, that our rights are entirely subordinate to the discovery of the will of God. If we met occasionally to ask ourselves what the words in that sentence mean—"God," "God's will" and "discover"—and these bring us face to face with the ultimate problems of ethics and epistemology as well as theology, isn't that a worthwhile dialogue? It is certainly the inevitable one.

St. Paul said God made us that we may dwell on the whole face of the earth *to seek Him.* That's the essential thing.

McDONALD: Do you think American theologians are ready to converse on this level as they do in Germany, Catholics there with Lutherans? We seem rather cautious about doing so here.

WRIGHT: We're cautious for good reasons, but justified caution does not require total non-co-operation. We're cautious because in these matters there are such titanic values involved, values with eternal implications. Then, too, as I have tried to say, we are really so far apart, so very far apart—and this fact imposes caution.

Caution is entirely called for, but some effort at dialogue is not less called for. The dialogue, however, must be on the ultimates, rather than on the proximates, because it is the ultimates which have become obscured.

We tend to assume that on the ultimates we all agree, and that it is only on these little practical applications—birth control, a Catholic President, etc.—that we disagree. Nothing could be further from the truth. We're more likely to agree on some of these than we are on the ultimates.

REV. JOSEPH FICHTER, S.J.

FATHER JOSEPH FICHTER, S.J., professor of sociology and head of that department at Loyola University, New Orleans, and author of numerous books and social studies, was born in Union City, New Jersey, in 1908. He entered the Society of Jesus at the age of twenty-two.

He received his Master's degree in sociology from St. Louis University and his Ph.D. degree in sociology from Harvard.

Father Fichter's perhaps most widely known and discussed book is *Southern Parish*, published in 1951 as the first of a projected series of four volumes comprising a comprehensive analysis of a typical urban parish. This report initiated the typology, now commonly used by sociologists of religion, which classifies communicants as nuclear, modal, marginal and dormant. The study was financed by the Carnegie Foundation and Loyola University, published by the University of Chicago Press, and acclaimed by social scientists as a reliable pioneering investigation in religious institutions. Nevertheless, resistance by "certain ecclesiastics" was strong enough to result in prohibition of publication of the remaining three volumes.

The story of the circumstances of Father Fichter's study and the fate of the book in New Orleans are told by Paul Courtney in an article, "The 'Southern Parish' Case," in the November 30, 1951, issue of *The Commonweal*. Since that incident, Father Fichter has published the results of two major parish inquiries, one a study of lay organizations in a German urban parish (made while visiting professor of sociology at the University of Münster), the other a thorough report on an American parochial school.

He was interviewed in one of the Jesuits' rooms at Marquette University after he had given a guest lecture to students and faculty on the subject, "Are We Going Secular?"

McDONALD: When did you begin getting interested in sociological studies of the Church?

FICHTER: Before I started graduate work at Harvard, I'd done mainly historical research. I had already published four or five books, mainly biographies—a study of St. Cecil Cyprian, one on Francis Suárez, another on James Laynez. My first book was called *Roots of Change*, a series of sketches on the great social thinkers of recent times. My doctoral dissertation at Harvard was a sociological interpretation of the Emperor Augustus' attempts back in ancient Rome to stabilize marriage, promote parenthood and halt the decline of the population. But the experience at Harvard was a kind of intellectual ferment for me. One of the sociological areas being explored while I was there was what we called "informal organization," focusing on the actual, rather than the expected or ideal, performance of functions in social groups. Research had been done in factories, in military groups, and other kinds of organizations, and the results were an exciting insight into the ways in which things really got done. It seemed to me that we could get similar results if we made this approach to the various kinds of religious groups and organizations in the Catholic Church.

McDONALD: Who were some of the influential social scientists at Harvard while you were there?

FICHTER: Sorokin was probably the best-known name there, and was certainly influential. He turned the chairmanship of the department over to Talcott Parsons, one of the leading sociological theorists in America. I learned a great deal from Gordon Allport and Clyde Kluckhohn. Carle Zimmermann was the one who opened up the possibilities of my thesis. But it was Parsons who suggested to me one day that I might do a research study of the Jesuit Order "from the inside," by which he meant the study of the informal organization of what he seemed to consider a tremendously effective religious group. We talked about this idea for a while, but I turned it down because I think it's very difficult to keep an objective, scientific perspective when you are yourself deeply and personally involved in a group. But I began to realize that here was a potential approach to the study of Catholicism in America and that a lot of research could be done on the social structures of the Church. We know what the rules are, we know what canon law and the Catechism say, but we don't know clearly the empirical adaptations that make the organization work in this particular culture. We really haven't analyzed the inner sociological effectiveness of the Church in America.

McDONALD: You mean we don't know how things actually work?

FICHTER: When I say "we," I'm saying that Americans who are in social science know more about primitive tribes than they know about how the Catholic Church works in America. Robert Lynd, who did the Middletown studies, once said to me that Catholicism is to the ordinary American an impenetrable jungle, that there are a lot of misconceptions about it and that it would be helpful if we really knew something about it.

McDONALD: You didn't do that study of the Jesuit Order, then?

FICHTER: No, but the notion of such a study was the beginning of a lot of thinking I did and I felt that social science could be put at the service of the Church and at the same time be a real pursuit of knowledge in which the social scientist would try to find the truth rather than simply try to prove something. It was on this principle that I got a grant from the Carnegie Foundation when I got back to Loyola University and began an intensive year-long study of an urban parish. My research assistants stayed with me right through the summer and on to the end of the liturgical year. It was an exacting, time-consuming task, and we collected such a mass of data that I decided to make it a four-volume report. It took a year to analyze and write up the first volume, which the University of Chicago Press contracted to publish, as well as the three volumes that were to come.

McDONALD: After *Southern Parish*, you made different studies to supplant the non-published subsequent volumes, didn't you?

FICHTER: Yes, I was visiting professor of sociology at the University of Münster in Germany, in 1953-1954, and one of my functions was to demonstrate aspects of empirical research in America. We did this by a research project in the parochial societies of a German urban parish. That report was published in Germany and it takes the place of the original Volume II we had planned. Then in 1956-1957, while I was at Notre Dame University, we did the parochial-school study which parallels the third volume of the original series of the *Southern Parish* project. Perhaps it won't be too long before we can substitute for the fourth volume with a study of family life in the parish.

McDONALD: How does a religious sociologist differ from a sociologist? Or do you classify yourself as a religious sociologist? Some of the European sociological research scholars have been so classified when they have worked in specifically Catholic areas and in a context of specifically Catholic problems.

FICHER: Well, I have always resisted that term, "religious sociologist." I don't think we can talk about religious sociology any more than we can about political sociology or economic sociology or educational sociology. Actually what we have is a sociology of religion, which is a much clearer term. In other words, it's the sociologist seeing a phenomenon that is present in an institutional form, in patterns and roles and relations that are religious. Europeans use the term "religious sociologist," but I don't like it.

McDONALD: Your methods would be the same as those of any sociologist?

FICHTER: Any empirical American sociologist, yes.

McDONALD: What about the analysis of your findings? Would the fact that you are a Catholic influence your analysis?

FICHTER: Of course, this is the problem that has bothered some of my non-Catholic colleagues for years. They say that maybe you, as a person, are looking for truth, but that your Church doesn't want truth, it wants apologetics. . . .

McDONALD: Edification?

FICHTER: Yes. So this is a difficulty. Obviously values are involved in the very selection of an area for research. When a man
decides to do research in housing or in delinquency or in race
relations, he's got to have some basis on which he decides that
this is worth doing, or more worth doing than something else at
this particular time. So, clearly, my values as a Catholic and as a
priest will be involved, and also my intense belief that social
science can make a contribution to the Church and to society in
general. But this is very different from saying my values enter
into my analysis. I think they do not; at least I like to think
that the scientific approach is what is guiding me on what I consider the significance of the generalizations that can be made
from this kind of study.

McDONALD: It seems to me that such publications as *Journalism Quarterly*, which is almost exclusively sociological in its approach to the press in this country, bend over backwards to keep
value judgments out of their studies. They invariably will bite
off a tiny piece of a small fragment of a partial problem, measure
the press's performance there and carefully refrain from showing
any interest in what the press's performance should actually be.
But then maybe that would be the function of some other publication, not yet in existence—to measure the distance between
how the press performs and how it ought to perform. But, as
you say, by simply selecting areas for investigation you are already
making some kind of judgment.

FICHTER: It's pretty difficult to keep the value implications out
of such studies. You have to be careful even with the terminology
itself that you use. Back during the War, Myrdal's *American
Dilemma* made very clear the need for expressing what he called
the researcher's "valuations," and he claimed that this clarification helps to keep bias out of your scientific analysis. Generally,
American social scientists seem to be accepting this idea. There
is much more discussion now about values than ever before. I
think the Nazis threw a scare even into the social scientists.
Robert Redfield once said that it's very easy to anthropologize in
a "value-free" way some remote tribe that doesn't threaten us;
but when a whole modern nation like Nazi Germany begins to
interfere with your peace and security, you soon start to ask value

questions. "On what basis can we say that we were right and the Nazis wrong?" You're no longer satisfied that morality is simply the "outgrowth of customs and culture." When someone else's morality gets in your way, you begin worrying about the difference between local and universal norms of morality.

McDONALD: I can see that the social scientist who is merely measuring things and putting his findings down doesn't have to make explicit value judgments. But as a person, later on he should, I suppose, stand up and be counted when the chips are down. But that wouldn't affect his work as a social scientist, would it?

FICHTER: No, it wouldn't. Howard Becker at the University of Wisconsin is very interested in this. As a matter of fact, there's a group, mostly Protestants (Nash at North Carolina, Kolb who was at Tulane and is now at Carleton, Becker, Eister and others), who are talking about a re-evaluation of what they call "the image of man." They are concerned about the behavioristic, positivistic concept, in which man is considered a kind of plastic organism that responds in a relatively unfree way to various stimuli. In their minds this colors the social scientists' handling of data, and so they are asking themselves, "Can't we operate from a more reliable premise? Can't we perhaps go to Augustine and other traditional interpreters of human nature for a more valid model of man?"

McDONALD: These are Protestant social scientists?

FICHTER: Yes, yes, and this is a fascinating development among men who are genuine scientists as well as religious persons. They realize that they are here talking about a kind of meta-sociology, to use Furfey's term. It's a sort of intellectual platform from which you project yourself, and it would undoubtedly find objections in men like George Lundberg and Kingsley Davis, who have their own, and different, meta-sociological platform.

McDONALD: What is your definition of social science? Is it a study of the behavior of man? Or is that too simple?

FICHTER: Every definition we use we have to start explaining, and maybe that's why it becomes complex. I define social science as the study of recurrent uniformities of social behavior. In other words, you can't have a science unless you have generalizations that are based on repetition; and so this is about as basic as you can get—that people do certain things in the same way and tend to have the same kinds of ideas and attitudes. If we couldn't do this, we'd have to close up shop; we could never call it social science.

McDONALD: Is your work primarily a task of polling and surveying people's opinions? What are the other things you look for and work with in your studies? Your empirical research includes more than just gathering people's opinions and attitudes, doesn't it?

FICHTER: In our published report of the parochial school study, the introductory chapter explains the methods and techniques we used in that particular field research. One technique is called "participant observation." We had nine research assistants spending many days in that school, taking down notes of everything that went on in the relationship of teachers to pupils, of one pupil to another—the playground situation, the athletic games, the parties they had, their meetings, church services—everything that looked like social behavior. This was one large part of the data we collected. Then we administered the California Test of Personality and several other tests and questionnaires, trying to discover the children's social attitudes, in both the parochial and public schools. We also did a great deal of interviewing. We conducted interviews with all the parents of the Catholic children from this parish, whether their children were in the parish or public school. We had another set of interviews with the parochial school teachers, and we balanced this with the same number of public school teachers, asking the same questions of both.

Of course we made constant cross-checks to verify or correct our findings. For example, we got the impression that some teachers looked upon the family and the home as a kind of disorderly jungle, in which anything goes. (This helped them to "explain" behavior problems around the school.) In visiting the homes we found that all parents establish regulations for their children. But this too was checked. If the parents had rules about the use of TV and the time for going to bed, we asked the children themselves what time they normally went to bed. We asked them what their favorite TV programs were, and checked this against the time they and their parents said they went to bed, and the time that the TV program was broadcast. There are all kinds of internal checks of this nature that the research scientist uses, and the result is a remarkably accurate picture.

McDONALD: This is a part of social science, then, research to protect yourself, verify your findings by cross-checking?

FICHTER: Oh, yes. You check your data to see whether you're getting an abnormal set of answers along one line. If you do, you check to see whether you've asked the wrong questions, or whether you're asking the questions in the wrong way. Maybe they don't understand the question, or maybe a particular time of year has something to do with the way certain kinds of answers are given.

McDONALD: How long did you have to stay in the classroom before the children started to behave naturally, without inhibitions because of strangers in the classroom?

FICHTER: That is always the problem of the foreign agent in the eye, the irritation. We found that after the first couple of weeks everything settled down, although there were some teachers who carried right on as though we were never there and there were others who tried to involve us in the class procedure. There was no even pattern with everybody. Research techniques have been fairly well worked out, however, by anthropologists and sociologists.

There are a couple of other ways in which you can check your data and get more data. For instance, I conducted what I called "soirees," which were group interviews with four or five couples at a time. These were people, deliberately selected because they were most deeply involved in the school program, who knew the most about the parish, its priests, people and teachers. Some of these also helped, after the school year closed, by reviewing with us the first draft of our research findings. They raised questions, clarified doubtful points, provided additional evidence and data. This is an invaluable technique, widely used by scientific researchers in groups and communities, to assure the reliability of both the empirical data and the scientific generalizations.

McDONALD: You said at one time that there was one very important, unanswered, question running through your mind all during your research into the parochial school, and that was whether the whole thing, the parochial school system, is worth what we're putting into it in money, energy, human resources.

FICHTER: Yes, the question was never answered. I did an article on it and it was reprinted several places, asking the question: "Are parochial schools worthwhile?" I summarized what we had found in our study and the conclusion is that there is no testable way that I know of in which you can say the parochial school was responsible for any specific later effect in the lives of its graduates. Suppose we went back to that Midwestern parish ten years later, say in 1967, and looked up all the people who had been in the sixth, seventh and eighth grades when we made the study. We could test them on their Catholicism, their citizenship, on all the facets of knowledge and behavior they were supposed to have learned in their elementary parochial school.

McDONALD: A lot of other things would have happened to them in the meantime.

FICHTER: Exactly. This is my point—there are so many other variables: the associations they've had, the way in which their family developed, their father's occupation, whether their parents divorced, or somebody died, whether the students went on to a public high school or a Catholic high school, whether they had got married in those ten years, whether they had had military service. It's very difficult, then, to pick out one factor, like a parochial school—in fact I would think it's impossible to do that scientifically—and say that that factor had had precisely this effect and that.

McDONALD: You have mentioned social science as being of great potential service to the Church. Is the Church anxious to have this service?

FICHTER: I'm not sure that that's a fair question to ask of the research person himself. All kinds of groups and organizations in America are inviting social scientists in to do research, sometimes paying for it themselves, sometimes getting funds from research foundations. This is really a question for "management," the officials and administrators of the Church, to answer. The scientific worker starts out with the assumption that the search for truth is the highest function of the human intellect. I think that this is seriously what we are trying to do. I feel that social science in the service of the Church can never be a "cover-up job," nor an apologetical approach. It's a job that finds, filters, and focuses data that are pertinent to the maintenance and operation of the Church as an organization made up of human beings. Obviously, there are both negative and positive aspects in the social behavior or ideas of imperfect human beings. But we have here an opportunity to analyze—particularly in America where Catholicism is new, where the American society itself is new and where changes are occurring that have never occurred before in the history of the world. Maybe the Church can learn what to do, from some of these findings, in completing its job of converting the whole world. I don't think you can learn this by keeping your eyes closed, or by judging the present by something that happened in the ninth or the sixteenth century.

MCDONALD: If not enough use is being made of social scientists and their data by the Church, might part of the blame be placed on the social scientists? Maybe they haven't made sufficiently clear the help and the value their findings and research can be to Church authorities responsible for the welfare of souls. Has the value of the Dutch and Belgian social scientists to their bishops after the war been made generally known in this country?

FICHTER: Ben Gaffin, who died in Chicago last year, used to ask that some question. He and his associates did the well-known *Catholic Digest* studies on religion and race relations. We often talked about the prospect, the "vision," of a statistical research bureau, backed up by millions of Catholic dollars, that would supply sociographic and demographic data to the bishops of the United States. This job would be much more difficult than it is for the Europeans who have statistics on religious affiliation available from their national census. But Ben was convinced that a "selling job" could be done, and would have to be done, to persuade Church officials that such research would be extremely helpful. I didn't always share his hopeful enthusiasm, and anyway, I am committed more to functional research in the group life of the Church than to the statistical and demographic research that the Europeans do.

MCDONALD: The experience of the Belgian and Dutch sociologists after the war was interesting. They showed the Belgian and Dutch hierarchy which direction the population was moving, certain economic and cultural trends which had some obvious implications in religious life and pastoral care, and I've been told that the bishops there took all this data into consideration in planning new parishes, deciding which ones to abandon, and how best to distribute their priests.

FICHTER: That's downright useful to the Church; and that's good. Research and scholarship have been urged by the Popes and other Church leaders in modern times. But, you know, this takes a variety of forms and it's on all levels of practical utility, and degrees of subtlety. American social science is moving into the more sophisticated areas of culture and group life. We are doing more studies in social structures, functions and relations. For example, my present research is dealing with what I call the "professional functionaries" of religion. A lot of graduate students have done their theses on the social "backgrounds" of vocations—a relatively simple job of gathering questionnaires from seminarians, Brothers and Sisters. But, practically nothing has been done on the performance of roles, that is, the functioning of these people within the occupational career of the Church. I've been gathering material on this for over four years, and gave courses on it in the graduate departments at Fordham and Notre Dame. Right now I'm doing an intensive research project on the diocesan parish priest. In all of our parochial field work we find that the priest is the key person. The parish revolves around him; and we are trying to discover what he does and thinks in this important role.

McDONALD: By the way, where do you get your money for projects like this?

FICHTER: I got a couple of small grants for this project: one from the American Philosophical Society, and another from the Social Science Research Council. It would be great to have research funds available from Church sources. It would pay for itself, for example, if these studies could ultimately raise the efficiency of operation in the Church by just 2 or 3 per cent.

McDONALD: You have been talking in recent months about the need for a Catholic intellectual center in this country. Why do you think we need one? What would be its work, to take some of the findings of people like yourself and relate them to other data developed by other people?

FICHTER: I think that a center in which Catholic intellectuals, expert scholars no matter what their fields might be, could exchange ideas and analyze data and come up with conclusions would be of terrific utility to the Church—again, if its findings were made use of. I would think of this in very broad terms—in literature, history, anthropology, economics. We're in desperate need, for instance, of a real Catholic economist who will think through this whole capitalist system, what it's leading to, and the product, the technology, what that is doing to the American people. The whole problem of leisure is bound up with that, and it has hardly been touched by anybody. We should be getting some answers from the philosophers and theologians.

McDONALD: The center would be useful, I suppose, in that the various people at the center could cross-check each other—the theologians be checked on their data, perhaps, by the social scientists, the sociologists cross-checked on some of their analyses by the philosophers and theologians.

FICHTER: Right, right. And I think it should be located at a university. Not precisely like the Center for Behavioral Studies out in Palo Alto, but something more closely allied to a graduate school. There should certainly be graduate students in training there, but perhaps no undergraduates at all. A center of this kind would do several things. You'd have the interchange of knowledge, the re-examination of ideas, the constant correction of one field against another. In the classical sense of education, you'd be handing on the techniques and traditions to the younger scholars of tomorrow. Thirdly, out of this comes production—research reports and scholarly publications that could raise the level of our cultural and intellectual life.

McDONALD: This would be a group of wise men at such a center, but they would also be knowledgeable men in the sense that . . .

FICHTER: They'd be neither eccentric nor ego-centric.

McDONALD: Yes, their wisdom would be constantly verified by the data they possess and which they would share with each other. Do you think that because there is no such intellectual center, there is little meaningful contact between the various disciplines—the theologians, sociologists, philosophers, historians and literary people aren't in close enough contact?

FICHTER: There are other problems, too. I think some people tend to sneer at social science and sociology because they don't know enough about it. Perhaps some social scientists sneer at theologians for being troglodytes, concerned only with things that happened a long time ago. This word "dialogue"—which I'm getting real sick of—stands for something that could go on inside the Church in a very productive way. Catholics don't seem to think of scholarship in the United States except in terms of teaching. Somehow or other, it has to "pay off." And if we could ever sell to the Catholic educational leaders that they don't have to balance a budget in a university, I think this would be a great advance. A university is not a business enterprise.

McDONALD: It's like symphony orchestras; they never end up in the black. Maybe all the good things in life never do end up paying their own way, commercially.

FICHTER: Yes, this is something I've thought a great deal about. These are what you might call "service" activities, compared to "profit" activities where you sell so many items at 4 per cent profit. Service activities are very poorly paid. Take social workers, who do a tremendous job; take teachers, who do a tremendous job—all underpaid. Maybe we have to re-think the whole capitalist concept of what is an investment. These people are an investment in human beings. Do we have the economic surplus to pay them in the way they should be paid?

McDONALD: You have said that this is a unique time for American Catholics, a time of great opportunity for the Church because of the radical changes taking place. Can you identify some of these changes? You mentioned one or two—the new leisure, technology.

FICHTER: One of the difficulties is that we don't even know precisely and clearly what is happening to us. How does the Church approach this new American system? I think the whole switch from a peasant-thinking, traditional, rural-bound sort of culture, to this volatile, challenging, urban system is something we haven't begun to absorb. We complain about the city, and even about the suburbs, but we are using out-of-date norms that are unrealistic in this unique modern society. So also in our patterns of behavior, we're pulled in all directions. For instance, the whole liturgy of the Church is built around rural living that has little meaning to American Catholics. Even here, we have passed the urban stage and have become metropolitan. What's happening in the United States now is going to happen in Western Europe and probably in the rest of the world. The thinking of Catholic scholars here and now could eventually influence the whole world. For example, what is really the Christian concept of work, as applied in a social system where work itself has radically changed? For the first time in history we face the potential of almost complete automation. Is work a punishment for sin? Is it a privilege by which man expresses himself and co-creates with God? If the drudgery is taken out of work, how do we employ the release this gives us? The implications of all this are startling.

McDonald: Suburbanism and the general decentralizing trend in where people live would seem to be an introduction of an important new element in our culture. You have observed that one of the good effects of suburbanism is that Catholics are mingling more with their neighbors than they had ever done in the urban, metropolitan centers.

Fichter: One of the things that struck me among the data we picked up in our study of the parochial school is that Catholic men and women who took an interest in the Cub Scouts and Boy Scouts were accepted by non-Catholics as competent people interested in the welfare of the community. This was especially apparent in the city-wide organization which planned the larger annual programs and carried them through. A certain mutual respect between Catholics and non-Catholics developed and Catholics were seen as citizens really concerned about their community.

McDonald: The fact that this struck you and stuck in your mind seems to indicate that it is the exception rather than the rule so far as Catholics and community life are concerned.

Fichter: It varies from one part of the country to another. In the Middle West I think there is a more highly developed adaptation, as shown in the mutual respect of Catholics and other Americans, than there is in any other part of the country. It varies too, by kinds of organization. Catholics ought to involve themselves more in the problems of public school education. The League of Women Voters ought to have more Catholic women in it; the same goes for other civic-minded groups. Some years ago we made a little survey of the women's organizations in New Orleans—there are hundreds of them—and checked the names of officers that appear on the letterheads. We found remarkably few Catholic names, even though the city's population is well over half Catholic. When I presented this fact at a Catholic women's college, I was immediately challenged by the audience. "But, Father," they said, "you must realize that Catholic women are active in Church organizations, and are busy at home raising their families." So, we did the whole study over to investigate the non-Catholic women in these civic organizations. Were they active in their churches and synagogues? Were they raising families? And they were, they were. Well, whatever the immediate and local reasons for Catholic non-participation in civic and community affairs, I think we have been plagued with the notion of the "holding operation." Subconsciously we are probably still bothered by the Reformation. The feeling seems to be that you have to protect your own against outside hazards. Yves Congar has said that we do not really appreciate the secular, the "world," as contrasted to the other-worldly. Perhaps Catholics tend to huddle together in a kind of self-centered way. Will Herberg's thesis seems to be that the drawing of the religious lines is being done more sharply.

McDONALD: Perhaps people are frightened for other reasons, too, the Bomb, that kind of thing. Perhaps this is one way to secure reassurance, by huddling together.

FICHTER: The need to belong, the need to be identified with the group. This is discussed a lot by Protestants and Jews, the rootlessness and the alienation bothers them. People talk about the "loneliness" of modern life. Here again this is one of those major transitions we are going to have to come to terms with. Some of my psychiatrist friends are bothered about the anxieties and worries of our time. I myself feel that the human personality is tremendously adaptive, but that we need time, perhaps a generation or so, before human beings learn to live with this rapidly dynamic culture. Put a primitive on Broadway at Times Square, and you'll scare him to death. Perhaps many of us are still primitives in this age of technology. Some people think that human beings should not be submitted to such demands, that it is almost "against nature." I think we can learn here from St. Ignatius Loyola, who visualized the ideal Jesuit as a highly elastic personality who isn't thrown off his feet by unexpected demands.

McDONALD: Yet, humans can respond in emergencies, they can summon certain adaptive energies and resources.

FICHTER: Yes, and I think we've got to learn to do this. But there's a common notion that this is too much to expect and not have people consuming tons of Miltowns and taking to drink and drugs. I have just that much faith in the human being and the fact that God made us in such a way that we can adapt.

McDONALD: You have more or less questioned the thesis of some that technology and technological organization necessarily dehumanizes or depersonalizes man.

FICHTER: As we get more involved in this new culture, I feel that our ideas about personalism have to change. About five years ago the Pope talked in a Christmas message about depersonalization as a defect of the technological system, but he was not for a moment condemning technology as such. Now, the group-relatedness that William Whyte objects to in modern industry is really a corrective of that defect. It's the fad now to sneer at togetherness and belongingness, but this is essentially the basis of a sound social system. As the occupational system changes, other forms of personalization are built into it. All of the sociological pother about large-scale organizations and inevitable bureaucracies misses the basic fact that primary groups and relations have to exist everywhere. There are all kinds of informal and personal clusters of human beings, not only the family and neighborhood, but in office and factory and recreation —everywhere. A society would collapse—in fact, no society has ever existed—without these informal groupings of people.

That doesn't mean that you have to belong to the same circle of people all your life. Our kind of society demands that you frequently make new friends, grouping and re-grouping all during your life. Is this instability? Anyway, what's the value in being stable and unchanging in a culture that is challenging the alert and progressive person? The point I'm trying to make is that in spite of Taylor's original study of work efficiency—that the closer you get to the machine the more work you get out of people— all of this has been discarded by industrial sociology for years. It just doesn't work; and the corrective came with the re-intro- duction and improvement of human relations in the industrial system. It wasn't technology that dehumanized and deper- sonalized the work life of society; it was the people who mis-ran and misused the occupational system. Thank God that the social scientists have done the research out of which management has been able to make improvements. Technology is here to stay— and thank God for that too.

McDONALD: Do you see any hopeful signs on the horizon so far as the Church in America is concerned?

FICHTER: One of the most hopeful signs is the rising status of the lay people in the Church, the developing maturity among lay people. I think that we priests have to recognize this and I believe the younger priests are changing to meet it.

McDONALD: Is this maturity visible mostly on the level of education?

FICHTER: Education, social status, competence, their psycho- logical security, a lot of things like that. And along with that is the general American value of having a voice, of participating, in one's organization.

McDONALD: Does this mean the laity are perhaps going to have to be given more of a voice?

FICHTER: Yes. In our studies on stratification and upward mobility, it seems to me that a Catholic can achieve status almost every place except in the Church. You have a closed structure. All of the functions that have prestige are tied up in the clergy. In the Protestant church the layman can go pretty high. I sus- pect that in other times in the history of the Church the Catholic layman could feel that he really belonged, that he was really doing something of importance. I think the whole fear of lay trusteeism in the Church in the United States is a false one and has to be dissipated.

McDONALD: Lay trusteeism went wrong for reasons that probably wouldn't be pertinent today.

FICHTER: Right. I think it was a misinterpretation, an attempt to understand the structure of Catholicism from the point of view of some sort of liberal-democratic voting system. As a matter of fact, in our studies of the parish in Germany, I was astonished to find that in that so-called authoritarian society, the layman had much more to say in the operation of the parish than does the "democratic" American Catholic in his parish. German parishioners are elected to a kind of board of directors who vote on whether the pastor can spend money, and even whether the bishop can divide the parish.

McDONALD: Is this true of parishes throughout Germany?

FICHTER: Yes, everywhere. It's an outcome of the *Kulturkampf*, and it has continued to the present time. Oh, there are other hopeful signs in our own country. I think that people are being a lot more intelligent about marriage and family life and child-raising than they used to be. And I think that the people in the Young Christian Students and Young Christian Workers and the Christian Family Movement are a tremendous promise for the future. We'll see adaptation coming out of that. Generally speaking, I would say that the American laity is willing and competent to work for and with the Church, not merely as a sacrifice or obligation, but as a positive action. But you can't have all authority at one end and all responsibility at the other. That is, you cannot have all the authority reserved to the clergy, and then expect initiative and responsibility from the laity. Multiple groups with multiple functions have to replace the large, all-purpose parish organizations. You can have everything from a St. Monica Guild of eighth-grade girls that baby-sit during Mass to theology classes for adults. All kinds of spiritual and secular activities can be promoted under the aegis of the parish.

McDONALD: I'm not too enthusiastic about having a great many of these activities. They tend to pile up on you. Everybody in the family seems to be going to meetings. After an evening meal they just scatter, one to a basketball game, another to the

CYO meeting, and a third to a Scout meeting. Sometimes you wind up with two meetings to attend on the same night.

FICHTER: I've sometimes said that the family is broken by divorce, by death—and by parish organizations. Yes, this is a real problem if you have the same people trying to do everything and belonging to all of the organizations. You bring up a real question here of surplus activity, of doing things that perhaps are not always the best things for you to do. The whole question of where we should put our educational resources is related to this. Some think that all of our educational effort should be thrown into the high schools rather than dividing it up between parochial grade schools and high schools. I'd like to see some real research done on this which would actually point out the direction for us.

McDONALD: Personally, I think they should be concentrated most heavily at the high school level. I think that in the first six years or so, the child is still pretty much under the control of his parents, but that it is at adolescence when he needs more systematic guidance of a religious kind. It's then when they begin to show a natural rebellion, natural independence and begin breaking away from the parental ties. I don't think the parents' responsibility ends at that time, by any means, but I do think that the teacher's moral and counseling responsibility increases tremendously at that point. The teaching Brother, priest or Sister can play a tremendous part in gaining the confidence of the teen-ager, guiding him.

FICHTER: This brings us back to the beginning. You have opinions and impressions and experiences—and so have I. So have all the other people who are involved in or interested in the Catholic educational system. The decision to focus our school resources on the adolescent can be intelligently made if it rests on the findings of systematic research. But this is only one of our social structures in the American Catholic Church. We have a gigantic social organization here, and a gigantic responsibility too. Can we afford to be less realistic in studying its maintenance and operation than people in less important forms of organization?

II

Encounter

REV. GUSTAVE WEIGEL, S.J.

FATHER GUSTAVE WEIGEL is professor of ecclesiology at the Jesuit seminary, Woodstock College, Maryland.

A foremost Catholic representative in what has come to be known as the "religious dialogue" in this country, Father Weigel has taken part in numerous symposia and seminars with Orthodox, Protestant and Jewish leaders, in which the motivation on all sides has been the desire to achieve greater mutual understanding.

A native of Buffalo, New York, Father Weigel was born in 1906. He received his doctorate in philosophy from the Gregorian University, Rome, in 1931, and his doctorate in theology from the same university in 1938. He taught dogmatic theology at the Universidad Católica de Chile and was dean of its theological faculty from 1942 to 1948 when he returned to the United States.

Father Weigel has contributed articles to many magazines, including *The American Scholar, Thought, America, The Review of Politics, The New Republic* and *The Lutheran World.* His books include *A Survey of Protestant Theology, A Catholic Primer on the Ecumenical Movement,* and *An American Dialogue,* the last written with the Protestant editor and theologian, Dr. Robert McAfee Brown, to appear in the fall of 1960.

The interview with Father Weigel was held in his hotel room in Chicago, where he was scheduled to take part, the next day, in a program for the Catholic clergy of that archdiocese which was to include, in addition to his own lecture, those of an Orthodox and a Protestant clergyman.

McDonald: When did you get interested in Protestant-Catholic relations?

Weigel: That interest has been with me all my life. But when I came back to this country in 1948, after having been away for thirteen years, and especially on reading the work of Paul Tillich, I began to realize that this was something more than sheer academic curiosity on my part. It was very important for Catholic theology. Likewise the ecumenical movement meant that this was important, not only for Catholic theology but for Catholic life in general.

McDonald: To what extent do you think your own interest in the dialogue between Catholics and Protestants is shared by other Catholics?

Weigel: Before the Second World War, Catholics were just beginning to realize that they were both Catholic and American. They never had doubted their Americanism, but they seemed to want to pull themselves together into something more than a mere federation of Catholic communities, into one general Catholic community. After the war, American Catholics, particularly on our college and university campuses, felt that American Catholicism had fused into one solid group and it seemed to me, as I traveled and moved around on university campuses from coast to coast, that Catholics now wanted something more from their community. They wanted to see a vigorous Catholic intellectual life which would be scientific according to the true sense of that word, in which a method is understood and one searches for truth for its own sake. They also wanted, I think, to speak on a plane of friendship with the other communities of the nation. They no longer looked at the other groups as hostile forces preventing Catholic growth and maturity. This was a feeling I had: the American Catholics did not want to live with the phantasms of the past but with the reality of the present. They wanted to understand and they were very anxious to be understood.

McDonald: Was there a corresponding feeling on the Protestant side? Are they also anxious to understand and be understood?

WEIGEL: Yes. Once I was in this action, I discovered that the Protestants and the Orthodox were also anxious to enter into the famous thing now called "dialogue." I think that word has already been beaten to death and so it doesn't speak all that it should say. An equivalent would be: let us meet each other and talk. That's what dialogue is. There is a strong desire on the part of Christian and Jewish bodies to come together and talk, not to knock down, not to triumph in a debate, but to achieve real understanding.

There is one difficulty in it from my point of view. The Protestants are anxious to make this ecumenical. The best manifestation of the ecumenical movement in Protestantism has been the World Council of Churches. It's my opinion that on its tacit postulates we cannot enter into the dialogue yet because there are working hypotheses in the Protestant ecumenical movement which seem to make it impossible for the Catholic to enter into it.

McDONALD: You mean it is an ecclesiological thing.

WEIGEL: It's mainly ecclesiological. Nevertheless it is evident that for the good of all these communities, the coming together for understanding should be practiced.

McDONALD: Would you say that that understanding could be a terminal good, a justifying terminal good of the dialogue, even though the ecumenical effect did not follow?

WEIGEL: This is my whole point. What is needed is not the ecumenical dialogue but the para-ecumenical dialogue, or, if you want, the pre-ecumenical dialogue. Before we discuss the question whether we shall become one church it is necessary to talk to each other so that we know where we are. The very hypotheses working on both the Catholic and the Protestant side make a union of the two into one church impossible. But we do need what I call the para-ecumenical conversation which goes on alongside the ecumenical conversation. The big thing now is to understand each other and to approach one another in the spirit of friendship, of affection. This may lead to a true ecumenical conversation at some future unknown date. But even if it doesn't, it is still highly worthwhile. It will make our living with the other communities a much more friendly thing, much more serene and much more efficient.

McDONALD: You're thinking of its effect on the political order?

WEIGEL: I wouldn't say "political." I avoid that word because it can be misunderstood. I say "civic." The para-ecumenical conversation gives grounds for common action in the civic order.

McDONALD: Though the para-ecumenical conversations are not immediately and directly concerned with ecumenicism, would they be concerned with positions on dogma?

WEIGEL: Yes.

McDONALD: From the Catholic standpoint, then, only highly qualified people should take part in such conversations.

WEIGEL: That would be equally true for all who are engaged in it. The first step will have to be among those who are experts in the field. From there on, it will have to move down and become more general. But in the moving down, there must always be present an expert who can say, with responsibility, not infallibility, the Catholic dogmatic position is thus, the Lutheran dogmatic position is so. Thus we wouldn't have people who don't know making false statements in all good faith and making promises which are entirely contrary to the spirit of the community to which they belong.

McDONALD: I suppose that by and large the meetings you attend are not exclusively theological discussions, because we haven't progressed quite that far yet in this country.

WEIGEL: In most of the meetings in which I take part, involving Catholics and Protestants, the problem is not directly or immediately religious. It will be some civic or secular concern which derives from certain religious commitments. I'm thinking of a meeting held at Columbia University's School of Journalism a few years ago. There were representatives from three religious journals—*The Christian Century*, *The Commonweal* and *Commentary*. They were discussing the problem of how religious journalists should conduct their journals for the benefit of the whole American community. This was not, immediately, a theological or doctrinal question. But in handling it, the question of doctrine arises.

McDONALD: That would have been similar to the Fund for the Republic's Religion in America seminar a couple years ago.

WEIGEL: Yes. They were interested in the problem of the relationship of what they call Church and State, although I consider that a completely unfortunate tag. It's not a question of

Church and State; it is a question of the sacral and the secular. It foreshortens the thing too much to refer to it as "Church and State." The State is only one aspect of the total secular order, and the Church, as an institution, is only one aspect of the sacral order which is, after all, an order of humanity, a dimension of man.

MCDONALD: There seems to be considerable difference between these conversations from country to country. Do the "rules" and the form of the dialogue more or less take shape and definition from the conditions and traditions within each country?

WEIGEL: That's right. Actually there are general norms for Catholics, given by Rome in the *monitum* of 1948 and the instruction of 1949, but those norms have to be applied by the bishops in the different countries according to the needs and possibilities of the country. Until very recently, the nervousness on the part of the Catholics in this country over this kind of conversation was almost extreme. It is tapering off.

MCDONALD: Is part of that nervousness due to a feeling of incompetence, of inadequacy on the part of American Catholics?

WEIGEL: No, I don't think so. But in the days in which Catholics were building themselves up as a community their focus of attention was inside. When they looked at the outside, they were looking at "the enemy." There aren't too many Catholics engaged in the conversation even now, but those who are do not feel at all insecure.

MCDONALD: It has been said that if American Catholics are separated, from kindergarten through university, in a Catholic school system, they will be unfitted for this conversation and perhaps even unaware of their responsibilities in this area.

WEIGEL: There's even more to it than that. The Catholics never did live completely in a so-called ghetto. They worked with non-Catholics. They did many things together with non-Catholics. They served in the Army and Navy with non-Catholics. So they obviously mixed with these people, but they always bracketed their specific religion in those instances. It was considered good form not to raise the confessional question. Now, many of the professors in our Catholic colleges and universities have themselves studied at non-Catholic schools and consequently they are producing an entirely different mentality in their Catholic students. They are able to approach the non-Catholic mentality with greater serenity.

There is an impatience in our action. We think things can be changed from night to morning. They can't. This is a problem which faces a generation. One generation brings it to a certain point. The next generation takes it a bit farther. We must always think in terms of generations. I consider myself a member of the middle generation. The older men before me, the generation on its way out, certainly did not have the same point of view that my generation has. But, consolingly enough, they are not hostile to what's happening, though they are reserved. In my generation, yes, we began to go out more, to meet the non-Catholic. It was kind of pioneer work. But in the next generation what we did will be taken so for granted that they again will go out farther. This much we can prophesy without fear.

McDONALD: You have said that the question of truth is relevant to all discussion of unity and that the question of the quality of love is also relevant. Some Protestants, you have said, think that love alone is sufficient to unite, but your point is that there are different kinds of love, some of which are non-unitive. You have also said that non-Catholics are impatient with you when you bring up the question of truth. Reinhold Niebuhr recently showed such impatience in a review of Christopher Dawson's most recent book because Dawson insisted on the hypothesis at least of one true Church. What is the reaction of Protestants when you speak and say these things?

WEIGEL: Oh, they know this is what Catholics think and say. They don't get angry. But they do feel it's too bad. Theirs is the Anglo-Saxon, pragmatic point of view. They say, let's not worry about those things; let's get together in spite of that. It really doesn't make much difference what you do believe as long as we have enough to go on. That is their attitude and it is quite in accord with the theological basis of the World Council of Churches. Those churches are qualified for membership which profess faith in Jesus Christ as God and Saviour. That is the only dogmatic statement in the constitution.

McDONALD: As a matter of fact, do they all believe that?

WEIGEL: They do. They can all say that much. Of course,

they would understand it differently. Now this is what I call their "principle of comprehension." This is very appealing to the Anglo-Saxon mind. It's not at all appealing, though, to the Germans or the French.

McDONALD: If understanding is the only possible objective that Catholics at this point can strive for in these conversations, because of the ecclesiological presumptions of the World Council of Churches, it's possible to achieve a good measure of such understanding. Would the conversation just continue then and be concerned with social and civic questions?

WEIGEL: No. It might be that the working postulates of ecumenical conversation of the Protestant might change. If they did, then, of course, a new situation would be here and it might mean that Catholics could then enter into formally ecumenical conversations. I can't, at the present moment, foresee such a change, but I see it as possible and I refuse to say we cannot ever get into a wide-scale ecumenical dialogue.

McDONALD: Is it possible that what we hold can broaden, church by church? Lutherans apparently are now coming back to sacramental interest and they're talking more and more about the liturgy.

WEIGEL: Let me interrupt. There are, indeed, in the dogmatic positions of the different churches, elements which, if considered in isolation and given a verbal formula in isolation, seem to be the same. But when you see them in their own organic reality as part of a constellation they're different, really.

McDONALD: I know they're not the same. But they are looking for things which they seem to feel they have lost, or which were abandoned by their fathers before them.

WEIGEL: It's a mistake to think that the liturgical movement and liturgical interest in the Lutheran churches is entirely new. The Lutheran church in Sweden has had bishops uninterruptedly. Some Swedish Lutherans claim apostolic succession for their bishops. They also have what they call "High Mass." The Bach Masses were Lutheran Masses. In the Anglican churches, you had for well over a hundred years a liturgical revival. What is interesting is to see some Calvinist churches, the present American Presbyterians for example, beginning to take an interest in the liturgy. And Baptist churches in the North are being erected on the principle of liturgical structures. The Baptists may not have liturgy yet, but their churches are being built for it.

McDONALD: These stirrings of interest in the liturgy might give grounds for reasonable hope that they will serve ecumenical goals.

WEIGEL: The liturgical movement certainly has helped the ecumenical movement.

McDONALD: And Scriptural scholarship, too.

WEIGEL: There are three things that are distinctive of the Christian churches in our time. First, the liturgical movement. Second, the return to Scripture on the part of all. Third, what I call the "ecclesiological concern," manifesting itself primarily in the ecumenical hope. The Scriptural thing is very important. It started on the Catholic side with Father Lagrange, the French Dominican, back in the 1890's, the founder of the *École Biblique* and the *Revue Biblique*. He was farther ahead in his appreciation of Scriptural scholarship than were the Catholic leaders in his day. He realized that Catholics would have to do what is called the "scientific analysis" of Scripture. The non-Catholics had an even bigger difficulty with the Scripture. They were treating Scripture as if it were merely an historical source book. All this changed around 1920. By that time, the modernist experience of the Church was finished. And it was then that Karl Barth, the Swiss Calvinist, asked for a return to the Scripture, not as an historical source book but as a record of Revelation.

McDONALD: Did the Popes encourage this new Biblical scholarship?

WEIGEL: Lagrange, with the blessing of Leo XIII, started the new study of Scriptures. But it didn't by any means become universal in the Church. A certain amount of confusion was produced and Benedict XV, around 1920, came out with a document to furnish guidance. But the decisive Catholic document was *Divino Afflante Spiritu*, in 1943, by Pius XII, in which he blessed the Scripture scholars working in the new way. Well, the result was that when Catholics and Protestants went to Scripture as Revelation with philological analysis, they were doing the same thing.

McDONALD: With the same results?

WEIGEL: The same results and it's not at all surprising that they should. Consequently, today the Scripture scholars, Catholic and non-Catholic, depend on each other. They even meet together. The theologians of our time welcome the new Scriptural studies and all that they give, but they are also studying another kind of exegesis, the exegesis which the Fathers of the Church used, which is not the scientific exegesis at all. Read St. Augustine. In him, it's very clear. It's clearer still, though perhaps not as deep, in a man like St. Gregory the Great. The Fathers were not inventing a way of reading the Scripture. St. Paul likewise interpreted Scripture not in the light of scientific philology but by the rabbinical method which, of course, he knew. They were interested in the allegorical dimension of the Scripture, what Catholics call the "mystical sense." I prefer to call it the "ecclesiastical sense." It is not merely a question of what the words themselves say, but how the Christian community through the ages understood the text.

McDONALD: This brings tradition into it. To what extent are Protestants close to Catholics in this area of tradition?

WEIGEL: They have become very aware that it is impossible to pick up the book and find all truth there in a sterilized void. You approach the Scriptures with ideas which history and culture have given you. Albert Cook Outler, a Methodist theologian of Southern Methodist University, got out a book two years ago, which is an analysis of tradition. But the Catholic and Protestant notions of tradition are not identical. The Catholic notion is strictly theological. By tradition, we mean that teaching of the Church in the past, the present and in the future. For Protestants, tradition is not a theological notion, it's an historical one. By historical method, the Protestant finds out what the Church held in the past and this he believes should be guiding, but not normative, in Christian thought and life.

McDONALD: Apparently there is still an ultimate resistance to authority, then?

WEIGEL: No, no. We can speak of the genius of Protestantism, but I think it'd be very, very difficult to define it. Certainly Protestants do not define, but they will talk about it. I did attempt a definition in the book I have authored with Robert McAfee Brown. This—to quote myself—is the way I consider the Protestant principle for the Protestant genius: "It can be said

that the Protestant principle consists of three interrelated propositions. It is an affirmation that God must be experienced immediately in an experience which is non-conceptual and whose whole
intellectual content is not central, not specific. Because it is
primary it is self-standing and self-justifying. The second proposition states that the conceptual expression of the vague intellectual
content which will necessarily follow on the experience is a task
which the believer must perform in freedom. This freedom is not
absolute. Hence, the third proposition, which declares that there
is a check and that that check is the Biblical text. The conceptual expression of the epistemological content of this experience must be expressed in Biblical terms."

McDONALD: This is the way you would define Protestantism
after all your studies and all your experiences?

WEIGEL: Yes. This is what I consider Protestantism to be. I
know very well that Protestants will not take it just as it stands.
They do not believe that Protestantism can be defined, but that
it can only be lived.

McDONALD: I once interviewed a liberal Protestant minister
who frankly acknowledged that he was not particularly scandalized by the spectacle of separated Christian communities. He
rather thought it was good for Christianity that there not be one
church; he was, he said, afraid of the danger of a monolithic
power structure if all the churches became one.

WEIGEL: The formula that seems to be the one most used
now in Protestantism is "unity without uniformity." This is
what I call the "principle of comprehension." The principle of
comprehension is not rejected totally by the Catholic Church.
We see it so clearly in the matter of worship. Take all of the
non-Latin Churches: some belong to the Byzantine Rite, some
to the Antiochean Rite, and all these different Rites are within
the one Catholic Church. There is no uniformity of ritual. And
even local church customs vary. You have universal celibacy in
the West, but you have married clergy in the East, both equally
Catholic. But we do have unity—Orientals perform the same
seven sacraments, and they say the same Mass, but not in a uniform way. So there is a field for comprehension. The difficulty
for the Protestant is that he wants this comprehension to include
the doctrines of faith and the structure of the Church. You see

that best in the new Church of South India where, by a principle of comprehension, they have non-hierarchical Presbyterians accepting ordination, which comes into that church through the Anglican root.

McDONALD: Is the whole ecumenical objective retarded when some Catholics, as they occasionally do, picket a movie theater, for instance? Do all the old suspicions of Catholic intentions boil up again to the surface when such things happen in the community? What is the image non-Catholics have of us?

WEIGEL: Images are something that float in a community. Although they have a basic stability, they do undergo changes. If Catholics start a picket line outside of a theater, well, no great harm is done. Yet the action impinges on the general community. The Protestants have likewise seen their own people do similar things. Many Protestants are not too pleased with the militant anti-drink position which is one of the elements of the image of Protestantism in this country. I think these incidents are taken in stride by the total community. I don't think that, of themselves, they will hinder understanding if understanding is being sought. If you've a friend who's constantly blinking one eye, this distracts you and may even make you feel uncomfortable. But once you understand why he blinks his eye, you ignore it. You're well aware that he's blinking his eye, but you no longer concentrate on it. This is what I mean by understanding.

McDONALD: You've been in this dialogue, these conversations, for ten or twelve years now. Have you detected any change for the better in inter-group relations and understanding? Is the climate better now than it once was?

WEIGEL: The climate is better on the level where I move. With the non-Catholic intellectual, I feel that many of the crass and gross misunderstandings of twenty years ago have completely disappeared. You don't hear any more, for example, that Catholics believe every Protestant goes to Hell. That kind of thing is not believed on the level where I'm moving.

McDONALD: Are you ever surprised or dismayed to find somebody on this level, the intellectual level, who you think is friendly and even understanding, turning around and writing something very hostile to the Catholic Church?

WEIGEL: No, no, not at all.

McDonald: Is there ever any duplicity?

Weigel: No, no.

McDonald: You wouldn't call such attacks bigotry?

Weigel: Oh, no. I would never call it bigotry.

McDonald: They can understand and still attack you?

Weigel: Their understanding is not complete. They're like debaters, some of them. They want your formula and then of course they "go to town" on that.

McDonald: This raises a question of sincerity. Are they really searching for understanding?

Weigel: Everybody's sincere.

McDonald: You mean you have to assume that.

Weigel: No, I don't have to assume it. For me, it is absolutely clear. Sincerity proves nothing and sincerity is the one thing that everybody achieves. I never have trouble with people's sincerity. I am far more interested in finding out what they know. Frequently they know many things "which ain't so."

McDonald: What do you mean when you say "everybody's sincere?"

Weigel: I don't see how a man cannot be sincere.

McDonald: If somebody seems friendly and understanding in a dialogue situation, and then . . .

Weigel: A man can dislike Catholicism without hating Catholics. This is quite possible. Take a man like Niebuhr, a man like Paul Tillich. They're certainly very friendly and even respect the Catholic reality, but they are certainly highly critical of the Catholic idea. But this would not poison their relations with Catholics.

McDonald: I guess what I am getting at is that somebody may pretend that this is the Catholic position which he is attacking; he may even distort or misrepresent that position and you know, from your discussions with him, that he knows better.

Weigel: No, no, this is not true.

McDonald: You mean it doesn't happen?

Weigel: I don't think it ever happens. We have our minds made up on certain things. For example, what is the Jew? Now we talk to Jews and we find out that they don't actually believe what is an element in our concept of the Jew. We hear them say so. And we know they're being sincere and we listen sincerely, too. Now we understand that they don't hold this. But we continue with our old idea. We say: "Yes, he doesn't realize that Jews have to hold that. He is not logical. I know the real thing."

McDONALD: Is what you're saying, then, that there is a distinction here between one's notional and one's real assent to a truth?

WEIGEL: No, no.

McDONALD: People rationalize a reality to make it fit their conception of it?

WEIGEL: You always do that. In the example I gave, a man has defined for himself what Judaism is and he has accepted the general image of it. He's committed to it. The commitment is not too reflective. It is, however, strongly in his mind. He meets the Jew and the Jew tries to correct the image. But the man now adds to his image of the Jew a new element—"They don't hold it, which shows how illogical they are. They don't even realize what is in it."

McDONALD: You seem to be ruling out all possibility of malice when you say you haven't met anybody who isn't sincere, or that everybody is sincere.

WEIGEL: I believe that people can go counter to what they do believe to be good and true, but not in a matter like this. This is what I mean by a fellow knowing a "lot of things that ain't so." Merely by telling him they "ain't so" does not persuade or convince him.

McDONALD: What does persuade him? Experience?

WEIGEL: Experience, and not a single experience but a continuing experience.

McDONALD: Do you think our Catholic schools are doing enough? You once said you saw a preoccupation with apologetics in the philosophy classes of our colleges and universities rather than with the search for truth for its own sake and the adventure of learning.

WEIGEL: If the students are just being trained to be debaters then, of course, they cannot help the dialogue. Debate is exactly what is not wanted. Questions are not being debated. Questions are being subjected to scrutiny. It's not a question of one side against the other and then, by dexterous swordsmanship, one side cutting the other to ribbons. In current meetings, no one is debating. Even the man who puts forth his own position very strongly doesn't debate. He may try to justify his conviction, but he is not trying to persuade you. He doesn't expect, at the end of it, that you will drop your arms and surrender.

McDONALD: What's needed on the college and university level is perhaps no direct training for the dialogue at all.

WEIGEL: The dialogue does not want polemically prepared people. The preparation that's required is a psychological preparation, a readiness and a willingness and a friendliness to be with the other and to speak sincerely. Above all, we don't want "techniques" or Madison Avenue tricks. The motivation would come from the whole atmosphere of the school rather than from any "training" as such.

McDONALD: I suppose the theological virtues should motivate the students in the direction of the dialogue.

WEIGEL: I would say that the Catholic schools should see to it that the student knows the Catholic theological position, not as a professional theologian would, but as an intelligent man should. We must always keep the minds of the men and women open, not closed; not answer questions forever, because questions change their meaning as time goes on. A good answer in 1910 may be an awfully bad answer in 1960. There must be a readiness to accept the question as the question shows up, and not say, "Ah, *that* question. That is on page 96 in the book." No, no, no. It is a living question and must be approached by a living mind.

One of the most interesting developments, in Catholic men's colleges and universities, is that we have many laymen now teaching philosophy. It is no longer the exclusive preserve of the clergy. And even within the field of scholastic thought, there are many outstanding laymen. We need only mention a man like James Collins of St. Louis University, who stands way on top. I don't know of any clergyman who stands as high. I would say that we are evolving toward a Catholic college or university which is not going to be exclusively run by some Religious corporation. Little by little, the policy-making core of the college and university is becoming more and more general, with many laymen in it. In so many of the departments of our schools, laymen are already in charge and with very little meddling on the part of the high policy-making group.

McDONALD: Some Catholics believe the solution to our slender resources on the university and graduate school level will be for Catholic colleges, liberal arts colleges, to attach themselves to the large state universities, use their expensive scientific facilities and have the students take their science courses there. The set-up would be similar to St. Michael's College at the University of Toronto.

WEIGEL: On the American scene, the Newman Clubs are no longer conceived of as Catholic parishes for Catholic students at non-Catholic universities. The clearest example of the educational potential of the Newman Club is the University of Illinois set-up. I think out of sheer necessity, the Catholic center's function in a state university is going to grow. In such a center, courses are given in philosophy, theology and history and the university grants credits for them. All the rest is done in the university itself.

McDONALD: I have been interested in what you said at the beginning about preferring the terms "sacral" and "secular" to "Church" and "State." Relating to that, you once said that the secular community resents and is embarrassed by the prophetic function of religion. Do you think that there is any danger that the secular elements will ever swallow up or absorb the religious impulses? We hear talk these days of the idolization of democracy, for example.

WEIGEL: We have that danger already in this country. The secular never quarreled with the sacral here. It does worse; it tries to absorb it. The secularist says: "By all means, have a religion. This will make you a better citizen." Of course, this isn't the function of religion. One thing the secular will not accept from the sacral is the prophetic protest. For example, take one thing which Catholics oppose—pornographic literature. The general community doesn't like that Catholic position, not because the general community is in favor of pornography. It is just as much against pornography as are the Catholics. What the general community doesn't like is the sacral saying, "This is the will of God." It has to be *our will*. As long as your churches don't tell secular society what it must do, there's no scandal. If they merely preach what secular society ought to do, that's all right; it's up to you to decide whether to do it or not. This is our danger. We're in danger of becoming very Blanshardy. Blanshard doesn't object if the country goes against birth control, as long as it does it in a democratic fashion.

McDONALD: Morality by majority.

WEIGEL: It's terrible. Fifty-one per cent gives you the norm for all your action. Your views are to be gathered by a show of hands.

McDONALD: Is there any danger in any of this dialogue that Catholics, participants or observers, will fall into religious indifferentism?

WEIGEL: If the dialogue suddenly became general, if it is not prepared first by a group of experts, then the danger certainly would be there. That's why I insist that some experts be present always. Otherwise it can go into indifferentism, especially with the so-called common man who is not accustomed to think in terms of distinctions and who wants answers that are not "yes and no" but "yes" or "no."

McDONALD: Do you think the ordinary Catholic observer of the dialogue, the one who reads about such conversations, might fall into indifferentism over his religion?

WEIGEL: I think that generally his feeling is one of contentment with what is going on, because all the evil of hostility and closed anger on both sides has been for him a very unpleasant thing. He wants to get rid of it. I believe he is glad, when he sees these dialogues going on, and he thinks they may help us to push all this unpleasantness into the past. But I don't think it will make him indifferent about his religion because I don't think he thinks theologically. You must remember that indifferentism is a theological position. Yet most people refuse to essay any theological opinion. In this connection, I find that there's one theological question which is widespread, widely talked about and very misunderstood. People are always worrying about a concrete man's ultimate salvation and they always work on the basis that it's man himself who achieves it and that all that God does is to be a good umpire.

McDONALD: By "they," do you mean Catholic and Protestant?

WEIGEL: Yes. This is a widespread idea. In true Catholicism, the question of God's saving action is mysterious. And we claim, as the very basis of Catholic doctrine, that we don't know whom God saves. We never for one minute claimed that He saved everybody in the Catholic Church. And Catholics know this from the way the preacher pounds down at them. We also hold —and this was made very clear in the Father Feeney incident— that God can save those whom He wants to save, even if outside the Catholic Church. In saving them, He makes them somehow Catholic. This is our position. Protestants are very much worried by this, but Catholics are not. Whom God saves, well that, of course, is God's business and we pray and we hope that in His goodness He will save us. But salvation is His action. This is basic Catholicism. That is why the Church, no matter how sinful some of her members' lives may seem to have been, will still bury them and pray for them. What we insist on is a plan of God, salvific, a plan which does not strangle God. God can work outside of His plan if it suits Him, but He did establish a plan. That's what we're interested in, that plan. We don't tell God whom He is to save and whom He is not to save.

McDonald: There has been a "great debate" in some of our leading newspapers and magazines concerning America's affluence and its effect on our moral life. On one occasion you said that there are several things religion can do for secular society and, among these, you said: "At this moment of material abundance, religion can preach and live austerity." You feel, then, that there is a connection between affluence and moral softness?

Weigel: Yes. In theory there is no need for it. In practice, it will always happen that way. As I said in that same statement, if you haven't got much food, fasting is necessary. If there is plenty of food, fasting is a virtue and a virtue that's hard to practice.

McDonald: Marcus Aurelius has said rather ironically that it is possible for man to live well, morally, even in a palace.

Weigel: It's possible, but not probable. St. Thomas, I think, gave the real answer. A certain degree of prosperity, he said, is necessary to virtue. I would likewise say that a certain degree of prosperity is a menace to virtue. The Religious Orders have all seen this. Once they grow fat, the Religious Orders decay, decline and die.

McDONALD: What's the solution? Has this problem ever been resolved successfully historically?

WEIGEL: No. No one has been able to give the answer to this one. In the time of Emperor Augustus, you had a full-fledged, fostered propaganda on the part of the government to preach the old virtues. Horace was engaged in it. So was Vergil. But both worked under the pressure of the government. Yet the emperor was at the same time doing everything possible to make the empire richer and stronger. The people were asked to practice the ancient virtue, but it just didn't work.

McDONALD: Does it take a catastrophe? Must man start all over again?

WEIGEL: I agree with Toynbee that there is no necessity for a culture to die. If a culture does not fulfill its own promise, then it will die; it has to die. The thing that kept it alive was the promise. I am afraid this probably is one of the great dangers of our own culture. We fought for a hundred years to give to all men a great degree of material well-being—not just for some; it was for all. We worked on that basis and, God knows, we worked hard at it. By working hard at it, we did achieve not universal prosperity—there's plenty of poverty in this country, plenty of want, plenty of misery—but we did achieve a widespread prosperity; not universal, but almost general. We have now got what the country promised and what can it say now? "Let's keep what we've got and make it even better." Well, you can't sacrifice for that. Our basis is to keep what we've got and to sacrifice nothing.

McDONALD: Do you think our moral level is depressed?

WEIGEL: I don't think so, no. I do think that the community, instead of rigorizing and stiffening its moral vision, has definitely relaxed it. I do not say that this is good morality or that is bad morality. But the moral demands have been loosened. Relaxation of moral vision, at some moment, is going to become immoral. I don't know where that moment is. I don't want to state that what we have is good morality or bad morality. All I am saying is that the moral demand is being relaxed continuously. At some point—maybe we've reached it, maybe we still have to reach it—the moral demand will no longer be a moral demand. It will be a complete license in matters moral.

McDONALD: Relaxation, then, corresponds to a descending curve.

WEIGEL: Yes. At some moment, somewhere on that curve, morality as a public concern is no longer effective.

JOHN COGLEY

JOHN COGLEY, forty-two, a director of the Fund for the Republic's Center for the Study of Democratic Institutions at Santa Barbara, California, is a native of Chicago, where he attended Catholic schools, including Loyola University.

In 1938, he became associated with the Catholic Worker movement and ran the Worker's House of Hospitality in Chicago from 1938 to 1942, when he got married and entered the Army.

Following his military service, Cogley returned to Chicago where he helped found and edit *Today*, the national monthly magazine for Catholic high school and college students. In 1948, he went to the University of Fribourg, Switzerland, where he studied for a year.

In 1949, Cogley became an editor of *The Commonweal*, and in the autumn of 1954 he took a leave of absence from that magazine to gather the data and write the Fund for the Republic's widely discussed Report on Blacklisting in the entertainment industries of this country.

Cogley was appointed to the executive staff of the Fund for the Republic in January, 1956. His weekly column, "Here and There," appears in *The Commonweal* and is read closely by Catholics and non-Catholics alike.

He was interviewed on one of his many visits to New York. The interview took place in the Brooklyn Heights apartment of his old friend and a former *Commonweal* editor, William Clancy.

McDONALD: Would you say that your experience with The Catholic Worker in Chicago was decisive or pivotal?

COGLEY: The Catholic Worker was the really important thing in my life in Chicago. I was about nineteen or twenty and had run across a copy of *The Catholic Worker* in the back of a church. There was a little note in that issue saying that any Chicago reader interested in The Catholic Worker should go to 1841 West Taylor Street. The following Sunday, with my friend Tom Sullivan, I went to 1841 West Taylor Street and was involved from then on. That was in 1937. Most of the people there were older. Tom Sullivan and Ed Marciniak and I were among the younger ones.

McDONALD: Was it just curiosity that brought you there?

COGLEY: For me it was a whole new world. I think I was attracted to The Catholic Worker at first by two things: one was Ade Bethune's drawings in the paper. I had had saccharinity in Catholic religious art up to my ears, so much of it that I thought some kind of natural law required it. Ade Bethune's drawings, then, came as a welcome shock. Second, there was Dorothy Day's writing in *The Worker*. She wrote about concrete things, simply and directly, and about actual people. I had suffered from the parochial notion of Catholicism which every other little Catholic boy in Chicago had grown up with, but Dorothy Day and the *Worker* writers stretched out this world by relating the Catholic religion to the whole world around them. I had known, by some kind of instinct, I guess, that there was a larger world; I had always felt unhappy with the club notion of Catholicism. And remember, too, there was a lot of social ferment at the time.

McDONALD: Wasn't Monsignor George Higgins more or less a contemporary of yours then?

COGLEY: I knew George Higgins then. He was among the Chicago seminarians at the time who used to come around to the Worker house on their vacations. Monsignor Reynold Hillenbrand had influenced that whole generation of seminarians at Mundelein Seminary, made them aware of the social question. It didn't take with all of them, but it did with some, with Daniel Cantwell and George Higgins and some others who have since distinguished themselves in this field as priests.

McDONALD: What did you do at The Catholic Worker in Chicago? Was it like the New York house?

COGLEY: We opened a House of Hospitality in Chicago and ran it from 1938 to 1942, early in 1942. It was the straight Catholic Worker type of thing. We had two breadlines a day. We had a house full of people. I was there the full four years while others came and went, so that I had that experience first of all.

McDONALD: John, it seems to me that after the war and after your experience editing *Today* and *The Commonweal*, the really pivotal thing in your life was that Report on Blacklisting that you did for the Fund for the Republic. That was a turning point, wasn't it?

COGLEY: The other day I saw the current issue of the *London Times* and the *Times* referred to the end of a period in American life marked by the "death of McCarthy and the appearance of the Fund for the Republic's blacklist study." I didn't know it had that kind of significance for anyone.

McDONALD: Were you surprised by the nature of some of the reaction to the blacklist report?

COGLEY: No, no. I knew exactly what was going to happen.

McDONALD: I suppose the worst thing, from the standpoint of your reputation, was Congressman Walter's reaction to it.

COGLEY: He finally backed down on the whole business.

McDONALD: Yes, but the net effect was not calculated to enhance your reputation, and you were attacked savagely, particularly in some areas of the Catholic press.

COGLEY: I am sure that the people involved in what is called right-wing anti-Communism are very sincere. There is a right-wing movement that is broader than the Catholic section of it, but the Catholic section is very important because it is a letter-writing crowd and that's considered important because letters spell power. One can whip up letters through certain Catholic papers much more easily than through the same kind of secular papers. This kind of Catholic paper has trained its people to get in there and *write*. And not only can they write and argue and express themselves well; they can do it in the name of Christianity, God, the Church, the Bible, Christian culture. The shadow of the picket line or the boycott is behind every letter.

McDONALD: Do you think the situation is better now than it was ten years ago? I mean insofar as all these fears, emotionalism, voluntarism, phobias and anti-intellectualism are concerned?

COGLEY: Do you mean in the community at large, or among Catholics?

McDONALD: Both. You're working now in a broader field than just among Catholics.

COGLEY: I think there is a trend in American life toward withdrawing from complexity. Take the Broadway musicals that have been big successes recently—they're usually set in the period about 1912: *The Music Man, My Fair Lady*, the new one based on a Eugene O'Neill play, *Take Me Along*. All of them are about the simple American life in which the old virtues were respected and rewarded. There was another world "out there," even in 1912, but it really didn't make much difference to Americans. Then suddenly we had to face up to ideological complexities abroad and a growing complexity at home brought about by the growth of the country, by technology and all sorts of developments. Many tried to reject this new, complex life; they feared it, hated it and tried to find somebody to blame for it. I think this reaction, in one sense, speaks well for the country. It showed we had some kind of ideal of peaceful simplicity. But I think that this ideal is no longer possible. Now if you tie that rejection and fear in with something else which is specifically Catholic, you have a hatred of modernity. There is a whole group of Catholics, remember, who have never really accepted the modern world.

McDONALD: Is part of their problem one of vocabulary? Is it that they are unable to understand the historical reason for the Syllabus of Errors, or the special meaning of modernism in the nineteenth century?

COGLEY: The more sophisticated among them have heard about the Syllabus and can talk about it at great length.

McDONALD: But I mean there is a certain ambiguity in some of these words, like "liberalism" and "modernism." Some of these Catholics either will not or cannot see that the meaning of these words has changed considerably from the nineteenth century to our day.

COGLEY: I think there are two groups of Catholics concerned. The first is represented by the person who instinctively rejects modernity, at least as it is expressed by the intellectuals. He has

his problems adjusting his Catholicism to the world. And the
Catholic intellectual has a problem adjusting the world to his
Catholicism and his religious beliefs. Neither of them is without
tension.

McDonald: You don't feel uneasy, do you, or troubled in your
work?

Cogley: Yes, from time to time, I do, sure.

McDonald: You once wrote in *The Commonweal* that a Catholic, working in a "pluralistic" situation, must be willing to take
some of the criticisms without reading too much into them.

Cogley: During the last three or four years in my work with
the Fund I've been involved with a group that cuts across the
intellectual community. It's a fairly small group but it represents
all kinds of views. There are several Catholics involved in it,
including Father John Courtney Murray. I think that there is
rarely a time when I say something, or when Father Murray says
something, that some of the other people sitting around the table
aren't thinking, well maybe he's got a trick up his sleeve. One
time Father Murray was stating a position and he wanted to
state it logically, explaining how, step by step, he arrived at it.
"We will start off with A," he said. "Do you accept A?" "A"
was some perfectly unexceptionable statement, like black is not
white. One of his fellow Fund consultants said he would accept
the unexceptionable proposition but he wanted it known that he
had been on that kind of a train before, and he also wanted to
make clear that he was not getting on an express train but a
local so that he could get off at the next stop. . . . Well, this
is what I mean. There's this fear or doubt about where "Catholic" logic is leading and because of it the Catholic is not quite
accepted, sometimes for good reasons, sometimes for bad reasons. To say that the Catholic is completely at ease in such a
situation just isn't true.

McDonald: I didn't realize there was still this reservation on
the part of non-Catholics.

Cogley: There is. It would be foolish to say that the non-
Catholic intellectual is completely at ease with the Catholic.
He isn't. He may respect the Catholic as a person, but he still
has his doubts. The stereotype of the Catholic which one finds

among non-Catholic intellectuals doesn't come out of nowhere. It's reaffirmed time and time again in diocesan newspapers and elsewhere. So when the so-called "liberal" Catholic appears in public, the non-Catholic thinks one of two things: either here is one Catholic who is not a very good Catholic, or he must be playing some kind of game, he's going to trick us. This isn't always explicit, of course, but I think it's in the back of a lot of people's minds.

McDONALD: The lay Catholic is criticized, fairly to some extent, for not engaging himself in community and political affairs. And yet when he does get involved, he might be quite innocent or even make some honest mistakes, but he will be instantly pilloried in some very loud sections of the Catholic press and no voice is raised in his behalf with the exception of a dissenting editor or two. It seems to me that occasionally authoritative spokesmen should come out, not to give testimonials for individual laymen, but to affirm the need for lay engagement in the temporal affairs of the community, affirming that this engagement is necessary, that mistakes may occasionally be made. Of course, that can cut both ways. If churchmen do that, the seculars will think the Church is grinding an ax.

COGLEY: There's no objection to laymen participating in the social and temporal order, provided they do so in a kind of party-line way. If you barrage your Congressman with letters on an issue which has become a "Catholic" cause, that's marvelous. So long as you act as part of a Catholic bloc or a cadre. For instance, in the labor field, there's not too much criticism now of ACTU [Association of Catholic Trade Unionists] because it operates as a Catholic group.

McDONALD: You don't think there is much awareness, then, of Maritain's notion of participation in the temporal order for its own sake.

COGLEY: Maritain's important point is the autonomy of the political, temporal order. It's a complex idea and I don't think it's understood very well. He doesn't mean autonomy from principle or autonomy from doctrine. But he does mean there has to be an autonomy of judgment in a given temporal situation. You can't be calling the bishop, or have a chaplain at your side, every time something comes up.

McDONALD: The temporal order has its own legitimate ends and methods.

COGLEY: That's right, and that's where the error and the possibility of mistake come in. It's interesting to me that when one wants to get a spokesman for the Catholic tradition on a general subject, one has to go to a few priests. The same three or four priests seem to be carrying the whole burden. They're always being called in. I think that it is necessary to get more Catholic laymen involved in the temporal problems of the day. It is also necessary to get more Catholic priests capable of taking their place at a pluralistic round table, more Father Murrays, more Father Weigels, more Father Ongs. What I'm trying to get at is that the autonomy we have spoken of is not so much the autonomy of the layman but the autonomy of the temporal order, in which the priests may also play a part.

McDONALD: It would be easier for the layman, though. The clerical collar is a symbol of ecclesiastical authority.

COGLEY: We've reached the point where people think the priest expresses the Catholic cultural tradition by virtue of the fact that he wears a Roman collar, whereas he may not be doing it very well at all. The priest is just as subject to error here as anybody else. George Shuster, whom I consider a pioneer in this kind of thing, represents the Catholic culture better than most priests. He understands basic theology and he understands the "world" better because he's been out in it, involved in it. Yet I don't think the distinction is between priest and layman but rather between the temporal and the spiritual orders.

McDONALD: So far as function goes, though, the priest's function is more specifically spiritual.

COGLEY: I'm talking about the priest as a scholar. We've got a number of priests who, by profession, are intellectuals. They're listed in college catalogues as teachers and professors. So they have to abide by the rules of intellectual life in which there is exchange, controversy, dialogue. They can't suddenly pull the rug out and say: "Wait a minute, I'm a priest. I'm performing a spiritual function." In his role as a professor of English in a university, a priest is just like any other professor of English.

McDONALD: What I was trying to get at is that the priest is not ordained to be a professor of English, even though that may be his work in life. He's ordained to bless, to offer sacrifice, to shrive.

COGLEY: You're on a key subject, but a difficult one. I just feel the argument has been confused by distinguishing between laymen and priests rather than by distinguishing between two different orders of reality, the temporal and the spiritual.

McDONALD: Do you think the priests are taking their proper place as professional intellectuals?

COGLEY: A few are. I think there's a particular compatibility between the scholarly life and the religious life; they go very well together. The priest is free from domestic troubles. He's got other obligations, though, just as the lay scholar has the problem of being a husband and a father. But I think there is a special conformity between the priestly and the scholarly life. This, to me, would indicate that we should look forward to more good priest-scholars in this country. To the degree the priest is supposed to be a scholar, he's subject to the same criticism and the same kind of battering all scholars get.

McDONALD: Do you think he's unwilling to accept that?

COGLEY: Some, not all, are. Father Ong is willing to accept it. Some university priests, though they hold high academic office, don't consider themselves scholars. I think they, rather, consider themselves as pastors-in-the-classroom, saving souls in the lecture hall. This is a problem for priests, not for us. It's just an interesting thing, that's all. It's something that Orders engaged in teaching have to think more about.

McDONALD: To get to your work with the Fund, for a moment, and then maybe we can return to this. What is the general purpose of the Fund for the Republic and what is your function in it?

COGLEY: The Fund started in 1953, with a Ford grant, as a foundation specifically concerned with civil liberties. One of its functions was to make grants to other people doing work in the field of civil liberties. About a million dollars' worth of grants were made to Church groups in the South to keep the discussion going in the South, for example. The Fund also made grants to individuals and groups engaged in fact-finding projects in the area of civil liberties.

McDONALD: The ultimate objective was to enhance and to strengthen civil liberties?

COGLEY: Yes. The idea, and it seems like a naïve idea now, was that if people knew what was going on they would want to do something about correcting it. The presumption was that people were uninformed about the state of our liberties. Few knew, for instance, that some GI's were being given bad discharges, not for anything they had done in military service, but because they had belonged to an organization on the Attorney General's list before they had entered the service. Roland Watts did a study of it, showed what the facts were, and the Army changed its practice. Some things were more complex. The whole blacklisting business, about which there had been a lot of talk back and forth, turned out to be very complex.

McDONALD: Your assignment was to develop the facts in that?

COGLEY: Yes. It was to try to give the picture of what was actually happening in the entertainment industry. Due to a great extent to the blacklist report and the reaction to it, specifically to an article by Monsignor Francis Lally in *The Pilot* of Boston, the Fund began what we called a Basic Issues program. At the time the blacklisting report came out, Monsignor Lally wrote an editorial, saying these are the factual issues, what are the basic issues? He said there was a contest between freedom and security and he wondered who was concerning himself with the basic questions. When Robert Hutchins, president of the Fund, saw that editorial, it hit him like a ton of bricks. Ultimately, the board agreed that we had done about all we could do on the fact-finding level and that for the remaining life of the Fund we ought to work at this basic issues level, trying to clarify the issues and set up the terms for rational argument about them.

McDONALD: Who did the arguing on these basic issues?

COGLEY: We decided to organize a group of consultants who would reflect the pluralism of our society, not necessarily the religious pluralism, but the philosophical pluralism, reasoning that if society has got to come to some sort of conclusion about the basic issues and all these different viewpoints are found in society, then if we gather together a highly trained, disciplined group of people who will be representative of these viewpoints, they might together clarify the issues underlying the burning controversies.

McDONALD: Father Murray more or less has represented the Catholic viewpoint in these discussions, hasn't he?

COGLEY: Father Murray reflects the Catholic viewpoint, not the Catholic theological but the Catholic political-cultural tradition. The program, incidentally, turned out to be quite successful. At first, the group met about once a month. It was difficult because all these men were busy, had their own jobs; some were presidents of universities, for instance. But the idea was so promising that it was decided about a year ago to establish a permanent residence, setting up an institution for this kind of study as a permanent thing in American life. That is how the Center for the Study of Democratic Institutions began in Santa Barbara.

McDONALD: Before you moved out there, hadn't the Fund decided to study American life, the problem of democracy in American life, in terms of its major institutions, such as religion, labor unions, the press?

COGLEY: That's right. At first we thought we could get at the problems in terms of the freedoms guaranteed in the Constitution, freedom of speech, freedom of assembly, of religion, etc. Finally after long discussion it dawned on us that the problems we face today do not arise out of any attack on these constitutional guarantees as ideas, but rather can be traced back to the fact that there have been changes in American life, changes in American institutions. We have institutions today that either did not exist when the Constitution was written or are radically different from what they once were. For instance, political parties were not mentioned in the Constitution—nor labor unions. The corporation is a completely different animal from what it was then. American religion then meant Protestantism. Now we have a huge Catholic Church and a growing Jewish community in American life and a vast group of "secularists," so-called.

McDONALD: Have you been aware in these last five years of any contributions made by Catholics to the sum total of freedom or civil liberties, constitutional liberties? Or aren't you aware of Catholics as such in your work?

COGLEY: Not particularly of Catholics, but I am aware of a Catholic tradition.

McDONALD: Has it dismayed you that your fellow Catholics haven't been doing more in this area?

COGLEY: No, I think they're doing much better than they ever did.

McDONALD: Are they doing as much as the Protestants or as the secular humanists?

COGLEY: No, the secular humanists have taken over. They're the majority group in the intellectual community. It does seem to me, though, that there is a Catholic tradition in the temporal order, a tradition represented by Father Murray, for instance, who talks a great deal about the consensus of Western political thinking. I think this tradition has a great deal to contribute. As a matter of fact, I think that this tradition has been so badly stated in the past that people have never really understood it. When they do understand it, they think it's pretty good.

McDONALD: What do you mean by Catholic tradition? How far back would you go with that term?

COGLEY: I mean there is a notion of law, for instance, which has been preserved in the Catholic tradition. There is a notion of civic responsibility in that tradition. The notion of authority or the notion of freedom go back beyond the discovery of America. The consensus of the West which Father Murray talks about had its roots in Greek and Roman civilization. Then it had its medieval phase, its Renaissance phase and its Enlightenment phase. Now it has been given an American expression. It has taken a great deal from everybody. The problem, though, is that each group in our society, it seems to me, will accept only a part of this consensus of the West. The Catholics, by and large, would be delighted to stop at the medieval contribution—anything after that is of Satan. The secular humanists want to start with the Enlightenment—anything before the Enlightenment is reaction. The problem is how to relate all of these. Everybody wants to call off the search for consensus at the point where his group stopped being the leader.

McDONALD: Would this be related somewhat to something you wrote a year or two ago in your *Commonweal* column about

American Catholic theologians and the irrelevance of their theologizing, so far as the American political society is concerned? I mean, have the theologians, like so many of us, failed to come to grips with mid-twentieth-century reality?

COGLEY: I think there is a general feeling in America that Catholic theology is irrelevant so far as American problems are concerned. I've heard it said that Reinhold Niebuhr has had more influence on American foreign policy and thinking about foreign policy questions than any other individual in the United States. I don't begrudge Dr. Niebuhr this distinction. I know him well and admire him very much. I am very fond of him. But why is it that Catholic theology is considered so irrelevant? The Catholic theologian seems to see his role as one of pointing out error. Maybe the Catholic theologian thinks of his role not as that of a speculative thinker but as a defender of defined dogma. A book like Father Teilhard de Chardin's [*The Phenomenon of Man*] is speculative; it may not be without error, but at least it's speculative. We don't seem to have any speculative theologians around. We have dogmatic theologians. But dogma is only formed, it seems to me, after speculation has gone on in the first place. Father Ong brought this out very well, I think, when he was talking about the notion of person. He said that the philosophic notion of person was not explored at all until the theological problem of the Trinity arose. The impetus of theology, then, brought out the philosophic development of thought about persons with all kinds of implications that are very significant even today. That's what I was trying to get at in those columns. I hope I did not just seem to be whining and complaining.

McDONALD: I wasn't trying to maneuver you into a position where you inveigh, stereotype-fashion, against your fellow Catholics. . . .

COGLEY: No, I didn't mean that. When I talked about theologians getting relevant, I didn't mean relevance in the sense of the theologians saying this is wrong, this is right, this is a venial sin, this is a mortal sin. I was talking about the need for theological speculation on the problem of the times. We know much more about the universe than was ever known before. It seems to me the more we know about the universe the more we can know about God, and it is the theologians' job to make these discoveries.

McDONALD: Are we agreed that Catholics aren't participating as they should in the democratic dialogue? Nobody is, for that matter, I suppose, but what about Catholics as such?

COGLEY: My discontent is not so much that Catholics aren't participating. I have qualms, rather, about the style of so much Catholic participation.

McDONALD: That's true, we certainly had a lot of Catholic participation in the temporal order with the McCarran-Walter immigration act, McCarthyism and all the rest.

COGLEY: Some contribute well. In the Fund's Religion in America seminar a few years ago, I was surprised at the excellence of the Catholic participation. It seemed to me the Catholics there did very well.

McDONALD: But that was an elite group.

COGLEY: It was an elite group, but then by definition it would have to be an elite group. Well, if you want me to say Catholics don't participate enough, yes, they don't participate enough at the local, city level.

McDONALD: I don't *want* you to say it. I'm just asking you if we're agreed that they don't.

COGLEY: I think this is the finding of almost every civic organization, except the American Legion, that Catholics don't participate enough. But if you have a right-wing cause, then you have Catholic participation beyond the Catholic proportion of the population. Take Bill Buckley's magazine, *The National Review*. It's supposed to be a lay magazine, not a religious magazine, and not in any sense a Catholic magazine. But the percentage of subscribers who are Catholics, I would guess, is far higher than the percentage of Catholics in the nation.

One of the interesting things in this country is that the Church never lost the working class. But it did lose many of the intellectuals it once had. James T. Farrell, Fitzgerald—that generation either left the Church completely or became priests or Religious and became Catholic-type scholars who know all about the medieval period and could always be depended upon to dis-

tinguish between liberty and license, that sort of thing. We're
not in danger of losing the group of intellectuals who conceive of
their role as keeping the intellectual tradition alive *within* the
Church and articulating traditional Catholic culture, like the
Catholic Renascence Society. And we must keep the memory
of the old Catholic culture alive. But I'm talking about those
who are trying to relate Catholicism to the existing culture.
Whether they will stay in the Churdh or not, I don't know. I
may be overly pessimistic. But if the Church went to some
rather extreme measures to keep the working class in the Church,
I think the Church is going to have to go to some extreme
measures to keep the intellectuals in the Church. I think that is
the real problem of American Catholicism.

McDONALD: Isn't that strange? I'm sure the average European
Catholic intellectual would consider American Catholicism very
mild, quite unadventurous. Yet, the American Catholic intellectuals, for all their relative tameness compared to Europeans,
still scare off the conservatives and traditionalists in the Church
here.

COGLEY: I think the whole "Americanism" controversy in the
last century terrified the American Church. It was a kind of
trauma. After that there was an extraordinary conservatism in
the American Church. *The Commonweal,* for instance, is criticized for being so daring; actually it is very tame. In France I
don't think anybody would look on it but as a most orthodox,
even super-orthodox publication. What I'm really wondering
about, though, is if anybody cares whether or not the Church
loses the intellectuals. That occurs to me from time to time.

McDONALD: What evidence do you have to support your
opinion about the Church losing the intellectuals?

COGLEY: I don't want to mention any names. But in talk, in
private conversations, I know so many who are in a state of
tension. I think somebody in the Church has to start worrying
about losing the intellectual class.

III

Forum

III

SENATOR EUGENE J. McCARTHY

In 1948, thirty-two-year-old Eugene J. McCarthy, a tall, good-looking, dark-haired Catholic professor of economics and political science at St. Thomas college, St. Paul, Minnesota, decided, upon the urging of his friends and his own conscience, to run for Congress on the Democratic ticket in the St. Paul district. The House seat, long held by a Republican, was won—to the surprise of a good many people—by the soft-spoken McCarthy. He was subsequently re-elected in 1950, 1952, 1954 and 1956. In 1958, McCarthy campaigned for the Senate seat then held by incumbent Edward Thye and defeated Thye in a close, hard-fought campaign.

Senator McCarthy attended St. John's University, Collegeville, Minnesota, a Benedictine school, and completed graduate work at the University of Minnesota. He is married to the former Abigail Quigley and they have four children.

Senator McCarthy was interviewed in his room at the Hotel Pfister in Milwaukee, Wisconsin. He had come to Milwaukee to address the biennial National Catholic Educational Press Congress, sponsored by the Marquette University College of Journalism.

McDonald: Actually, you consider yourself a liberal. I realize labels are dangerous, but by your voting record and by your whole philosophy, you would be considered a liberal.

McCARTHY: That's generally accepted. I have my own definition of liberal and liberalism, but, with the limitations of my
own definition, I am quite willing to be called a liberal in the
context of current American politics.

McDONALD: Do you have the definition at hand?

McCARTHY: It's rather long. I think the basic distinction, if
we can make one, is in terms of attitude and of approach. The
liberal is normally somewhat optimistic, not blindly in the sense
that he believes things are inevitably getting better and better,
but that it is possible, through human attention and effort and
changes in institutions, and by being willing to make some effort,
that the general lot and the condition of living of mankind can
be improved. The liberal is not pessimistic; he doesn't say, "This
is a hopeless proposition."

He's normally willing to accept change, not simply for the
sake of change, but he says, "Well, now, we know at all times
there's need for improvement." He's willing to take some chances,
and he says: "I'll trust people, rather than mistrust them, and
I'll be a little bit generous rather than extremely selfish, and,
rather than betray people, I'll take a chance on being betrayed
myself." These are rather vague distinctions.

McDONALD: You say it's an attitude of mind, then . . .

McCARTHY: That's right. When you take these attitudes and
relate and apply them to action on a particular problem or a
particular issue, they tend to give direction to the issue, and to
the attempt to resolve the issue.

McDONALD: Would you include this in your definition of a
liberal, that he is less fearful of governmental action; not that he
is on the side of "big government" . . .

McCARTHY: He may or he may not be. I suppose you'd say
that so far as most of the domestic issues of the country are concerned—civil rights and labor and social welfare—that that would
distinguish him. But this is not fundamental to liberalism. There
could very well be a time when a liberal is the man who is
opposed to governmental action.

Take the case of a totalitarian regime. It was the conservative
support that was behind Hitler and the Nazi movement in Germany and it was the liberal who was in opposition. Actually in

recent American history the liberal position has been in support, for example, of the family-type farm, whereas the economic planner would be inclined to say, "While we don't want the government to take over the farms, we believe they must be built into larger units." Social and economic control over the lives of the people who work the land would be exercised not by the government but by a non-governmental power which might be just as destructive of freedom as if the government would do it. . . .

McDONALD: An area that is often talked about, sometimes not too clearly, is that of politics and religion. Did you encounter any religious bigotry in your recent campaign for the Senate? Samuel Lubell, in his pre-election articles, said that he had run into it in talking to voters and so he was not sure which way the election was going because . . .

McCARTHY: That's the kind of thing you can get a lot of talk about if you raise the question.

Of course, Lubell's thesis, I think, is that people vote religion and national origins, so when he goes out to make a survey, he's trying to prove his own thesis, you see, instead of going in to report objectively. I didn't see any more, so far as we were able to discover, any greater evidence of the religious issue in the statewide campaign than I used to find when I was running for Congress in my own district. It's my general opinion that if the issues are clear and if the differences are clear then religion is of relatively minor importance in a campaign. . . .

McDONALD: A question that is being asked, and increasingly so, now that Catholic Democrats are coming to the fore, usually goes something like this—and it's asked of a Catholic who might be a Presidential candidate—"If you had to enforce a law which was in conflict with the teaching or doctrine of your Church, to which would you be loyal, the law of your country or your Church?" . . . Will Herberg says that a man's first loyalty is to God, an answer that rephrases the question somewhat, changing "Church" to "God." Eleanor Roosevelt said a few weeks ago that she thought a Catholic could be elected President provided that on this particular question he comes out clearly and unequivocally and so that everybody knows his answer. This seemed to me an implied criticism, again, of the way some of the answers have come out.

McCARTHY: This is rather difficult, it's such a generalized question. It depends on the law itself and the content of it. For example, this is the same issue that was involved in the Nuremberg trials. We were willing to condemn Germans who had carried out what was the law of the land and the orders which were given to them. So we come round now and raise the same question and say, in effect, in principle: "Well, now, if you want to be President of the United States, you must act the same way as the people did whom we convicted and executed in the Nuremberg trials."

Let's take a divorce law, for example. We have it every day, the enforcement of laws relating to divorce in this country by Catholics and the determination by Catholic judges. I suppose you'd speak of the order in society which is involved in accepting what the majority of people at least, what the government and legislatures, have adopted in the country. This doesn't constitute a great problem. It's a question of the degree and the nature of the law itself. And you'd reach a point where you'd have to say, in effect: "Well, you could give up the office." This is what it would come to.

McDONALD: My own personal opinion is that it's kind of a phony question.

McCARTHY: I'd say there's no problem so far as the laws that we now have on the statute books are concerned, and this is all we really need to be concerned about. If the country changes why you'd say the man could resign, or, if he didn't carry out the law, you could always impeach him and you can vote him out of office in four years. This is more a practical problem than one of principle.

McDONALD: If Congress, by some strange mishap of history, were to enact a law requiring sterilization of the "socially unfit," as the Hitler regime did to some extent . . .

McCARTHY: I think a Catholic President would certainly be under obligation to veto a bill of that kind.

McDONALD: And not just because he's a Catholic . . .

McCARTHY: That's right. This would not necessarily be a

problem only for a Catholic. It could be a problem for anyone. This was the point that was raised by the Episcopalian Dean Sayre. He said we raise these questions as though they were problems only for Catholics and as though everybody else could do anything that the State ordered, and as though they were completely subordinate and subject to the determinations of the government, which is not true. Take Quakers, for example. You have almost a more serious problem with a Quaker President. What would he do with regard to the Department of Defense or a declaration of war? And you could find two or three other religious groups that are accepted in this country and the danger of their having difficulty is much more pressing and imminent than would be the danger of a Catholic running into this kind of conflict with government policy and determination. . . .

McDONALD: In the last two years, at least, there seems to be a sort of vagueness in the Administration, an indecision, and this criticism has come from members of both political parties. Senator Humphrey, your Democratic colleague from Minnesota, has said he felt it was very important that the Democratic majority in the Congress should assume, or provide, some of the leadership that seems to be lacking in the Administration in foreign policy matters and in some areas of domestic economic problems. How can the Senate do this constitutionally, or even logically? What things are "open" to Congress, what opportunities are present . . . ?

McCARTHY: It's quite difficult to do it. If we had a parliamentary system, such as the British have, then it would be relatively easy; but when the party in control of Congress does not control the White House and the State Department this is especially true in the field of foreign policy—it's extremely difficult to exert any great initiative or any great leadership.

In the last Congress, we did effectively move in the field of domestic economic policy, not as far as we should have, but in any case we were effective and I would expect a continuation from there. In the field of foreign policy I think there is one area in which we can be especially effective and that is in developing and I suppose you could say "putting pressure" on, if not providing, leadership to the Administration in the extension and in the improvement of the various economic aid programs, since these do not require the same kind of complicated and even secret negotiations that oftentimes are required in other diplomatic areas. I would expect and hope that we would be effective in that particular field of foreign policy.

McDonald: I think one of the things that could be said about Senator Humphrey's subcommittee on disarmament is that it did go out and develop certain facts and enlisted expert opinions which had an apparently discernible effect on some of the people in the Administration.

McCarthy: I'm not sure they developed facts that the Administration didn't have, but they took these facts to the public and they developed a kind of public mind and a public attitude, and a Congressional mind and a Congressional attitude which did have some effect upon the Administration.

McDonald: That's one case, I suppose, where investigation and the investigative function turned out to have a constructive and positive effect.

McCarthy: I think so. And I've proposed that we have joint committees in several fields, similar to the Joint Committee on Atomic Energy. This kind of joint-committee method has aspects of the cabinet and parliamentary system of government in which they don't quite take over the responsibility of administration in a joint committee, but indirectly they do. What they recommend is done and in certain cases recommendations by the Administration must have the committee's approval, so you'd set up almost a kind of direct veto power, a kind of reversal of the traditional roles whereby the legislature proposes and the President then says "Yes" or "No." In this case it works both ways and I would like to see something of the same thing done in the fields of intelligence and information, since I think Congress has a great responsibility there and there is reason to believe that either the intelligence service of the country is not adequate or that, if it is, Congress is not being given the measure of information they ought to have in order to pass properly on many questions. . . .

McDonald: Senator, you've often said that frequently a legislator has no opportunity to choose between black and white on particular issues and that there are sometimes only several "shades of gray" from which he must choose when he makes a decision. And I think you cited the McCarran-Walter immigration act as an example in which the choice was between what you considered a poor immigration law or no law at all. Now, I wonder, after hearing you say that and after watching Congress in action from afar, have you been subjected to criticism for the way you have had to make these tough decisions? And if so how do you handle such criticism?

McCARTHY: Let me say, it wasn't a choice between McCarran-Walter and no law, it was a question of the McCarran-Walter act and the existing law which had some inadequacies. Yes, of course, one is criticized for voting for what would be considered compromise proposals. The McCarran-Walter vote would be one in which this was involved since there were one or two things in it which were in the nature of an improvement. But since the great issue related to the question of national origins and other matters of principle involved in the debate, I felt it was better to support the position taken at that time by President Truman.

McDONALD: By that you mean you voted against the law.

McCARTHY: Yes, I voted against the passage of the McCarran-Walter act and, as you know, President Truman vetoed the same act.

Take the question of amendments to housing legislation, for example, amendments relating to segregation. This is an issue that has come before the Congress a number of times. You have to face a question as to whether or not, if you add an amendment of that kind, it would have the effect of defeating the whole program.

We had it in relation to the school-aid program, I think it was two years ago, in which it was argued that if this amendment were added Southerners would then vote against the school program and in consequence you would do nothing to advance the program of desegregation and of course so burden the education bill itself that it would be defeated. Well, as a matter of fact, I think that the addition of that amendment probably did have something to do with the defeat of the bill. But the general feeling at that time was that since the Supreme Court had spoken on this issue and since the issue was raised in relation to the school bill, there was a kind of obligation on the part of Congress to say: "Well, at least this time we will add this amendment to show that the Congress sustains the position of the Court."

Now I was satisfied that the second time around on that, once we made that position clear, we should then say: "This matter of integration is proceeding under Court decisions and so it's not necessary for us to add this amendment, which had become in the nature of a gesture which accomplished no real good in itself, except that it would put us on record again and it might have the effect of giving those who are opposed to this program anyway additional strength to defeat the bill."

So in that case if you were among those who voted against the amendment there would be those who said: "You departed from principle," whereas in fact you hadn't; you had made a practical choice. You're saying: "We'll get something that we want, something which is good and necessary and we have given up really nothing in substance, we give up only the appearances."

McDONALD: Is the matter of criticism a real problem? Or do you think the people are beginning to understand these complexities? Are they becoming a bit more sophisticated about this?

McCARTHY: I think they are somewhat more sophisticated, but it's the kind of thing that comes up in every campaign. In this last campaign, for example, I was criticized quite continuously for one vote on the soil bank question, a preliminary vote against it. A majority of the House, really, voted against the extension of the soil bank program, insisting that we wanted two provisions in it before we would vote for it. One was a $3,000 limitation on the amount of payment that would be made to any one farmer (the purpose of this was principally to have the program restricted to smaller farm units and to family-type farms). The second amendment related to the time in which the payments had to be made. We had found in the previous year, 1956, that the payments had been made just a few days before election and we felt that it was not the intent of Congress that the soil bank payments should be used quite so directly as politically partisan aids.

And so when these amendments were not included we voted against the program but when it came back—well, it didn't come back . . . the Senate passed a bill and we took it up after they passed it, with these limitations written in. Then we voted for the program.

But the criticism against me was that I had voted against this program which meant some $20 million of income to the farmers of Minnesota.

McDONALD: Now is it difficult to explain that in a campaign, do you get bogged down in details trying to explain it?

McCARTHY: You do get bogged down in details, and about all you can do in that case is to say: "I voted for the program." What I did finally was vote for it and the farmers didn't lose anything. And as a matter of fact my vote helped because this was a political move. The fact that we defeated it in the House moved them in the Senate to put in these limitations and so the "No" vote we cast resulted in better legislation than if we had gone along passively and had voted for it in the first instance. But sometimes it is extremely difficult to explain a vote of that kind.

McDONALD: Senator McCarthy, you said in an address at the Newman Club at Iowa City two or three years ago that we had better not talk about a "Christian" or a "Catholic" politics, since there has been no specifically Catholic State to which we can point in history as best exemplifying "Christian politics" or "Catholic politics." You said that the real test of a politician is whether his actions promote the temporal good of man and are orientated toward justice. Doesn't one's philosophy and Faith help determine one's definition of justice and the temporal good?

McCARTHY: I would say the temporal common good would not necessarily be different if defined by a Catholic from what it would be if defined by a non-Catholic if in each case you have a proper conception of the function of the State. I would say this, of course, that in a practical situation you would expect that a man who was acting in what we would call the Christian tradition of political thought (although that is not really a religious tradition but a cultural tradition), such a man's approach to politics would be somewhat different. And the consequences of having Christians active in politics should be manifest in institutional changes and in the kind of political action and political programs that might be developed.

But to say that a particular form of political organization— a monarchy or a Christian democracy, or whichever form we might want to take—is *the* Christian form is, it seems to me, extremely dangerous. The testimony of history is that, whenever such claims have been made for any political institution, usually there has been regret some time later about the fact that the claim was made. Some might say, "Well, that was a mistake; that particular institution was not really Christian; they shouldn't have called it that; but the one that we're advocating is." But, again, it's likely that the testimony of history would show that this second claim is also wrong.

McDONALD: I could see, however, that you would have a definition or a notion or a conception of the common good that, because of your Catholicism, your Catholic background, would be different from that of someone else. Of course, that's hard to pin down unless you have some specific issues such as the immigration law or perhaps some phase of foreign policy.

McCARTHY: You might hope that a Catholic would have a deeper concern for justice, although this is not necessarily true. I mean one could conceive of the good man of Plato as being as deeply and profoundly concerned about justice in terms of the arrangement of the temporal affairs of man. You might say that as a matter of fact this particular Christian may be more concerned but it isn't inevitable that he should be so.

McDONALD: Would a Catholic have more motivation to work for justice and the common good? Of course, a Catholic did help to write the McCarran-Walter immigration act, which would be an exception to the viewpoint that Catholics should be distinguished by their concern for justice. But I should think that a Catholic who really understands, for example, that God created the world for the good of all the people and not just for this group or that group, that such a Catholic's approach, say, to such a thing as an immigration law would be to favor a liberal concept of such a law; not that all Catholics would necessarily favor this particular law or that law, but all would favor liberality in the law. And all Catholics should be on the side of liberality in such a thing as world law, the rights of the laboring man, etc. . . . I know you can find exceptions, you can find certain Catholic Senators and Representatives who would be very reactionary in such matters. I'm not trying to put a denominational stamp on politics but I should think that one's theology and philosophy would determine a man's general outlook at least.

McCarthy: I think that's quite right. I would say that in the first place you would expect to find some reflection of the whole great body of teaching in the Catholic tradition relating to government and politics and the question of social justice and, well, even the simple distinctions between commutative and distributive justice. If you don't have a conception of distributive justice it's extremely difficult to reason with regard to certain problems.

This point was really involved in the debate over wheat to India several years ago. One member of Congress took the floor and made rather an interesting point—that government had no right to carry on charitable works for the citizens; that our responsibility and our freedom to act was limited to those things that could be justified in terms of justice. I responded saying that really we should not establish that this was an act of charity, that all we were proposing to do could very well be justified in terms of distributive justice. I said that the question of the state of famine existing in India and the surplus production that we had, was really a question in terms of justice. This would be a rather isolated example, but an example.

There is a question of methods too. We say this all too often and too freely that "the end does not justify the means." But certainly in the methodology of politics you would expect the Christian to be particularly careful about being truthful, not to misrepresent. And beyond that—well, you can be truthful and still pervert the people; you might appeal to the emotions at a time when people should be extremely rational, extremely calm. One can cloud issues, the Communist issue for example, by bringing in emotional overtones or implications when what is called for is a deliberate kind of examination. Certainly a Christian in politics should avoid that kind of appeal, not that he should never appeal to emotions because there has to be a kind of balance here. But it's a question of prudence and restraint.

And also I think this was almost answered in your question, the matter of attitude in something like immigration. Sometimes you can't be quite sure just where to draw the line; you can argue and say there are dangers on both sides of this proposition. But the Christian disposition, it seems to me, should be one that when there is a measure of uncertainty, the Christian, if he is going to make mistakes, ought to make them because he has been somewhat too trusting of people, either in our own country or in other parts of the world; or that he would make mistakes because he has been somewhat too liberal or too generous rather than because of a narrow self-interest and the fear that by helping other people he might do harm to them or harm to himself. A kind of openness, a kind of outgoing approach, it seems to me, should distinguish the Christian in politics. . . .

McDonald: If some intelligent young man had a strong desire to "get into politics" as an elected official, what advice can you offer him as to procedure and the logical order of steps he should take?

McCarthy: I think that varies so much from state to state, and even within states, it's a bit hard to give general advice. Ordinarily, if he's very young, I tell him I think he ought to keep an interest in politics but that he ought at the same time to get himself established in some business or profession before he makes the big move to run for office.

McDonald: By "young," now, I mean a man who would be about the age you were when you first ran for Congress, say, thirty-two years old or so. Did you have to start at the bottom level of party politics and work up?

McCarthy: You see, this is something that varies so much. If this were in New York my advice would be quite a bit different from what it would be in Minnesota; if it were in Chicago I'd tell him he ought to see Mayor Daley, I suppose, or, if he couldn't get that far, to talk to the ward chairman; whereas in Minnesota the way was quite open, you just kind of moved ahead and . . .

McDonald: But he should identify himself clearly and take a position so far as party is concerned?

McCarthy: That's right, and it's really quite easy, I think, to become active and to be accepted in the parties anywhere in the country because they're all desperate for help; they need people who are willing to participate in politics. I'd just say: "Go ahead wherever you see the beginning of an opportunity to be politically active; just move ahead if you have the ability and the continued interest unless you're caught in a terrible sort of political-machine situation."

McDONALD: Ordinarily, I suppose, there aren't any "short cuts." There are the Rockefellers and the Willkies, but normally you have to stick to protocol and procedures and begin at the precinct level and work up.

McCARTHY: I don't think so. I think that generally in the American political system the political opportunities are quite open.

McDONALD: What about government service other than elective? Do you think, from your observation in Washington in the last decade, that the pay and the prestige are sufficient to encourage intelligent aspirants for civil and diplomatic service jobs?

McCARTHY: That is rather a difficult question. I don't know about the pay; I suppose the pay perhaps is inadequate. But certainly there is little prestige attached to civil service generally, although within the civil service itself they've built up some lines of respect and prestige which the outside world, so to speak, doesn't appreciate.

I'm seriously concerned about the whole matter of civil service in this country. Our attitude is very different from the attitude, for example, of the British toward civil service. In Britain there is a great deal of prestige in service to the government; such service stands as high as service in private enterprise. We have that in some measure at the highest levels of government here, but the British have it even at lower levels.

One talks about this and people say: "You're for the spoils system. You want to destroy the civil service." But that is not the case, really. I don't know the whole answer to it but I do hope that in the Senate I'll have a chance to inquire into this question because this is related to a point I made earlier, that one of the responsibilities of the Senate is the administration of the government. I think that that involves a special Senate responsibility for civil service and for civil servants, and if we can open this up at least in some areas, why I think it would make for a better public service.

McDONALD: I suppose it's partly a matter of tradition which is hard to establish.

McCARTHY: Yes, we don't have that tradition in this country, but we can open up certain areas and lay the foundation for the tradition.

DOROTHY DAY

DOROTHY DAY, co-founder, with the late Peter Maurin, of the Catholic Worker movement and newspaper, was born in New York City in 1897. As a child and young woman she lived with her family in New York, Berkeley and Oakland, California, and Chicago.

She attended the University of Illinois and worked on the staff of the old *New York Call*, 1916-17. She was a member of the Socialist Party, the IWW and, later, various Communist affiliates, and wrote for various Socialist and Communist publications, including *The Masses*, *The Liberator* and *The New Masses*.

In 1927, Dorothy Day was converted to the Catholic faith. Five years later, she founded with Peter Maurin the Catholic Worker movement. Members of the movement live a life of voluntary poverty, dedicate their lives to helping the poor and the destitute, and publish a newspaper, *The Catholic Worker*, setting forth their social philosophy and principles and detailing the work of the movement.

From this movement, Houses of Hospitality and Catholic Worker farms sprang up in various parts of the country. The Houses, located in the large metropolitan centers of the nation, offer beds to homeless men and women, two breadlines a day and clothes.

The Catholic Worker philosophy is pacifistic and anarchistic (some members of the movement refuse to pay income taxes on the grounds that most of the tax revenue is used for military purposes); it emphasizes the person and personal responsibility, the works of mercy, maximum decentralization of all authority and organization—political and economic, and rural living to the fullest extent.

Because of her beliefs and her willingness to act on them, Miss Day has been jailed frequently—in recent years for her refusal to participate in practice air raid drills in the city of New York.

Despite the fact that many of her fellow Catholics do not share Dorothy Day's position on pacifism and payment of taxes, she is widely admired both inside and outside the Catholic community for her dedicated work with the poor and the outcast.

Miss Day is the author of several books, including *On Pilgrimage* and the autobiographical *The Long Loneliness.*

The interview with Dorothy Day took place in St. Martha's House, one of two Catholic Worker houses in Detroit, where Miss Day was visiting on one of her "pilgrimages" across the country. This Catholic Worker house is a few minutes from downtown Detroit; the area is earmarked for slum clearance within a year or two.

McDonald: Any discussion of you and the Catholic Worker movement must involve, it seems to me, Peter Maurin. When did you first meet Peter and under what circumstances?

Day: George Shuster, who was the editor of *The Commonweal*, brought us together. I had written a series of articles from Mexico for *The Commonweal*, very direct and personal articles about Tamar, my daughter, and myself. Tamar was only three years old then. I had written several articles about government and politics and religion, but it was only after I wrote these very personal articles that I got any reaction. It was the kind of writing that was very much the forerunner of the writing we do in *The Catholic Worker* now. I met Peter after I had been in Washington covering the hunger march there. That was in 1932, about five years after I had become a Catholic. I prayed at the Shrine of the Immaculate Conception that some way would open up for me so that I could work for the poor and for the worker. I felt this tremendous nostalgia for the work I had done with the poor and the workers in the past.

McDonald: You had been involved or committed almost from

the start, then, with the workers, beginning with your Socialist days.

DAY: Yes, as a Socialist and Communist. I felt this great involvement with them. I began by reading Upton Sinclair and Jack London. It wasn't London's later romances, but the stories of his Socialist days that interested me. And Sinclair's books, like *The Jungle*, which I think is still a great book. It does give a picture of the worker and the poor and their struggles, and their fall, too.

Well, I prayed at the Shrine of the Immaculate Conception in Washington. That is very definite; it isn't something I thought about afterwards. I was there on December 8, the Feast of the Immaculate Conception, and I made this fervent prayer. You know, St. Catherine of Siena once said she prayed so hard for the Pope and for the cardinals that she sweat enough to "bathe" them in it. Well I prayed hard, I prayed with energy and vigor. I just felt I was being absorbed in this petition. And I came back to New York and Peter Maurin was waiting for me. George Shuster had sent him to my house.

McDONALD: And that is how The Catholic Worker got started?

DAY: Well, Peter would sit around and talk with us. I was living with my brother and sister-in-law then, neither of them Catholic. Peter felt that what I needed first was an education. He felt that as a Catholic I had only a very limited view of Catholicism. Remember those "easy essays" of his? He would recite all those essays to me and bring them to me to read. Then he'd bring synopses of books. The first one was *Fields, Factories and Workshops* by Peter Kropotkin. It was about the need for decentralizing industrial work and doing more work on the land. It fascinated me. I had know the anarchists of the old days, Alexander Berkman and others. I had never known Emma Goldman—I didn't care for her from her writings. She was always talking free love and birth control and neither of them appealed to me. Fundamentally I had a good, natural attitude, I think, to love and family life, due to my mother and father. They had made a good home for us, a happy home.

McDONALD: Had Peter just come over here from France at that time?

DAY: No, he'd been here since 1910 or so.

McDONALD: What did you think of Peter when you first saw him? And what did he think of you?

DAY: I think that one of the marks of his sanctity is that he was able, with all the disabilities of his accent, his almost unlimited enthusiasm and even lack of judgment of people, to make such an impression on people. People never forgot him. And they really did start doing things and are doing them to this day because of Peter Maurin. As far as what he thought of me, I think he thought at first I would be another St. Catherine of Siena. He would go to people like Thomas Woodlock and John Moody and say, "Here is another St. Catherine of Siena." I guess he thought I would go to bishops and cardinals and be able to have influence. My whole instinct was exactly the opposite. I wanted to begin at the bottom, and I think my instinct was a right one.

McDONALD: What was Peter's program? Can it be summed up in a few points?

DAY: Peter's program was a simple one. He wanted to get out a paper and call it *The Catholic Radical*. He wanted to start with voluntary poverty and the works of mercy; you'd be forced into the voluntary poverty, really, because you'd be sharing everything you had. He also wanted farming communes and roundtable discussions for clarification of thought. He always said the scholars should become workers and the workers should become scholars. But the Houses of Hospitality were what he proposed for the bishops. He said this was the work of the bishops, to start Catholic Houses of Hospitality which, besides sheltering the homeless and the down-and-out, would also be indoctrination centers to take up all the social questions. But it ended up by our starting the Houses of Hospitality. I said to Peter once, "Was this the kind of thing you envisioned?" And he shook his head sadly and said, "Well, at least it arouses the conscience."

McDONALD: What was the actual beginning of *The Catholic Worker* newspaper?

DAY: I went to my spiritual adviser, Father Joseph McSorley of the Paulist Press, and he suggested I go to Mr. Menendez of the Press to find out how much it would cost to bring out a paper. I had asked a number of Order priests whether I needed permission to put a paper out and they said, "Oh, no, never ask permission." Mr. Menendez said it would cost $57 for 2,500 copies of eight pages each. Well, $57 isn't very hard to raise. I had had some money coming in for an article I had written and I didn't pay the gas bill or something—you know. We got the $57 and brought the first issue out. Peter was disappointed when he saw it and he went back up to the camp he had been living at in the Adirondacks, I suppose to think it over. I wrote about the interracial situation and about unions . . .

McDONALD: In very specific, concrete language?

DAY: Yes, and also it was very personal, bringing out the personal approach. I said we had written this on the kitchen table and that we would present it to people on park benches. Peter was shocked. He felt it lacked dignity and that it should be devoted just to serious discussions of theory. So for a while he had his name taken off the masthead of the paper.

McDONALD: But he was reconciled shortly after that, wasn't he?

DAY: Oh, yes, he came back in a month or so. But on that first issue of the paper I went out myself with a couple of young Catholics and we went out on Union Square. It was May Day and the Communists were just flooding the Square. We stayed all afternoon, selling the paper at a cent a copy and meeting with rebuffs and ridicule. I saw a lot of my Communist friends there. They wanted to know what the Church had to do with workers.

McDONALD: Did you start getting support through the paper?

DAY: Immediately. People began writing in and sending money to help it along. The very fact that we wrote it from that point of view, that we were writing it on a kitchen table, that we had no office and were beginning from rock bottom made them immediately contribute. People like Father Wilfrid Parsons, S.J., and Father John LaFarge, S.J., sent in money. The clergy began immediately to help us. They realized that things begin in this way. Then we took a store downstairs for an office and began organized work on the paper. And we began feeding people that came in to us, people who'd come in with hard-luck stories.

McDONALD: Is that how the House of Hospitality got started?

DAY: The House actually started when an unemployed, homeless woman came in with her belongings in a paper shopping bag.
Peter had written in the fifth issue of the paper about what the
bishops ought to do in the way of starting Houses of Hospitality.
He said people ought not to be forced to go to municipal lodging
houses. This woman came in and said, "Where are these Houses
of Hospitality?" We said, "There aren't any." She said, "Why
do you write about them then?" We were so touched and
smitten by this that we went down the street, rented an apartment and then begged a bed and bedding and put her in it. She
was the first inmate of a House of Hospitality. Then we took
in other women. Then we took some apartments for men and
rented a house on Charles Street. After about two years, we were
given the use of a rear house on Mott Street and that had 20
rooms. We took in immediately a bunch of striking seamen, so
we had to rent more apartments in the front house. From then
on, we were very large—38 rooms, actually, and in 1936, three
years after the work started, the breadline started. Before that,
we just fed those who came in and sat down with us. The more
we gave away, the more came in.

McDONALD: That has been the history of your work all through
the years, hasn't it? Every time you're down to your last dollar,
more comes in.

DAY: Yes. You give all your furniture away, more furniture
comes in. You give your blankets away, some more blankets
come in. You give every bit of food away and food comes in,
or money comes in. You give everything away and it just returns.
We've always had bills. Pope Pius XII said, "Never be afraid of
running up bills for the poor." So we just charge things at the
grocer. Listen, a bag of beans, what does that cost? A sack of
potatoes . . . I remember some meals we'd have mashed potatoes
with mushrooms on top. You'd buy a few pounds of mushrooms
and chop them up and make a big, rich gravy, flour gravy, and
put them on top of a big dish of mashed potatoes. You can
imagine what a wonderful meal that was. You go down to the
fish market and you go late in the morning, after their work for
the day is done, and you ask, "What fish have you got left
over?" For a dollar they'll give you a hundred pounds of fish.

Can you imagine? There's always the possibility of getting food. You can beg food from neighbors. But the rent, that's the hardest part, finding shelter. It's our biggest problem. When we were forced out at Chrystie Street last year—more urban development —we had to pay $800 a month in rents. I don't know how much we're paying now, I haven't figured it up. We're paying $100 a month for the loft on Spring Street. We're paying from $25 to $45 a month for each apartment, we have eight apartments. We're paying $10 a night, $300 a month, on the Bowery for beds.

McDONALD: Then you're not all under one roof.

DAY: No, we feed people in the big loft and have meetings and clothes rooms and offices there. It's the biggest space we've ever had and cheerful and comfortable. But it's two flights up and hard for the poor and the crippled to get up there. But the apartments are very cheerful, they're small and homelike and the staff is scattered amongst the apartments so that each one is responsible for a few people. It's much more like a family than an institution. We still own the house on Staten Island which is a farm and that houses about 25 people and can be used for retreats and conferences. And we still have two beach houses to house families in need.

McDONALD: It seems to me that there are two things which you and Peter and the whole Worker movement have done. One is to be a witness to Christian principles among the poor and the other is the indoctrinating of your philosophy. Can you have one without the other? Do you expect everyone to go along with your indoctrination and philosophy?

DAY: It was natural for Peter to indoctrinate, he was the agitator and the teacher, that was his job. But all of us are more or less forced into indoctrinating by the work we do. No, we don't expect everybody to live in Houses of Hospitality. But we do expect everybody to perform the works of mercy and to make personal sacrifices, whether you're visiting the sick in the hospital, whether you're giving some of your week's salary to someone who is down and out, whether you're helping a friend pay his rent— everybody's obliged to perform works of mercy. But for us, it all goes together. The works of mercy are feeding the hungry, clothing the naked, sheltering the harborless, visiting the sick

and the prisoner. And what is war? It is the opposite of the
works of mercy. War lays waste the fields, it destroys homes, it
wounds and makes people sick. It is absolutely the opposite of
the works of mercy. So you're driven into the position of
pacifism by the very works of mercy. You don't do all these
things and then patch everybody together again.

McDONALD: But many people help you in your work even
though they don't share your views on pacifism and anarchism.

DAY: One reason they help us is that, in spite of all the
propaganda against personal charity and in favor of State aid,
in spite of the fact that they're always being told not to give to
beggars but to give to organized charity, they are drawn to do
personal works of mercy. The natural feeling in their heart is
that they should perform these works of mercy. They love God
and they love their brother and so they go ahead and do the
works of mercy themselves and help us do them.

McDONALD: What were some of the other points in Peter's
program, I mean, besides pacifism and anarchism?

DAY: Peter emphasized liberty and voluntary co-operation. He
said the destitute should never be asked to give something for
the food and shelter we gave them. The fact that they were in
need was the call they made on us. We weren't supposed to say,
"Here, work for your bread." Work, he said, should be voluntarily given. Man should not bargain with his labor over a
counter. And he believed in changing the social order and that
is why he didn't like social workers. He said they tried to make
people adapt themselves to society, but that we were to try to
change society. And he used to say there is no unemployment
on the land. People would write in and say, "What do you
mean, there is no unemployment on the land? Look at all our
farm labor people unemployed." What he meant was that if
we had farming communes, which he first called "agronomic universities," where the worker would be a scholar and the scholar a
worker, there would be the security of the community. People
wouldn't be looking for insurance or pensions or wages. Everybody would have what he needed. There would be no unemployment because there would be work for the aged. Nobody would
ever be too old not to have some kind of contribution he could

make. He could sit by a roadside stand, selling tomatoes, or he could feed the chickens or open up the gates for the cows to come through the field. He could do all kinds of little things. So the old would have employment and the young would have employment. And that was another thing: Peter believed everybody should have work to do, the work of their hands. He said there would be fewer nervous breakdowns if men used their hands more.

McDONALD: Then the anarchism and pacifism and non-payment of taxes is all a kind of protest?

DAY: No, Peter said he liked to shock people, it made them think. So he used words like anarchism. But the theory in back of the philosophical anarchism is that of decentralization, of communes, of voluntary co-operation and mutual aid, without the State control and without centralized power. An anarchist society would be made up of a whole group of free associations. Suppose every parish in a city would go ahead and get a farm outside the city. There would be employment for the unemployed. There'd be food for the poor of the parish. There would be work for young people to do. There would be a center for indoctrination and discussion. There'd be a place for folk dances and music and cultural activities. There'd be all the things that Roosevelt very beautifully did in the way of dealing with the problem of unemployment. When you think of all he did for young people . . .

McDONALD: You mean the CCC camps?

DAY: That and the work projects, the artists', writers', actors', music projects. Young people were looked after and their various abilities were developed.

McDONALD: But that was the government stepping in and you would not consider that an ideal, would you?

DAY: No, but the depression was a great emergency. The ideal is that these things should spring up in the neighborhoods and in the parishes. You hear people say, "Well, given human nature as it is, no matter how ideal the social order, don't you think greed would enter in and class war and all the rest?" They always want to discourage you. They always point out that this "can't be done." My reply always is that we are a redeemed people—I'm speaking now just from the standpoint of Catholics. I say we are a redeemed people. We receive all the help necessary through the Sacraments. We participate in the divine nature. But you say that to a whole student body and they don't know what you're talking about. When you say we are participators in the divine nature and that we have the divine life of Christ flowing in our veins, that we "put on Christ" when we receive Communion and that we should be Christ to others— they don't understand that at all. But they are very interested and they are looking for work and for the ideals.

McDONALD: Then idealism isn't dead among the young people?

DAY: Absolutely not. One of the things I noticed on this trip was that young college students are giving themselves to the missions—some of them for a vacation, for the summer, or for an entire year. Gonzaga University sent about ten students to the Jesuit mission in Alaska last year. It's just the way the Mormons and the Seventh Day Adventists expect their people to go out and give a year to the church.

McDONALD: You have said in your writings that you must have a lot of faith to do the work you do. Have you ever been tempted to despair in your work?

DAY: St. Teresa of Avila said that when her nuns got discouraged she would "feed them steak." If you get discouraged, sometimes there is a physical reason for it. Maybe you just plain need to take a day off and read or go to a show or a good concert. I think you're constantly renewed every day by the Sacraments. I think daily Mass and Communion is essential, absolutely essential. I don't think I could continue to live without that. I think when people go to daily Mass and receive Communion daily they're happier, they're readier and more alive to what God wants of them.

McDONALD: How many times have you been put in jail, Dorothy?

DAY: I think about seven times. I was jailed twice before I was a Catholic, the first time when I was working with the suffragists down in Washington, not because of the vote but because of the rights of political prisoners. That was part of our radical activity at the time. The second time was a raid on IWW headquarters in Chicago; I was kept in jail over the weekend. Then in New York it's always been on account of the air raid drills. This will be the sixth year.

McDONALD: What are you trying to accomplish by these demonstrations against air raid drills? Are you trying to make people consider your position by these protests?

DAY: You're not obliged to obey a law that is against right reason and air raid drills are against right reason. There is no defense against hydrogen bombs. And we do believe in nonviolent resistance to evil. It's not easy to defy the law. All of us have an innate respect for the country and for law and order. It's difficult to go ahead and face the condemnation of people who say, "Who do you think you are, having this pacifist point of view?" But you do reach people with your protests. Last year, I had a big placard quoting Pope John who has said that war is "massacre and suicide."

McDONALD: You want to make people think and reflect, then?

DAY: Yes, and there is a second objective, it is to visit the prisoner, which is one of the works of mercy. That comes about incidentally, but it is very rewarding to be able to be so close to people who are in extreme destitution, to see their needs and to be able to help them in some way. The very fact that a policewoman in the New York jail has started a Legion of Mary group which meets on Monday nights, and that they are making some effort now to bring religious literature into the jail, and that they have made three pleasant dormitories to replace some of the hideous cells—these are all changes for the better.

McDONALD: Have they been done because of your influence when you were in the jail?

DAY: Oh, yes, I am sure of that. If you go into the jail in a spirit of friendship and love you're going to get co-operation. One of the first attitudes we saw in jail came from the policewomen and other officials who asked us, "How can you bear to come here and share the company of such degraded and terrible people as these women are? Do you know that this woman hired somebody to kill her husband and that woman poisoned her children?" And when we replied that we should find Christ in everyone, that these are the poor and that we are supposed to love the poor and go to them and visit the prisoner, regardless of their guilt or innocence, the superintendent of the prison wanted to know if we were Christian Scientists. He thought we were denying the existence of evil.

McDONALD: Have you seen any of the effects of these changes inside the prison so far as any of the prisoners are concerned?

DAY: The last time there was a touching incident. A young Negro girl was in the dormitory right across from me. She was the mother of two little children and was a drug addict and prostitute. She prostituted herself to get money to buy the drugs. One day she brought a book over to me. It was the autobiography of St. Thérèse, the Little Flower of Jesus, and this girl said, "Oh, if I'd only had a home like the Little Flower had." Imagine a little drug addict, a little prostitute, identifying herself with the Little Flower and saying that if she had had such a home life she could have been more like the Little Flower.

McDONALD: And how sad to think that she would be going back, though, into that world of drug addiction and prostitution.

DAY: Well, God's grace is such that we don't know what will happen to her. Do you think she will ever forget this book? And as long as they keep trying and keep trying. She may fall another seventy times. But that book she read in jail may be her way to final salvation. Another incident was a woman kidnaper waiting trial kneeling down with seven other prisoners each night saying the rosary.

McDONALD: If I were inclined to differ with you, Dorothy, I would think your most difficult argument would be in this matter of pacifism. Wouldn't it be foolhardy for a nation to disarm unilaterally, to lay down its arms out of pure love for one's fellow man when another nation is bristling with arms and makes no secret of its aggressive intentions and objectives?

DAY: I should think that that would be so clear, though. I mean, on the one hand you can't do evil that good may come of it. You have to go ahead and follow all the principles laid down by St. Thomas, the conditions for a just war—and all those principles are now violated. So we can't possibly keep up with the Russians with the kind of weapons now being used—nerve gas, poison gas, germ warfare, indiscriminate killing of civilians, women, children, the aged and sick. We're not permitted to go out and commit even one venial sin to bring about the salvation of the world.

McDONALD: But you can defend yourself.

DAY: You can defend yourself, but what about the means used to defend yourself? You are not permitted to use any means whatsoever.

McDONALD: Of course, your "limited warfare" people would argue that it is not necessarily true that hydrogen weapons would be used, or that germ warfare would be used. I am not so optimistic about that, however.

DAY: Yes, and they talk about using the "clean bomb." Isn't that an awful deceit though? And how could we use limited warfare and Russia not use limited warfare?

McDONALD: Are we faced, then, with an impossible dilemma, in which on the one hand we leave ourselves wide open to possible annihilation and on the other hand we employ immoral means to defend ourselves?

DAY: I think it's an impossible dilemma unless we think in terms of non-violent resistance. There are many, many ways of resisting the aggressor. There has been a long history of how the conquered overcame the conquerors, again and again. And besides, during the war we were content to have Russia as our ally. Now we've got Germany and Japan for allies. We shift around all the time. Next thing you know, we will be having Russia as our ally against China. So I would say right away that that is an argument against war.

McDONALD: Undoubtedly it's true that the conquerors eventually are overcome by the conquered, but that's small consolation to the immediate generation of people who may have to live in slavery.

DAY: In the long run, non-violence does win out and it's not always such a long run either. You see, I have a very strong feeling that Our Lord is right over there in Russia, too. All the churches there have the Blessed Sacrament—they're a schismatic not a heretical church. They have the Blessed Sacrament all over Russia, in all the churches. Religion is rather strong there.

McDONALD: Certainly at a moment of great crisis in Russia, when Hitler's armies were at the gates of its great cities, the rulers didn't appeal to the people's allegiance to Marx or Lenin or scientism, they appealed to their loyalty to Holy Mother Russia.

DAY: Yes, and if we're all brothers, then the Russians are our brothers, too.

McDONALD: You think there are ways, then, in which passive resistance can win out?

DAY: I certainly do. We do not ever call it *passive* resistance. We have good examples of non-violent resistance among the Negroes in the South right now. And in Mexico, there are still anti-religious laws on the books which are all more or less openly violated without any punishment from the State. Look at the French Canadians, conquered by the English. The French in Canada have remained unconquered. They have their own language and religion and culture.

McDONALD: You have been working all your life with and for the poor. You have seen many people and observed a tremendous variety of social and working conditions over the past thirty years or so. Would you say that despite our present prosperity people are more restless now than they were, say, during the big depression?

DAY: I'd say we have *more* poverty. For one thing, we have more of what they call "unemployables" today in our kind of profit-motivated economy. During the war, when they needed manpower, they hired epileptics and men with ruptures and cripples, but when the war was over, all those men were fired. Now all kinds of men are considered unemployable. A man over forty-five—you can't imagine how hard it is for him to face unemployment, especially if he has any disabilities whatever. And look at the living conditions. In this urban redevelopment, people say, "Aren't you in favor of doing away with slums?" I say, "Not the way they're doing it, no, not at all." In St. Louis, where I came through last week, they have torn down 250 acres of slums. Where have all these people gone? No provision has been made for them. People are all doubling up. Same thing here in Detroit. And if people have to live under those circumstances, don't you think they're bound to become more neurotic? There's no quiet, no peace, no space. And they're more rushed than they ever were.

Listen, the first need is for some living space for ourselves and our families. In New York, they're taking four-room apartments and dividing them up into two-room apartments and getting twice the rent for them. Look at the rent the Negro and Puerto Rican pays. I've seen people pay $80 a month rent for two-room shacks, just hovels. Helen Caldwell Day, out in California, had her last baby in her doctor's office and still paid $225 for his services. Can you imagine? She had her baby, picked up the baby and went home. We had a Legion of Mary meeting at her home shortly after that and I said to her, "Helen, do you suppose it's because you're a Negro that you were so overcharged?" Another woman said, "Why, no, not at all. That was not discrimination against her. I've had to pay the same fee and I do the same thing. I prefer to have the baby in the delivery room at the doctor's office and go home, I want to be home with my family." In New York, a whole family will be taken out of a slum apartment which is to be torn down and they will be put into a single room of a rooming house. There may be one toilet for four families in that house and half the time it doesn't work; it runs all over the floor. The filth and the squalor are unspeakable.

McDonald: The usual criticism one hears is that these people in the slums wouldn't be there if they didn't want to be there.

Day: They say, "Why did the Puerto Ricans come to this country anyway?" Well, one of the things we do have in New York is free medical care. These women can go to Bellevue Hospital and have their babies for nothing. And they have clinics. I know one young girl who is an epileptic. All she has to do is go every other week to the hospital, the epilepsy clinic, for her free medicine which has done away with the five fits a day she used to have. It is magnificent medical care given by the city. It isn't by the state or by the Federal government.

McDonald: But you would consider such aid less than ideal, also, wouldn't you, because it is governmental.

Day: But it's the community, the city.

McDonald: Where would you draw the line between desirable

and undesirable organization and organized effort? The ind
ual on his own cannot do everything for himself, can he?

DAY: We're not against organization as such. A community
or a village is an organization. A family is an organization. Peter
used to talk about the need for organizations of employers to
work with unions and Don Luigi Sturzo talked about the corporative order as opposed to the corporative State—that is, a series of
corporations of unions, businesses, doctors' groups, lawyers'
groups. That would be a community of communities. It's the
"third way." You've got the American way and the Russian way.
And the communitarian approach with emphasis on personal
freedom and personal responsibility, all organization decen-
tralized so far as possible, that would be the "third way."

McDONALD: Then you are not opposed to such charitable organizations as the Catholic Charities in our large cities, or the
St. Vincent de Paul Societies?

DAY: No, but these should not be highly centralized.

McDONALD: I suppose centralization comes in in the name of
efficiency, managerial efficiency.

DAY: Yes, but it's not really efficient. As a matter of fact,
Catholic Charities groups are known as "referral agencies" now.
In other words, they study a situation and then refer you to the
appropriate governmental agency. They'll take care of you tem-
porarily until you can get to a governmental agency.

McDONALD: Do you think the parish is the logical instrument
to restore some of this person-to-person charity among people?

DAY: It begins with the family, then the neighborhood and
parish.

McDONALD: So many of our metropolitan and even suburban
parishes are vast and impersonal, with thousands of families in
each of them.

DAY: Ade Bethune says that we should have many little
churches, that, instead of one large parish with six priests, there
should be six small parishes, each with a priest.

McDONALD: Dorothy, you wrote in one of your books that
you once woke up in the middle of the night, on one of your
trips, and that you were on the verge of tears, you felt so un-
wanted and unloved and lonely.

DAY: That was when I was on a long trip and I was homesick. I asked myself why I was wandering around the country talking. That was out in Kansas. I remember it very plainly. But then I had the most wonderful feeling—I suddenly thought how important I was, you know. I was a child of God and of great importance. My Father was a King, I was the daughter of a King. I felt a great sense of how important we are, that each of us has a mission.

McDONALD: Do you feel that what you're doing is almost inevitable so far as you are concerned, that you're bound to do what you do?

DAY: I feel it's a vocation. It isn't everybody's vocation to do this. It *is* everybody's vocation to love, however, and we all want to love. Each of us has a vocation but a different way to accomplish it.

McDONALD: You're doing it the hard way?

DAY: No, it's easy for me because that was my background, you see.

McDONALD: When you first came into the Catholic Church, did you feel you could no longer work with the poor as you had done before?

DAY: Yes, I did feel that. I felt there was no place for me. And when I went out to work in Hollywood, writing dialogue, I thought what a dishonorable vocation this is!

But I had become a Christian from working with Socialists and Communists. Peter was the first one I met as a Catholic who talked about the social order. I think a lot of converts have a rather lonely time of it. I think one of the functions of The Catholic Worker is to build up a real sense of community among people. A young man came to one of our meetings last winter. You felt he hadn't found himself yet, that he was at a loss. That young man did one of the sweetest things I have ever seen done around The Catholic Worker. I had put in the paper that poor John Pohl had lost his radio and he loves music so. He lost his wife, he is an unemployed printer and he has been in and out of a mental hospital, but he loved his radio and somebody had stolen it and it was the greatest loss in the world to him. I said in the paper that if anybody had a radio to give, they should bring it and give it to John Pohl, to nobody else. Well, this young man was working in an old people's home, a nursing

home—it's usually the last ditch; when you can't find any other
job, you can always get one at a place like that—and out of his
salary he bought a brand-new little radio and gave it to John
Pohl. Wasn't that a sweet and wonderful thing to do? But he
felt such a sense of belonging to a community that he wanted to
help him.

McDonald: You have also mentioned in one of your books
about one's need for companionship and you related the story
of how one priest asked what you knew about marriage and
family life since you had none. You were thirty-eight at the
time, I believe, and you said this started you thinking and reflect-
ing on a woman's need for family.

Day: I remember feeling to myself that I resented the fact
that Tamar and I were not considered a family. I think a woman
always wants a family. I think my work is a vocation, though,
and when you have a vocation, you give up some things for
others; not that the things you give up aren't very good. As a
matter of fact the better they are, the greater your sacrifice when
you give them up for something else. But, down at the beach
we have these two small houses. Last summer we took in a
family who were awfully nice and I used to like to be with them.
In the evening, we'd sit around and we'd bake bread and pies.
It was wonderful. They were a delight to have with you and I
had that sense of family then. We did all the nice things together, as a family would.

McDonald: You have said that you rebel against talk about
"sanctifying" one's surroundings because if something is not good
to begin with, you cannot "leaven" it.

Day: Do you think you can sanctify a Madison Avenue advertising agency or a public relations firm in the hire of Trujillo?
Imagine! I think there's lots of things we just have to walk out
of. You may think you're going to be able to make some dent.
You may go out to Hollywood and think you're going to be able
to produce good movies, but how many get produced?

McDonald: I know you are not a sentimental romanticist, in
fact, you have said that one could not have gone through the
twenty-eight years you have gone through with just a romantic
motivation or idea.

Day: You know how young people have a romantic attitude

about St. Francis and his poverty. It all sounds wonderful. Then they come down to The Catholic Worker and they think they're going to be another St. Francis and they see the greed on the part of the poor, some of them pushing themselves forward and they get discouraged with the poor and they get discouraged with themselves, and they see all our faults and get discouraged with us.

McDONALD: You couldn't sustain yourself on a romantic notion, you had to have faith and a real sense of vocation.

DAY: We don't have any illusions. I had my illusions knocked out of me before I became a Catholic.

McDONALD: In your book, *On Pilgrimage*, you said that it is always a "terrible thing" to come back to the Catholic Worker House in New York after you've been away for a while. Why do you say that?

DAY: It is a terrible thing and it will be terrible to come back now. For one thing, there are so many calling upon us for help. We have more than our share. It shouldn't be as crowded as it is. We shouldn't be as overwhelmed as we are. I mean, there's never a moment, from morning until night, when there are not people coming in and making demands on you. One case of human misery after another, one crisis after another. We've even had people sent to us from South America, from Mexico, from Chicago, from Binghamton and Ireland.

McDONALD: By whom?

DAY: By people who feel they can't do anything with the situation. They say, "Let's send them off to The Catholic Worker." You have a priest calling you up from Brooklyn and saying, "Have you got room to put up a woman tonight?" Well, how many families has he got in his parish? Isn't there one Christian family in his parish that he can call up and say, "Can you put up this woman for the night?" No. He has to call up The Catholic Worker. I said to him, "Don't you think it's pretty terrible to send a woman through these slums at this hour of the night to come over and have a bed? Isn't there even a little boarding house where you could pay for a bed for her? Isn't there a family that will take her in?" I mean, great numbers of people have not been taught anything about the personal obligation to practice the works of mercy. If every Catholic parish had some kind of a mutual aid center then everything wouldn't be piled up on top of one group. Once there were two veterans who had their pensions and they started a little House of Hospitality in Washington. Well, many of the Religious Orders down in Washington began sending people who appealed for aid to them. Every time a beggar appeared at the door, they'd say, "Oh, there are two men down there starting a House of Hospitality. Go down and see them." The two veterans got terrified and gave up. We are a large staff but overloaded with work, so that when I go back, that . . .

McDONALD: That's what depresses you.

DAY: It's just too much at once. If you're in the routine, you can in a way take it.

McDONALD: In all of your travel across the face of this country, you've had a chance to compare people now with what they were in the 1930's and 1940's. Would you say American Catholics are more aware of their social responsibilities now than they were in your early years?

DAY: I think they are. And yet there are still very few Houses of Hospitality. They turn to the state instead. And they're not aware of the peace problem at all. In England there was a demonstration this Easter in Trafalgar Square, 75,000 people all demonstrating for peace and against nuclear weapons. But America and Russia are the countries most involved. All the others are terrified about what we're going to do, both sides. And when the Popes speak against war, they speak about both sides, not just about Russia.

McDONALD: So many Catholics think that our biggest problem is the problem of the relationship of Church to State and the relationship of Catholic to Protestant and the condition of our Catholic educational system. Yet in all our discussion here you have not mentioned those problems. You would say, then, that the major problems, as you see them, are those of peace, of work, of the works of mercy that should be practiced?

DAY: Those and man's relationship to the State, his attitude toward the State. He's turned himself over to the State. I spoke up at Boston College and the other colleges in that area and the feeling on the part of the students is that "we owe everything we have to the State." They felt a great sense of allegiance to the State, as though it were Holy Mother State. We've just gone Marxist, to that extent, without realizing it. Man and the State and war and peace—those are the greatest problems of the day because they both come down to man's freedom, his personal responsibility and his freedom. We're given free will, free choice. It is a gift—this freedom to choose good or evil, or to choose the better rather than the good. And I think one of our greatest evils is greed. We want everything and I don't mean just money or food. We want everything. We have such enormous appetites. We want to experience everything. We don't exercise our choice. I see this in a lot of young people.

McDONALD: But one does have to have certain wants to drive him to certain accomplishments.

DAY: You have to have wants, but you have to make a choice between those wants and say, now which do I want most? After you choose your objective, you have to eliminate a lot of other things. You have to do without a lot, and not only do you have to do without sin, you have to do without many good things, and I'm not just speaking about the spiritual order now, in order to choose God.

McDONALD: You have said that "we are still trying to work out a theory of love, a study of the problem of love so that the revolution of love, instead of that of hate, will come about and we will have a new heaven and a new earth wherein justice dwelleth." Do you think, then, that your work is still incomplete?

DAY: You have to keep on writing and talking about these things until people begin to see what you mean. If they can't understand you, it just shows you haven't been clear enough about it. The first point to make to one's self and others is that we begin with ourselves in this life work of growing in the love of God and the love of our fellow men.

McDONALD: Are you willing to revise any of your positions if somebody can prove to you they are wrong?

DAY: About peace, and about all these things?

McDONALD: Yes, about the basic fundamentals of your position?

DAY: Oh, how could they be wrong? It's the Gospels, how could the Gospels be wrong? I could say we've probably stated our convictions badly. I do think I understand far more than people think I understand of their predicament, of their objections. I am not a simplist, a spiritualist. Sometimes I make myself clear. Other times I'm not able to convey ideas. But I understand the situation a man is in, for instance, if he is harboring a Negro and a mob of people is at his door demanding the Negro. The question is a real one: how much force would we use, how much would we battle for this person we are protecting? I think the answer to that, though, is how far have we developed our spiritual strength so that we can overcome, by moral force, those forces of evil represented by the mob? I read a story once about a mob which had gathered at a Southern jail demanding a Negro prisoner and the one officer at the jail went out on the steps and quelled that mob. He had moral force. Others might have been terrified and just given way. That officer might just have been contemptuous and have possessed armed strength, I don't know. But the thing we need to emphasize is that tremendous force of love so that people come to be convinced what it means to be a son of God, that they are but dust, yes, but that they are also a "little less than the angels." These are the things we have to keep trying to bring out. Remember those quotations from my favorite epistle of St. John— "There is a stronger power at work in you than in the world," and "If we love one another, then we have God dwelling in us."

MONSIGNOR GEORGE G. HIGGINS

MONSIGNOR GEORGE G. HIGGINS has been a member of the Social Action department of the National Catholic Welfare Conference, Washington, D.C., since 1944. He has been director of the department since 1945.

Monsignor Higgins was born in Chicago, in 1916. After completing his training for the priesthood at Mundelein Seminary, Chicago, where he came under the influence of the then rector,

Monsignor Reynold Hillenbrand (a man intensely interested in social action and reform), Monsignor Higgins went on to the Catholic University of America for postgraduate work in economics. At Catholic University, he specialized in labor economics under Monsignor Francis Haas (later Bishop Haas of Grand Rapids, Michigan), a pioneer in the field of social action.

The Social Action department at NCWC is primarily concerned with labor-management problems, the conditions of workers, particularly minority-group workers (migrants, Mexican "wetbacks," et al.), and with the general problem of relating economic activity to the common good of American society.

In addition to attending and taking active part in numerous labor, management and joint labor-management meetings throughout the country, Monsignor Higgins is a member of the Public Review Board of the UAW-CIO, a final review board empowered to adjudicate certain grievances brought before it. Monsignor Higgins also writes a weekly column on social action problems for the Catholic diocesan press in this country.

The conversation with Monsignor Higgins was recorded in New York where he was attending a meeting sponsored by the Foreign Policy Association.

McDONALD: I have often thought that something like a conversion accounts for a person's interest and participation in social action. I know that in my own case, I wasn't really concerned with social problems until I read Pius XI's encyclical, *Quadragesimo Anno*, years ago. For me that was an eye-opener.

HIGGINS: My interest in labor started in the seminary, I think, and partly because of my father's interest in labor and unionism. I remember he took me downtown in Chicago one time to hear Monsignor John Ryan give a lecture on labor; that made an impression on me, though I was only in grammar school at the time.

McDONALD: I sometimes wonder why it is that some people, when exposed to *Quadragesimo Anno* or to a lecture by a Monsignor Ryan, get the fever, get all excited about social problems, while others can remain quite indifferent.

HIGGINS: To me, that's an insoluble problem. I have oc-

casionally said, rather facetiously, that it must be a matter of
temperament, but obviously that's not a serious approach to the
question. I think that we sometimes, unconsciously perhaps,
assume that if we can get a person to read the encyclicals, or
attend a certain number of courses, he will seriously concern
himself with the problems. I don't think it necessarily follows
that he will. I am inclined to think that the specialized technique of the Young Christian Workers and Young Christian
Students and the Christian Family Movement—while not the
only technique or always the "best" technique—may be psyscho-
logically more effective than our reliance on the straight study
approach. What YCS and YCW and the CFM do is to get
people interested first in a specific problem and then show them
the relevance of Catholic teaching in that area.

McDONALD: You are not suggesting a de-emphasis of study,
merely that it should follow rather than precede personal involvement.

HIGGINS: Yes. And I would add a footnote to what I said
about the specialized movements. I think you can exaggerate the
technique and turn your group into a sort of "group dynamics"
thing by which people who do not know very much are expected,
simply because of the group context, to be able to instruct people
out of their own ignorance. There has to be some intellectual
content.

McDONALD: Do you have any knowledge of the extent to
which seminarians are being exposed to the thought and teaching
in the Papal social encyclicals?

HIGGINS: My guess, and it's a sheer guess, is that perhaps a
fourth of the seminaries have a specialized and rather systematic
course on the social encyclicals. I would suspect that the remaining seminaries pick up the social problems in some way or other,
perhaps under special ethics. I don't think that's sufficient.
Father Joseph Munier's work at St. Patrick's Seminary in Menlo
Park, California, is outstanding in this regard. Not only does he
give the seminarians an adequate course in the social encyclicals
and Catholic social teaching, but he also spends a good deal of
time discussing the lay apostolate and the function of the priest
in training lay people. He's trying to prepare them psychologically

and intellectually for the formation of lay leaders in the social action fields. I think that is important.

McDONALD: Is the curriculum in our seminaries too crowded in most cases for a special course in social problems and the Church's social teaching?

HIGGINS: Seminary professors in this day and age are expected to give a smattering of knowledge in so many fields that it's difficult for them to find the time to cover all of them adequately. I have great sympathy for them in the problem they're facing in the curriculum. I'm personally not as critical of the seminaries as some people are. I'd like to see more social action studies, naturally, but under the circumstances I think it would be almost sufficient if the seminaries succeeded in doing this much—helping seminarians realize that serious social problems exist, that they should be interested in and concerned with those problems, and that they should develop an appetite for serious reading in the field which will continue long after they have left the seminary.

McDONALD: You implied a division of responsibility between priest and layman in the social field. Do you conceive of the priest's role as one of guide, who would exert a formative influence on the layman? Some priests have been much more active than that; some have walked the picket line in a strike and exhorted the workers at company gates.

HIGGINS: The general principle, and this is quite clear from Papal teaching on the matter, is that the primary role of the priest in social action is one of helping to educate the layman and above all to form lay leaders spiritually. Normally, priests should not be expected to enter directly into the affairs of the labor movement. But, having said that, I would want to make allowances for exceptional cases. You mentioned priests on picket lines. I would say that, first they were a minority and, second, in most cases I am familiar with, there was a reasonable justification for their action. Circumstances at the time might have been such as to convince them that that was the only effective way to carry out even their educational role. That kind of dramatic action, by the way, is almost ancient history now. It occurred during the depression when labor's right to organize was being openly and vigorously defied.

McDONALD: What has been the social-minded priest's relationship to unions, a sympathetic advisory one?

HIGGINS: The success of American priests in the labor field can be attributed, to a great extent, to the fact that the vast majority of them did not become involved in the political affairs of the trade union movement. In the best sense of the word, they kept their place. They were never, with very few exceptions, suspected or accused, by either Catholics or non-Catholics in the labor movement, of interfering in the internal affairs of the unions. I think the majority of priests involved in this work are highly respected by the labor movement on that score, among others. The priests, perhaps by instinct, have played it very correctly, I think. They have carried out their own primary function of encouraging lay leadership, of defending labor when labor seemed to need defense, but of not getting involved in the internal affairs of the union organization. I think labor leaders, by and large, feel the priests have been in this thing for very disinterested motives, that they were not in it to advance what you might call the institutional interest of the Church, but to encourage the labor movement itself.

McDONALD: It seems to me that the unions, at least on the leadership level, have been and continue to be interested primarily in what have been called the "bread-and-butter" problems, the *ad hoc* problems, and haven't shown much insight or perception so far as long-range problems are concerned. Nor do I see a great deal of understanding of the relationship of unionism to the common good. One manifestation of this is the almost complete lack of attention paid by union leaders to something like the industry council plan, which some Catholic social thinkers have been discussing for years. As recently as the last steel strike, for instance, we had a settlement based, again, on very immediate considerations—another wage increase for labor, another ultimate price increase for management, and no regard for the common good. I know there have been exceptions. Walter Reuther, right after the war, wanted to negotiate with General Motors on a "let's-look-at-the-books" basis, something which begins to get negotiations out of the narrow wages-and-profits consideration and into the area of the common good.

HIGGINS: This is a difficult subject on which to generalize. The charge is frequently made that American labor unions are too exclusively concerned with bread-and-butter issues, that they have too limited a philosophy, often described as pure business unionism. And to an extent that's a valid criticism. But so-called business unionism has certain virtues which may be a good foundation for our going into something better. The American unions have placed major emphasis on collective bargaining. Unions in Western European countries have tended to look down on the American unions; the European unions are more concerned with a broader social philosophy. But now that American unions are established and, in most cases, securely established, at least in the big industries, they have a solid, healthy foundation on which to expand the whole concept of collective bargaining, the collective determination of issues in an organic, natural way, even into something that might lead to an industry council plan.

McDONALD: Do you see any indication among union leaders of an awareness that there are deeper and more fundamental issues than the *ad hoc* issues?

HIGGINS: Yes, I do. The awareness is not always or clearly articulated and it is more apparent in some unions than it is in others. Let me give you just two current examples which show at least the beginnings of that awareness. To me, the most hopeful part of the steel settlement was that clause written into the contract calling for the establishment of a joint labor-management-public committee, two committees: one to study the problem of work rules, the other to take a joint look at the economics of the industry. These committees are advisory, but they are a step in the right direction. Now I would rather see the unions and management grow into the industry council plan by that natural, organic way, than to try to get the ICP, as some Europeans are trying to do it, by legislation, or by some doctrinaire, ideological approach. The other example is the recent contract between the Armour Packing Company, and the Packinghouse Workers. Automation is an increasingly serious problem in the packing industry. The company and the union agreed to establish a joint committee—labor, management and public representatives—to study, first, the problem of automation in the company and the matter of re-training workers who may be hurt by automation, re-allocating jobs and that sort of thing. Again, that's only a straw in the wind, but it is growing out of collective bargaining and there is a recognition on the part of both union and management that automation is too big a problem for either one of them to solve, that it has implications that go beyond the immediate contract and situation.

McDONALD: How can the common good, the general welfare, however you want to phrase it, be represented in labor-management relations? I suppose the problem is to give the common good a voice without sacrificing some other values that we already have on both labor's and management's side?

HIGGINS: I think we're a long way from the day when labor and management will agree to have a third party sitting in at collective bargaining negotiations. I think the problem is too complicated to hope for that as an immediate answer. What I think I discern, and perhaps I'm too optimistic, is a growing awareness that it *is* a problem that must be thought through. These joint committees I've mentioned are steps in the right direction. Another factor that will push us in the right direction, I think, is the common fear on the part of labor and management that if they don't find some way of working together more sensibly than they've done in the past, they can expect more government intervention in their affairs. The temper of the country being what it is, and our international situation being so perilous, I think it goes without saying that no Administration in Washington is going to tolerate major breakdowns in any of the major industries. So if labor and management cannot voluntarily find some way of solving their problems more effectively, we're liable to find the government trying to do it for them. They know that and I think that may hasten them in the right direction. At least, that's my hope.

McDONALD: What are some of the major problems facing the labor movement?

HIGGINS: I'd say that obviously number one is the problem of organizing the unorganized, primarily in those areas of the South, industrial areas, which are not organized. Then there is the whole field of white-collar employment. I would expect that

within the next five to ten years that will be the major center
of attention, organizing drives by the unions in the white-collar
field. I think that's going to take time, but I think it should be
done, at least in the larger institutions, commercial and manu-
facturing institutions which employ large numbers of white-collar
workers.

McDONALD: You would say that even though the workers are
receiving just wages and enjoy good working conditions?

HIGGINS: Yes, I would.

McDONALD: In other words, organization is good for its own
sake.

HIGGINS: I think we have done less than justice perhaps to
Catholic social teaching over the years, for understandable reasons. We have put too much emphasis on the negative reasons
for organizing, that workers have a right to organize to protect
themselves. And that's perfectly true. But I think the time has
come to put a great deal more emphasis on the necessity of
organization as the normal means through which people carry
out their responsibilities to one another and to the economy as
a whole. It seems to me that white-collar workers are no different in that respect from blue-collar workers. Waiving for the
moment the whole question of whether, in fact, white-collar
workers are receiving just wages (in many cases, I think they
aren't), the best short treatment of this question of the nor-
malcy of labor organization is the statement by the French
Canadian bishops in 1951, I believe. It is a masterful summary
of the philosophical basis for the Catholic approach to labor
organization.

McDONALD: If the union organizers take a negative, hostile
approach, would that not tend to alienate management? The
owners and managers would look upon unions as an intervening
thing, something coming between themselves and the white-
collar workers, and resist it. If you could get this other idea
across, that union organization is the normal and ordinary way
in which workers can fulfill their social responsibilities, there
might be less opposition from management.

HIGGINS: I would hope that there might be less resistance if
organization were presented in this full perspective.

McDONALD: Yet organizers, by and large, take the negative, hostile approach, don't they?

HIGGINS: Yes, I suppose inevitably so, unfortunately so. But opposition on the part of management is still substantial and it seems to be almost inevitable that union organizers will fall into the usual pattern of trying to convince workers they need this protection of their interests, which, of course, they do. That's one side of the coin. I was only suggesting the other side to round out the picture.

McDONALD: Are labor unions well established, well accepted by and large? We have had in recent years this whole "right-to-work" controversy, this push for anti-union-shop laws in the states. Is that a real threat or a receding one?

HIGGINS: I think these laws, which are on the books in seventeen or eighteen states, will slow down organization of new workers, but I do not subscribe to the theory of some labor leaders that the labor movement is going to be put out of business by them. The mystery to me is why the powers that be in big industry haven't spoken out against the "right-to-work" people. I think big industry knows unions are here to stay and even wants unions, needs unions for the orderly handling of industrial relations problems. Yet few, if any, of the leaders of big industry have taken a public stand against this anti-union legislation.

You asked what some of the problems of labor are. One, I think, is sheer bigness of some unions and how to preserve democracy in a big organization, how to get a reasonable amount of participation by the rank and file members in the affairs of their union. The common stereotype in some segments of the press is that labor leaders are power-hungry, that they don't want rank and file participation and will obstruct it. I think most labor leaders—and I know most of the important ones in the country —are just as concerned about rank and file participation as anyone else is. Frankly they don't know how to secure it. I think we moralists have tended to oversimplify the problem. We have asserted on a number of occasions that a trade union member has an obligation to attend all his union meetings, or the majority of them. It seems to me that that's an obligation we don't impose upon people in any other area of life. We say a man has an obligation to vote, but we don't say he has an obligation to attend all the meetings of his political party. If he's a stockholder he is not expected to attend all the meetings of the corporation. I don't think we're going to solve the very real problem of rank and file union participation by a utopian emphasis on complete attendance and participation in all union meetings. I think the unions are rather going to have to find some way of securing adequate representative democracy.

McDONALD: Would that be comparable to our delegating of political responsibility to our representatives in Washington?

HIGGINS: Some sort of delegation, yes. The majority of labor leaders are very much concerned about this. They're baffled for the same reason that people in other organizations are baffled by the problem of bigness, the mobility of the American population, the distractions of modern life, the multiple demands on their time, the increasing emphasis—and a very good emphasis—on participation by men in family life. All these changes are taking place in American life.

McDONALD: The fact that a worker no longer lives close to his place of employment, that he may live a half-hour or an hour away, would affect his inclination and even his ability, I suppose, to attend union meetings.

HIGGINS: Yes, there is a completely different problem. George Meany once said that when he was an apprentice plumber coming up he would no more have thought of missing a union meeting than he would of missing Mass on Sunday.

McDONALD: Perhaps attendance at meetings in those days was a way of identifying oneself. Then workers were just numbers on a payroll or on a time-clock ticket. Today they belong to other organizations in which self-identity is possible.

HIGGINS: That's right. That was particularly true in the case of the mine workers. By the sheer fact of their geographical isolation, membership in the union was, next to their attendance at church, the most important thing in their whole social and civic life. And they lived in towns in which there was nothing else to do. There were few automobiles, few distractions, so that the trade union hall became an important part and center of their life and activities. That day is gone forever. Miners today frequently live in towns ten or fifteen miles from the mines.

McDONALD: Do you think automation is a serious problem in labor's future? Will it be an increasingly intensified problem?

HIGGINS: I don't have any expert knowledge on the subject of automation and I become increasingly more cautious in anything I say on it. I suspect that automation has been somewhat over-dramatized and perhaps unnecessary fears have been engendered by this overdramatization in popular magazines. There was a spate of articles a few years ago which would lead you to believe that within the next twenty to thirty years we could run the entire economy with just a handful of men pushing buttons. I'm told by experts in automation, and I gather from reading an occasional article or book on the subject, that we're not likely to see anything too drastic, that there will be a steady, gradual increase in the introduction of new processes in industry. Nevertheless, it will create problems. I would only hope that labor and management in the big industries would follow the approach taken in the Armour contract, of realizing that this is a problem that must be worked out jointly. The unions cannot and, I think, in most cases will not attempt to stand in the way of automation. But they have a perfect right to demand to be consulted, so that they will have some protection and so that individual workers will not have to suffer unnecessarily.

McDONALD: One of the problems that keeps bothering me is this matter of the creative instincts, the natural creative desires of all men to make things. People like Eric Gill have written about this problem in somewhat extreme fashion. But other people like Father Gerald Vann, O.P., in his *The Heart of Man*, have pointed out that man is intended by his very nature to create and to make rather than to just "do." The assembly line would be the most dramatic example of this contrast between making and doing in modern work. On the line, the worker has only one fragmentary operation to perform. He "does" something all day long, but he never really "makes" anything and so this natural desire to create and make is constantly being thwarted or frustrated. I know that Henry Ford has attempted to remedy this to some extent by rotating his workers, giving them multiple jobs to perform so that they will see more of the wholeness of the thing that is being made. But that doesn't really solve the problem either. Is there any way out of this dilemma in modern work?

HIGGINS: Again, I am not an expert on the subject. But it would be my impression that there are only limited solutions to that problem. I think that, for better or worse, we are going to be stuck with a considerable number of jobs which will be frustrating. But I don't know what effect increased automation will have here. Some of the experts claim that automation will actually eliminate many of the more frustrating jobs, the drudge jobs, and people will be released for more interesting work in service occupations and other trades. We have reached the stage —we reached it a few years ago—where we have less people in blue-collar jobs than we have in white-collar jobs. Of course, a great many of the white-collar jobs are worse from the standpoint of frustration than are the more manual jobs. The picture isn't entirely black. But I see no way out of the problem, no way to solve or eliminate the heart of it. If we want, as we seem to want and as our culture seems to demand, an economy which produces an abundance of material goods at low prices, then we're going to have to settle, I think, for assembly-line mass production.

McDONALD: We haven't even touched on the problem of "labor racketeering," as the business press invariably describes it. Somebody said the other day that the union which has been most democratic, from the standpoint of rank and file participation, the Teamsters union, has had some of the worst elements of labor unionism and racketeering, while some of your most "autocratic" unions have been the cleanest so far as racketeering elements are concerned.

HIGGINS: I am not sufficiently familiar with local practices of the Teamsters union to comment on that. However, I think the point has a certain amount of validity. It comes back to what I said earlier about our oversimplifying the problem of rank and file participation in unions. We have said that union leaders, as a group, are just no good and that the rank and file have a monopoly on the virtues. It's my opinion that in many unions the rank and file has better leadership than it deserves. This is the type of statement that can be misunderstood. I've said it as a sensational way of stating the case for the integrity of most labor leaders. I think that they are ordinarily decent people doing a very difficult job under difficult circumstances. Regarding your broader question about labor racketeering, I think it was a real problem; it was neglected too long by the labor movement and perhaps too long by the friends of the movement.

McDonald: Was there a reluctance on the part of labor priests and other friends of the labor movement to criticize the unions on the grounds that criticism would give ammunition to bitter, long-time enemies of unionism?

Higgins: I think that was true to some extent. The record will show, however, that a fair number of the so-called labor priests did, from time to time, rebuke labor publicly for some of its abuses. The bigger problem is that labor and students of labor didn't know the extent to which racketeering had gone in unionism. Therefore, while I have some very serious reservations about the manner in which the McClellan hearings were conducted, I think they served a useful purpose, they dramatized an issue which had to be faced up to by the labor movement. The response of labor to the racketeering problem has been very good. The action of the AFL-CIO, for example, in expelling the Teamsters is, it seems to me, an almost unprecedented action in the history of voluntary American organizations. This was the largest affiliate and it cost the AFL-CIO a sizable portion of its income; that was a very remarkable action. Another good result has been the adoption of the ethical practices codes, very involved, very detailed—perhaps too detailed—codes. The Public Review Board established by Mr. Reuther's union a little over two years ago—another remarkable action. That board is empowered, under the revised constitution of the Auto Workers union, to act as a board of final review on certain types of appeals brought either by individual members or by affiliates of the Auto Workers union against the international union.

McDonald: Who is on that board besides yourself?

Higgins: There are seven members—six at the moment. The chairman is Rabbi Morris Adler, a prominent Detroit rabbi. Another Detroit member is a Negro judge, Judge Wade McCree. There's a Canadian member, a magistrate in Windsor, Magistrate J. A. Hanrahan. Professor Edwin E. Witte, retired professor of labor economics at the University of Wisconsin, is on the board. And Bishop G. Bromley Oxnam of Washington is on it. Sometimes cases can be handled by a panel of three members; we're authorized to use panels of three. However, if it's a case of unusual importance, every effort is made to get the entire board to sit on the case and, if necessary, public hearings are held.

McDONALD: How many cases have you heard?

HIGGINS: We've handed down some 32 or 33 decisions. The experience of the board has demonstrated the validity of the idea of public review boards. The union, I am convinced, is very sincere about it. It gave the board a considerable amount of authority.

McDONALD: Does this represent a big step forward in labor unionism?

HIGGINS: It does. I think it's a very statesmanlike move. I'm not sanguine about the possibility of its being copied by a great many other unions in the short run. However, they may take another look at the idea after they've had a chance to see our board in operation. I am sorry that when Congress passed the labor bill in the last session it didn't give more attention to this approach. It seems to me that if they'd taken their time in trying to handle the problems they were confronted with, if they'd gone about it in a more leisurely way and had looked for alternatives, it might have been possible to encourage the growth of public review boards.

IV

Worship

REV. GODFREY DIEKMANN, O.S.B.

FATHER GODFREY DIEKMANN, a member of the Benedictine Order, has been the editor of *Worship*, the leading Catholic English-language periodical on the liturgy of the Church, since 1938. He edits this monthly magazine, published by the Benedictines' Liturgical Press, at St. John's Abbey, ten miles from St. Cloud, Minnesota. He is also a theologian and heads the theology department in the college at St. John's and teaches patrology, or the study of the Church Fathers, in the seminary there.

Father Diekmann was born in 1908 at Roscoe, Minnesota, which is thirty miles from the Abbey. He attended high school and college at St. John's and took his theology at the International Benedictine College in Rome, where he was ordained in 1931. He then spent a year of study at the famed Maria Laach monastery in Germany, source for much of the progressive liturgical thought and action inside the Catholic Church today.

The interview with Father Diekmann took place in one of the first-floor parlors in the central administrative building of St. John's Abbey. Outside, construction workers were busy on the massive new Abbey church being built as part of the long-range master plan for rebuilding most of the monastic and university facilities at St. John's.

McDONALD: I hadn't realized until recently that your work, as a teacher, has been more in the field of theology than in

137

liturgy. Somehow I had thought liturgy was your whole work.

DIEKMANN: Yes, I am a trained theologian rather than a liturgist in the sense of an historical liturgist. But I would not say that liturgy is not my whole work either. If you define liturgy as the public worship of the Church consisting of the Mass and Sacraments, then Sacramental theology is just as much a development of liturgical thought as are other studies, say in the sources or in the history of the development of rites. Actually the basic thing in the liturgy is the theology of the Church.

McDONALD: The fact that you teach patrology calls to my mind some of the work of Father Henri de Lubac, the French Jesuit, who is relying more and more, it seems to me, on tradition and the teachings of the Fathers as he elucidates and applies his theological thought.

DIEKMANN: Yes, that is, I think, simply a part of a modern phenomenon, a going back to the sources—Scriptures and the Fathers—in order to rediscover ourselves. I am convinced we are living in very good times. Every period of reform has been accompanied by a return to the roots. If the Church goes back to her roots to re-study her real nature, her real being, her real strength, it is bound to be beneficial.

McDONALD: So long as this going back doesn't become mere antiquarianism; so long as the modern applications continue to be made.

DIEKMANN: Surely. But at the same time I think there is a danger in our time of the pragmatic spirit, a danger that we will think of reform only in pragmatic terms, a danger of asking only, "How will this help the people?" instead of looking always for what is essential and necessary and searching for the principles that underlie the great achievements of the past.

McDONALD: You think we may get too impatient for useful results?

DIEKMANN: Yes. If there's a reform, let us say, of the missal that will last for the next several hundred years, and if that reform isn't based on very careful study of the whole history of the principles and development of worship, we'd be stuck with a missal of only inadequate value.

McDONALD: Yet if the progressive theologian or liturgist says such things too loudly or too publicly, the traditionalists who oppose any changes could pick that up and use it for their own purposes.

DIEKMANN: I saw a definition of tradition the other day which seemed to me very apt. It described tradition as that which our forefathers would have done had they lived in our own time. That applies to worship and it applies to other things, such as architecture and to our ideas of spiritual life. Sometimes you hear the complaint, "But we don't find this in the Rule of the Order." The question is not simply what the founders of the Religious Orders wrote in their time, but also what they would write if they were alive today. The founders of the Orders, by definition, are people who were alive to the needs of the Church in their time. They were alive to what was happening and they made changes accordingly.

McDONALD: The problem in all reform, then, is to know what is essential, what one must keep.

DIEKMANN: That's right. And that's why in the field of the Mass we are so grateful to a work like Jungmann's *The Mass of the Roman Rite*. The same thing is true of other areas, for example the Scriptures: today's Scriptural studies have only been possible because of our other knowledges, of archaeology, language, neighboring and parallel cultures and all the rest. In the liturgy, today's studies of the history of the liturgy put in the shade everything else in the past so far as scientific analysis of historical development and the various contributing influences are concerned.

McDONALD: Are these studies being published?

DIEKMANN: There is a flood of such studies, and the genius of a man like Father Jungmann lies in the fact that he is not only an original researcher himself but has been able to gather all of the various studies and present them in a form that is meaningful to the non-specialist. His work on the Mass will, in many ways, be the standard for years to come. Actually reform of the missal is now possible because it can be based on an exact knowledge of the past. I doubt whether the same thing is true of the breviary, the Divine Office recited by priests. There have not been parallel studies of the breviary.

McDONALD: But there *is* a change coming up in the breviary.

DIEKMANN: I've seen a newspaper report of a change and I'm just a little fearful that perhaps it might be too hurried a job. The history of the development of the breviary, the essential meaning of the breviary and the meaning of the public prayer of the Church—these things have not been studied sufficiently. We hear it said, for example, that the priest recites the breviary in the name of the entire Church. Well, for almost a thousand years the public prayer of the Church was considered to be the public prayer of the whole community, including the laity, with the priest, of course, leading them. Now it's completely clerical. A few years ago, at the international liturgical week in Assisi, the big meeting with all the Cardinals present got all the publicity. But in some ways an even more important meeting was the three-day preliminary study sessions which brought together specialists on the breviary. These men came to the conclusion that the whole field of the breviary is still pretty much of an unknown area so far as present practices and historical development are concerned.

McDONALD: I was interested in something you said earlier about the intimate relationship of theology and liturgy. One accepts the fact that there is a connection, but you apparently see that relationship as a very organic thing, which I suppose it is.

DIEKMANN: Actually theologians have the most to contribute to the liturgical movement, and to the development of the liturgy itself. Historians are necessary and, thank God, they are available. But I think, so far as the ordinary pastor is concerned, unless liturgical reform and liturgical thought are presented in a theologically meaningful fashion, we can hardly expect him to consider it as an essential part of his priestly ministry. The longer I've been in this field and the more I get in contact with priests, the less temptation I have to be impatient. I've given quite a few priests' retreats the last few years and I've been tremendously edified by the work of the priests in various parts of the country. Now if a priest has gone through four years of seminary theology, in a seminary he considers quite good and where he had good professors whom he respects, and if he is then told that his seminary training was deficient in a major area of capital importance for the entire spiritual life of the Church, namely the liturgy, well, he is not too inclined to accept that very readily unless it is explained clearly and in theological terms. Certain areas of theological thought have been obscured. This isn't a question of dogma; dogma remains the same. It's a question of theology, which is the presentation of dogma. The liturgical movement ultimately involves a re-thinking of theology. This recasting of theological thought and teaching is quite a challenge. There is a certain danger, almost, in the fact that when some of these things, the results of recent theological studies, are taught on the college level and our young married couples accept them eagerly, they don't find, perhaps, a sympathetic audience in their parish priest who may have come from an earlier generation of seminary training. It could lead to bitterness and resentment. The first task of the liturgical movement is to reach the priests and other teachers.

McDONALD: College people do have to make an adjustment in many cases when they leave college and must find their liturgical life in a parish which has not kept up with liturgical progress. It seems to me that any discussion of the liturgy could be divided into two parts, one on the liturgy itself and a second on the liturgical movement, the more or less organized effort to make the liturgy better understood and participated in.

DIEKMANN: Through the years I have become more and more convinced that the liturgical movement is nothing else than the Sacraments being exploited to their fullest capacities as intended by Christ. It is the theology of the Sacraments translated into spiritual life and into action in terms of both the individual and community life. I am convinced that the movement is really a rediscovery of Christ. That is obvious enough in our awareness of the meaning of the Mystical Body of Christ, that Christ is not merely the historical Christ of 2,000 years ago but that Christ lives in the present, that He is, as Cardinal Suhard said, "incarnate in every generation." The liturgical movement is the next step. The greatest contribution of Pius XII's encyclical on the liturgy, *Mediator Dei*, is its stress on the presence of Christ the High Priest here and now, on the fact that His principal activity in the Church, in and with ourselves, is the liturgy. The liturgical movement, then, is the rediscovery of Christ and Christ's activity, to which we are privileged to join ourselves and by which we are saved. The redemption of Christ is not something that was accomplished historically and now we get its fruits, but rather the redemption of Christ was accomplished by Him insofar as He is the head of the human race and we are ourselves brought into that redemptive work by virtue of our reenactment of it in the Sacraments, particularly the Eucharist.

McDONALD: There was a lack of realization of these truths before the liturgical movement began?

DIEKMANN: A lack of the full realization of Christ and His mediatorship operative in the total Church, yes, very definitely.

McDONALD: When did that start, roughly?

DIEKMANN: Jungmann, in an article that appeared in the theological magazine published by the seminary at Innsbruck, traces it back to the anti-Arian controversy in the sixth century. Arianism was the great heresy of the fourth century which denied the divinity of Christ. It was originally an Eastern heresy but the West was affected by it through the barbarian tribes which overran the West, most of whom were Arian or semi-Arian. In fighting Arianism, the Church insisted on the divinity of Christ and so effectively did she insist on it that His mediatorship became obscured. As a matter of fact, Christianity means that the Second Person of the Trinity became man, it means God-manhood, it means that God became one with us and unites us to Himself in worshiping and leading us back to the Father. But if we stress the divinity of Christ exclusively, that tends to put Christ into the Trinity and just leaves Him there.

McDONALD: That would withdraw Him from humanity.

DIEKMANN: Withdraws Him from humanity, so that emphasis remains on man in a sinful state. Christianity becomes, then, largely a moralizing rather than a sanctifying religion, and our whole notion of grace becomes affected by that. For a thousand years we have been thinking in terms more of actual grace than sanctifying grace. And the liturgy itself has been affected. The liturgy was formerly *ad Patrem*, to the Father. Everything was in and with Christ to the Father. But from the sixth century on, the emphasis began to shift to the Trinity, and Trinitarian prayers and prayers directed to Christ as God began to appear in the liturgy. From that time, too, we had the so-called "apologies," of which the Confiteor is a part. It meant also that the Mass became detached from "sinful humanity" and only the ordained priests could play an intimate part in it as the ministers of Christ-God. This in turn meant—and I think it one of the most important developments—the beginning of the separation of the clergy and laity, that is to say, a clericalization of the Church.

McDONALD: Until now the laity have been withdrawn from active participation in the liturgy. You have mentioned that several times, so you obviously consider it an important point.

DIEKMANN: I consider it of the utmost importance. The reason why the laity did not participate in the liturgy is precisely because, theologically speaking, they were not considered to have any right to participate. The Eucharist was the Holy of Holies and the laity simply had to stay their distance. The laity were merely to have pious thoughts and to receive the benefits from the Eucharist, namely, from Holy Communion. Again, if you emphasize one-sidedly the divinity of Christ and the sinfulness of man, the laity tend to be frightened away from receiving Communion.

Along with the anti-Arianism emphasis, there was a parallel development, the Western theory of redemption and the purpose and meaning of redemption. St. Paul says that Christ delivered Himself up for our sins and rose again for our justification. In other words, there are *two* aspects to redemption—the forgiveness of sin is one aspect but that is only for the purpose of the second aspect, the sanctifying and elevating of man. Louis Bouyer has pointed out repeatedly that there is only one mystery in Christianity and that is the mystery of Christ's death and resurrection, that the two belong together. They are one mystery, death *and* resurrection. The death is for the purpose of the resurrection, it leads to it. Now the Church in the East, echoing Scripture more closely, has always emphasized the resurrection; that is the great feast in the East. All the Eastern Fathers spoke of God becoming man that man might become divine; some use the traditional image of light—that God is light and transfigures us with His light, so that the whole being of man, body and soul, is transfigured. The West has always been more moralistic in its attitude. In the West, as early as Tertullian, which goes back to the third century, the emphasis was on satisfaction, on paying for sins committed, on the fact that man had sinned and was unable to atone for his sins and, therefore, that Christ, the Son of God, came and atoned in our stead. The emphasis was not on the resurrection but on the crucifixion. The West has always inclined to the juridical and has therefore put more stress on merits.

McDONALD: You are saying that the merits are a continuing thing?

DIEKMANN: It's true that Christ merited only during His life and that He merits only up to His death. But that is quite a different thing from efficient causality. St. Thomas is very clear in stating that Christ by His resurrection, not simply by His crucifixion, was exercising efficient causality on our redemption. The resurrection is an essential part of the whole process of redemption. If, therefore, we consider Christian life as a sharing of the life of Christ and if we put the emphasis on resurrection, we will get that new dimension of our sonship which, until now, has been obscured to a great extent. So, the whole liturgical movement means, in many ways, a rediscovery of the meaning of Christ and the Christian life. This movement is a big thing. It is not a question of liturgical "practices"; it is a question of the rediscovery of the full dimensions of Christianity.

McDONALD: When did the current rediscovery start?

DIEKMANN: From the standpoint of theology, I think Johann Möhler of Tübingen, Germany, was the initiator with his book called *The Unity of the Church*. And then, much more important, is Matthias Scheeben, undoubtedly the greatest theologian of the nineteenth century and, some think, the greatest creative theologian since St. Thomas. His book, *The Mysteries of Christianity*, has many of these ideas. He was a good Scholastic, he knew his Scholastic theology, but he went back and brought the Eastern tradition into conjunction with the West, the Eastern concept of redemption through resurrection and all the rest.

McDONALD: It seems to me that all these currents are found

on the theological level, among theologians and historians, rather than among the people themselves.

DIEKMANN: I think it has to start on the theological level because it is a question of understanding Christianity and unless that penetrates into the seminaries it cannot penetrate into the catechisms.

McDONALD: Do you think the liturgy, in its forms and expressions, should correspond to the popular demands? Hasn't it been historically true that what the people want almost determines what the Church does about its liturgy? For example, we hear that the Church will poll her bishops on a particular point and her inquiry invariably is couched in some such wording as this: "What do your people think? How do they respond to this?" Do you think it is valid to consult and look to what the people need?

DIEKMANN: What the people need, or what the people think they need? Don't you think it would be the primary obligation of the bishops, as the leaders of their flocks, to interpret the needs of their people to the Holy See? The reform of the Holy Week liturgy several years ago took several countries by surprise, including the United States to a very large extent. But it didn't take France and Germany by surprise. The French bishops and priests were very realistic after the Second World War. They faced the fact that the people, by and large, had lost any need of Christ, any need of the Church. How were they to get back to the fundamentals? And to the French clergy and hierarchy, the fundamentals meant the liturgy, because the liturgy means contact with Christ and with the life of Christ. So, when Pius XII said that he thought the restored Eastern Vigil would be the beginning of a great spiritual transformation of the Church, what meaning did that have to most of us in America? But he saw deeper, as the French and German bishops saw deeper, that basic contact with Christ is with Christ in His resurrection. Once we begin to understand the resurrection of Christ and to take part in it, things begin to open up. Then Sunday, for instance, becomes meaningful again, since Sunday is nothing else than the renewal of the resurrection, the renewal of the Easter feast. Sometimes a priest will say, "Well, I have no time for this liturgy, I have to do the essential, I have to take care of the people and give them the Sacraments." Once you understand the liturgy as simply the great life activities of Christ in the Church, then these things become, in fact, essential.

McDONALD: It seems to me that running all through this thing, both the liturgy and the movement itself, are two elements which need to be kept in balance. Bouyer, for example, talks about relating the subjective to the objective in your prayer and in your liturgy. Corresponding somewhat to that are the individualistic and the social elements in the liturgy, and those, too, have to be kept in balance, don't they?

DIEKMANN: I was about to say that the liturgical movement is ultimately an effort to personalize religion in the best sense of that word. The answer to these tensions, the balance we're looking for, is to be found in the Trinity where you have three Persons forming a community and still there is only one God. In the Trinity, the meaning of personality is not self-centeredness but, by definition, a person in God is a *relatio ad*, the relation to another. They are persons in relation to another. If we use God as an exemplar, and we must, then we will be able to balance the individual with the social and the community if we realize that the individual as a person develops his personality most fully by a relation to others.

McDONALD: That would be true even on the level of human relationships, wouldn't it? We see a personality grow and develop in love or friendship, but seldom when it is isolated from all social relations.

DIEKMANN: Exactly. And personalizing religion means that the Church is becoming personalized. I think it means, for instance, that the Sacraments must be personalized. To my mind, one of the greatest obstacles to anything like ecumenical understanding with Protestants is the misunderstanding of our system of the Sacraments. Protestants emphasize their personal relationship to Christ, to Christ as their Saviour, and that's a thoroughly Catholic emphasis. But Protestants feel that the Sacraments are a machinery which is somehow interposed between Christ and the people, that they are a mechanical process, like turning on a faucet and getting grace, that sort of thing. I think the Protestant feeling is, to a large extent, our fault. I am convinced that if the Sacraments would have been presented in the sixteenth century in personal terms, in terms of Christ, if they had been seen as the saving acts of Christ and that by them Christ was here and now drawing us to Himself, then the Sacraments could not have been rejected by the Protestants. They rejected what they did not know. They wanted to get behind the "machinery" and into personal union with Christ. They didn't realize that it is precisely in the Sacraments that Christ is personally active and unites us to Himself.

McDonald: From what you have said and from some reading I have done in this field, I would gather that the liturgical movement and the problems of the liturgy are closely tied up with psychology. It seems to me one would have to be a pretty fair psychologist to understand what types of prayers are best, for example. Some of the liturgical specialists have said that if you ignore this personal dimension in prayer, you do so at your own peril. Psychological perceptiveness, then, would seem to be highly useful in our thinking about the liturgy. For example, Guardini talks about the dangers of over-emotionalizing the liturgy and he says one of the after-effects of such over-emotionalization is a "post-emotional sluggishness." Another danger, I suppose, is to try to evoke emotions in prayer which the people do not feel. Of course, Guardini is always on the side of the rational and the cool.

Diekmann: He calls it the "primacy of the logos over the ethos," but that, of course, must not be to the exclusion of emotion.

McDonald: Well, does the psychological problem take care of itself in this matter of the liturgy?

Diekmann: Definitely not. And I think that is part of the problem of adaptation to our own times and to our own needs. We have now a worship which is magnificent and impressive, but it hardly takes into sufficient account the emotional needs of those who worship. It's become too impersonal, too "objective," in the sense that the people were excluded from it.

McDonald: Well, then in one sense you can say the liturgy is "for" the people rather than for its own sake, and therefore the forms and expressions of the liturgy have to be popular.

DIEKMANN: I wonder whether this isn't the same problem as when one asks the purpose of Christ's coming on earth. We could say, simply, He came to save mankind. But He came to save mankind from sin in order to lead mankind to God and to worship God. Just so, the liturgy is for the purpose of redeeming mankind, of stirring up our Faith, of deepening our Faith, of bringing about a closer union with Christ for a higher purpose. But unless the immediate purpose is achieved, that higher purpose cannot be achieved.

McDONALD: On this immediate level, then, is where one must adapt to the people's need and to the conditions of the time.

DIEKMANN: There has to be that amount of adaptation so that it becomes meaningful, otherwise the signs of the liturgy will not signify and will not be properly effective. Take the Eucharist: until we begin to realize that the sign of the Eucharist essentially connotes community, the bread, the meal, the many grains, etc., we can hardly expect the Eucharist to achieve its result. The people will go to the Eucharist merely to receive graces for themselves, never realizing that that gift creates social obligations in terms of community and fraternal charity. Unless a sign is significant and its significance is explained, it is self-defeating. One of the most important developments of our own times is the awareness of the Sacraments as signs. For centuries, we emphasized the simple causality of the Sacraments and that brought with it the danger of implying there was a kind of mechanical causality, the sort of thing that scandalized Protestants. Now we're going back to the importance of the signification, that only insofar as they signify do they cause, that the signification is prior in time and importance. That is getting into the field of Sacramental theology and that is very strong in our own time.

McDONALD: How do you reconcile this position—i.e., "unless they signify they cannot cause"—with the *ex opere operato*, that the Sacraments, of themselves, are sufficient to exert causality?

DIEKMANN: You can go to the Eucharist, to Communion, and it is capable of giving us grace by itself. But unless you receive devoutly—with the whole openness of Faith and the openness of yourself to your neighbor—you will not receive the grace of the Eucharist in the way that Christ has intended. I think it is sound that the sign or signification of the Sacraments is very much to the fore now because it involves the question of the receptivity of the faithful.

McDONALD: Guardini has said that it is on the plane of liturgical relations that the individual experiences the meaning of religious fellowship. It seems to me that what we have been saying here is that he *should* be, though perhaps he isn't, experiencing that fellowship.

DIEKMANN: It follows, I think, that if the liturgy is so "dignified" and staid and set that it takes a major effort to understand it, then it does not adequately fulfill its function of signification. Also it does not fulfill its function of grasping the whole man in worship, and that means man with his emotions. We have something to learn from our non-Catholic brethren. A couple of years ago, I was in the Bahamas and attended some of the services of the "Jumpers," as they are called down there. Well, that's the opposite extreme, of course. But, at the same time, you felt, well, perhaps they have got something which we have lost. I think we have always been afraid of the word "religious experience" because some Protestants have identified it with a particular event. But religious experience is something Catholic. Man has a right to religious experience and if he does not get it in his Sunday worship, if he does not experience the sense of community with others, if he does not feel that this is a family of God worshiping with Christ, he's been cheated.

McDONALD: That leads us, it seems to me, into this problem of language, and the use of Latin in the liturgy. To what extent does the language difficulty relate to the general problem of the intelligibility of signs? I guess I am a vernacularist, with reservations. It does seem to me that if meaning is critical here, then language is certainly critical.

DIEKMANN: The purpose of language is to communicate. All ritual is in some way language. It's a delicate problem. Pope Pius XII, toward the end of his life, became somewhat alarmed at what he considered excessive emphasis on this particular phase. Frankly I sympathize with the alarm. I think that in the long run there is no other answer except that those things meant for the people should be in the language of the people. I think that

that is the only logical and meaningful answer to this whole problem of divine worship.

McDonald: But you think there are reasons for delay?

Diekmann: Yes. One of them is that the language aspect has become a sort of shibboleth, a panacea for all the ills. Some of the people who agitate for the vernacular don't realize the vaster problems involved. If we get the vernacular without a corresponding Biblical culture and a deepening of theological awareness of the Mystical Body and of our membership in Christ, of our fellowship in Christ, of the purpose of the Eucharist, then we are preparing a terrible disappointment for ourselves.

McDonald: How are the people going to get a deeper awareness of the meaning, say, of the Mystical Body of Christ and all these other things that might be broadly grouped under the heading "liturgy"? Will it be on a multiplicity of fronts, this instruction and learning? Will it be from sermons, from education, from articles and books, from the prayers themselves?

Diekmann: In his encyclical on the Mystical Body, Pius XII said that the renewed emphasis on the Mystical Body came through the whole liturgical movement. I think he means by that that through the use of the missal, through at least a partial understanding of the mystery, the truth of the Mystical Body gradually opened up and became an obvious background to all that they were doing. Pius XI once stated that the most important organ of the ordinary magisterium of the Church is the liturgy itself. That's saying much. The liturgy is, then, more important than ecumenical councils or pronouncements of the Holy Father. But in order to have this organ speak, I would think it is up to the priests to break the bread of the liturgy to the faithful. Unless the priest himself has some broader theological background, he might pick out small items which are merely moralistic or merely pietistic and fail to see the full impact of these larger truths.

McDonald: In order for the liturgy to form you theologically, then, you have to have some theological formation to begin with, at least some theological background.

Diekmann: It goes hand in hand, yes. It is interactionary.

McDonald: We seem to have left out of consideration another teaching instrument, your own magazine, *Worship.* It is the only magazine of its kind, isn't it?

DIEKMANN: Oh, no, no. These things have their repercussions in a lot of other magazines. You have *Theology Digest,* for instance; they have done a fine job of keeping their readers abreast of the various developments in theology, in Scripture study, in patristics. The same is true of several other magazines such as *Theological Studies.* Very important, too, has been the educative effect of the Notre Dame summer courses in liturgy and the work of the National Liturgical Conference and its Liturgical Weeks —and, more recently, the encouragement of the national Episcopal Commission on the Liturgy. A magazine like *Worship* would have very little effect if these same ideas were not being presented from a lot of other angles. Otherwise we would be a small group of specialists or "hobbyists." The same thing is true of the seminary. No matter how good a liturgy class you might have in the seminary, if you don't also have a professor of Sacramental theology who teaches his subject according to the new insights of the last twenty or thirty years, and if you don't have a Scripture professor who presents his material in what is now called the "history of salvation" form, and if the dogmatic theologians don't go along with all of it, then your liturgy and religion courses won't be very successful in liturgical formation. Unless a magazine like *Worship* is supplemented from all sides, it couldn't hope to have much effect.

McDONALD: How many subscribers do you have?

DIEKMANN: About 14,000.

McDONALD: Mostly priests?

DIEKMANN: About 40 per cent are lay people. A source of great satisfaction, too, is that we have many hundreds of Protestant ministers who subscribe to the magazine. The importance of the liturgical movement, so far as ecumenical understanding is concerned, is one of the great hopes of our time. Many Protestants are rediscovering the key role of the Eucharist, which, on the basis of Scripture, some are now even willing to call sacrifice; for they understand it is not simply a mental or psychological "reminder," but the re-activation for the present assembly of that same covenant that was ritually established at the

Last Supper. The writings of Thurian, Leenhardt and Cullmann are very enlightening along this line. Otto Karrer, in a recent issue of *Cross Currents*, talks about this. According to him the only real point of division between Catholics and Lutherans in Germany, those Lutherans who have been meeting with Catholic theologians for the last twelve or fifteen years, is the question, "What is the Church?" Here, again, if we go back to some of the sources, we find that the early Fathers spoke of authority as an expression of charity, which is what Pope John XXIII has said, again and again.

McDONALD: What reading would you recommend for the Catholic who is coming to this for the first time?

DIEKMAN: We published a series of articles in *Worship* many years ago by Father Clifford Howell, S.J. I am ashamed to say that at the time I thought they were too elementary. But I did publish them and there was a very good response. They became the booklet, *Of Sacraments and Sacrifice*. For a lot of people that is an excellent beginning. Right now, two books are proving to be very useful to a lot of people on the college graduate level. One is Bouyer's *Liturgical Piety* and the other is *The Liturgy and the Word of God*, a symposium published last year by the Liturgical Press. It's on the relationship of Scriptures and liturgy. One of the most important books to come out in many years is *Theological Dimensions of the Liturgy* by Vagaggini. It makes some demands on the reader, and only the first volume has been translated into English so far, but it is recognized throughout the world as one of the most significant books in the field. Of course, Jungmann's book, *The Mass of the Roman Rite*, is basic for the Mass. The volumes of Proceedings of the National Liturgical Weeks also contain a wealth of good material.

I should like, however, to return for a moment to the Protestants and the Eucharist. Most of these people have *The Last Supper* and they are in good faith, we must certainly take that for granted. They are celebrating what they think is the Last Supper of Christ. They're trying to do what Christ did. Could that be something like receiving the Eucharist in desire, as we say a person can receive the Sacrament of Baptism in desire? It has its grace effects. I think we should welcome these things.

The more they approach the Eucharist, the closer that does bring them to the Church. The Eucharist, by definition, is a Sacrament that creates unity. That is the purpose of the Eucharist; it creates the people of God, it creates unity. Therefore, if Protestants celebrate what they consider the Eucharist with good intention, I am sure they receive the grace that leads to union with the Church established by Christ. So I welcome the fact that these people are rediscovering the Sacraments.

One other area of theology that is promising, I think, in addition to the incarnational awareness, is the eschatological emphasis, the realization that we are citizens of Heaven. The doctrines of Purgatory and the Private Judgment by God are part of our essential Christian faith. But if we go back to Scripture, we see that the over-all emphasis was on the second coming of Christ and that has importance in many ways, including the idea of the essential dignity of the human body, and the totality of man, body and soul, which will share in the risen Christ. I wonder if it would be right to say that three-fourths of all the heresies in the Church have come from hyper-spiritualization, from angelism, from an ignoring of the incarnational principle in Christianity.

McDONALD: How does all this fit in with the idea of spiritual life for the individual, and the need for spiritual directors and spiritual direction? I know that is not strictly the liturgist's concern, but . . .

DIEKMANN: Yes, but if we understand the Sacraments as Christ-acts, we've taken a big step. Christ is the principal minister of every Sacrament. He unites us to Himself and we worship the Father with Him. These are the vital activities of Christ and the Church. So, by definition, this is the spiritual life. These are the foundations of the spiritual life. So that, some modern authors can say that the whole of spirituality is essentially Sacramental. Action follows being. The Sacraments give us the being of Christian, they transform us into Christ, they give us the reality, the divine life, and our effort can be nothing else than simply to be worthy of that, to let this thing become operative and show itself in the virtuous life.

REV. ALFRED LONGLEY

FATHER ALFRED LONGLEY is pastor of the Church of Saint Richard in the Minneapolis suburb of Richfield, Minnesota. The parish, and Father Longley, have been described in a number of newspaper stories, in an article in *Worship*, in *America*, and in a book by Father Leo Ward, C.S.C., called *The Living Parish*.

At St. Richard's, Father Longley has attempted to put into practice the results of the immense amount of contemporary scholarship by both American and European experts in parish and liturgical life. As such, St. Richard's is one of a small number of Catholic parishes in the United States which are in the van of the most progressive thought in this area of Catholicity.

Father Longley was born in Twin Falls, Idaho, in 1913. He attended St. Paul Seminary in St. Paul, Minnesota, and was ordained in 1939. After three years as an assistant pastor in Faribault, Minnesota, Father Longley entered military service in March, 1942, as an Army chaplain. In January, 1952, he left the military service and, at Archbishop John Gregory Murray's request, became the pastor of a new parish to be formed at Richfield.

The conversation with Father Longley took place in one of the rooms of the St. Catherine's parish rectory, Milwaukee. Father Longley had come to Milwaukee to give an address at the annual Wisconsin Catholic Action Convention.

McDONALD: All through your ten years in military service, did you have the time to form some ideas and convictions as to what a parish should be, how parish life should be formed? Did you have time to do some reading and thinking about it?

LONGLEY: Yes, it was mostly by observation and conversation. I was particularly impressed by the fine parochial spirit in Europe, especially in Germany. I became very friendly with Father Johannes Pinsk, a Berlin pastor, who had done a lot of work in the parochial-liturgical apostolate and who had done a great deal of writing, especially on the importance of sacred Scripture in worship. Also I was able to go to Maria Laach monastery. We had arranged to have a spiritual retreat there for American chaplains and I rediscovered an old friend there who had visited us in the St. Paul Seminary back in 1935, Dom Albert Hammenstede. Dom Albert was the retreat master and I can assure you the retreat was unique, to the American mentality, and very effective.

McDONALD: You were familiar, then, with these liturgical thinkers and writers who had been appearing in such magazines as *Orate Fratres* before you entered military service?

LONGLEY: Oh, yes, because in the St. Paul Seminary we were under the influence of Father William Busch, and our present archbishop, then the rector, Archbishop William O. Brady. They encouraged us by doing many good things, such as introducing Prime and Compline for the official night and morning prayers in the seminary and doing dialogue Mass (and this in the mid-'30's).

McDONALD: I suppose there will always be some mistakes in a new parish.

LONGLEY: At the time, Archbishop Murray said that establishing a new parish is like having a new baby—"you can raise it any way you want to." Yes, the parish went through and is still going through its infancy. We're making mistakes and I'm right in with them, I'm responsible, actually. The faults start with me. We've had changes and have had veerings in order to preserve the important, the essential, things, the deposit of the Faith.

McDONALD: What did you have in the way of a parish when you started St. Richard's in 1952?

LONGLEY: We had some land. It was winter and the land was covered with snow, so we planted a big sign saying, *The Church of St. Richard.* We bought a small Rambler, a one-story suburban-type house, and used that for a temporary rectory close to the land we had bought. We met the first Sunday in the auditorium of the public school that is now across from the Church. It was the feast of St. Blaise. I remember that because it gave me a good personal contact with the people. I explained that there is no reason to celebrate a Mass as a solo performance on the part of the priest, that we had formed a community for the purpose of worshiping God. I went on to say that most of the parishioners had been to parochial school and had learned how to sing at Mass and that many of the men had been acolytes and that putting together these various experiences I was sure we could do a dialogue Mass, as of now. I said, "So when the priest says, 'Dominus Vobiscum,' what do you say?" And I can recall it came out loud and clear, " 'Et cum spiritu tuo.' " I said, "There is no use in having any further rehearsal or practice. I realize I am fortunate in having a young, eager congregation. Let's take advantage of our youth and our enthusiasm and make ourselves known to God this very day as someone who wants to worship Him in the best way."

McDONALD: How many families did you have in your parish at the start?

LONGLEY: About 300.

McDONALD: Were you alone when you started?

LONGLEY: Oh, yes. The shortage of priests in the archdiocese of St. Paul was, and still is, critical. At the present time, our parish has 1,200 families and I have one assistant priest to help me. We have 600-plus in our grade school. We have the Sisters of St. Joseph of Bourg, France, whose Provincial house in this area is at Crookston, Minnesota. We have five teaching Sisters, a Sister-principal and ten lay teachers.

McDONALD: That lay teaching-salary load must be a heavy financial burden on the parish.

LONGLEY: Yes, it is. It's a burden. Many other people, bishops and pastors, have similar loads. What's going to happen? I don't know. Something's got to give. It's a very grave financial obligation. So far, we've been able to keep above water, just.

McDONALD: Did you ever take a census of your parish? How do you keep up with new arrivals and departures?

LONGLEY: At the beginning, we had census cards from the other parishes out of which our parish was carved. We have kept what I hope has been a very accurate census ever since, thanks to the Legion of Mary in our parish. The Legion is outstanding; I couldn't do without them. We subscribe to a directory service, a mimeographed sheet which indicates all the people, Catholic and non-Catholic, who move in and move out of our territory. The Legion calls on everyone reported as having moved into the parish area. If they are non-Catholics, the Legionnaires, without any apology, say, "We're just trying to find out who the Catholics are. But on the other hand, we're glad to welcome you to the community and if there is anything we can do, as individuals or as a parish, we'd be only too happy to help. It is part of our duty, as Catholic Christians, to be interested in everybody." If it's a new Catholic family, the Legionnaires register the family and leave with them a letter from the pastor explaining the financial policy of the parish and assuring them that a priest will call later to discuss in detail what this family perhaps should do, what the parish problem is; weekly contribution envelopes are wrapped inside this letter. The Legionnaires then explain that if the new family wishes, a priest will come soon to bless their home. They go on to explain the idea of consecrating a home as a sacred space wherein the Sacrament of Marriage is celebrated, even as the church is the sacred space in which the whole community—namely, the "family of families"—worships God. This is outlined by the Legion and the priest continues this development when he comes later on.

In the meantime, one of the girls makes a specific appointment for us, so that on a given night—usually it's Thursday for me, Friday for Father Gerald Kenney—one of the men of the Legion of Mary picks us up and takes us from house to house, where they're expecting us. We sing a Gelineau Psalm—"May the Lord Watch Over This House and Keep Us in Peace"—and we use the ritual of the blessing of the house. We explain what we're doing and we give a special blessing to the bridal chamber. This also affords an opportunity to the people to ask us about the way Mass is celebrated in church and their own participation in it, their singing at Mass, the commentary at Mass and the reading of the Scriptures in English. This is a good time to discuss and to explain these things.

McDONALD: Is your idea of the parish that it is divided up into prayer and spiritual life in one area, intellectual life in another, social life in another?

LONGLEY: Oh, no. I try to think of the parish always as a

unity, as a miniature Mystical Body in which everything that concerns the people of God is of interest. It begins around the altar and goes right down into every detail of a man's life, his social life, his business and professional and work life and then what he gets in the forum he carries back to the altar and offers it to God and it's sanctified. There is a marvelous interplay here. The parish membership got together a couple weeks ago and went to the Knights of Columbus hall for a dance. Everybody that could fly, creep or crawl was there and they had a marvelous time. That's vitally necessary. We pray together and we play together. Somebody had a house burn down a couple of months ago and the rest of the parish got clothes and furniture for them; another family took them in—it was a parish project.

McDonald: That would seem to be a direct result of the spiritual unity you are talking about and trying to nourish.

Longley: Yes, and that reminds me of the series of lectures that Father Karl Rahner, S.J., of Innsbruck gave a year ago. They're in a book called *The Parish*. He's the head of the theology department at the seminary in Innsbruck and has tremendous insight. In that book he asked the question: "Where does the Mystical Body achieve placeness? Where does it become event? . . . Not in the convent chapel. . . . Not in communities of priests or monks or friars. It does become event there but not in the real Mystical Body sense. But it does become event in the parish church where there is a baptistry and an altar." We try in our parish to develop a consciousness that we must pay respect and bend every effort to make true in our own place and day the prayer of Our Lord at the Last Supper, the prayer that is found in the 15th, 16th and 17th chapters of the Holy Gospel according to St. John, whose theme is, Father, I pray that they may be one in love in Me as I am one in love with Thee. It's the unity of the community.

McDonald: Is that the central, over-arching idea of the parish, the thing you are always trying to convey?

Longley: Yes. That's the antiphon that's sung over and over again in our homilies and in all our dealings with the people, for where charity and love is, there is God. And the nourishment of it comes in the Eucharist. We've tried in every possible way to impress upon the faithful that the Eucharistic banquet is the renewal of oneness in love which began in Baptism and that if they are going to receive Communion, they must just grow in love for one another.

McDONALD: The idea being that if you have anything against your brother . . .

LONGLEY: Don't come to the altar until you've made peace with him, absolutely. But we put the thing even more positively. We explain that *there* is the reason for participation in the liturgy, rather than everyone coming into church and putting his nose into a missal. The missal is fine, but it's only a crutch. It was never intended to be done that way but because of language difficulties, we have to have missals. The reason for active congregational participation in the Mass is so that what we are— a community—becomes reality, achieves placeness here and now as we pray aloud together. We're listening to a common proclamation of the Word of God.

McDONALD: What are some of the actual practices that you tried? Which ones succeeded, which didn't?

LONGLEY: Several years ago, we made arrangements with the monks at St. John's Abbey to publish our own edition of their Short Breviary as a parish prayerbook and we called it, *God's Children Pray and Sing.* Among other things, it included prayers of the Divine Office and we tried to introduce public recitation of the Office in the church every day. We had Matins and Lauds and Prime before the early Mass each morning; we had Sext before the children's Mass at eleven; and Nones at noon; Vespers and Compline at eight in the evening. It just didn't register too well with the people.

McDONALD: Was it too monastic?

LONGLEY: I think priests might criticize it from that point of view. But the people would say, "It's all so strange. We never saw these strange prayers before." Well, we shifted the emphasis to recitation of at least Compline and Vespers at home and I understand that that has had a good success. That prayer links the folks at home with the parish church. And then we asked that only a token force come to the recitation of the Office in church. The only parts of it that we do publicly now are Lauds and Vespers—Lauds after the early Mass and Vespers before supper, at a quarter to six. And after Vespers every night, we're available for the Sacrament of Penance.

McDONALD: You mean you have time to hear Confessions every evening?

LONGLEY: We do it every morning, too, before Mass.

McDONALD: To what extent do your parishioners participate in Sunday Mass?

LONGLEY: We had participation before the Vatican Instruction in September, 1958. All our Sunday Masses are participation Masses. All are at least dialogue Masses. But we have a variety and the people can choose. The first Mass in the morning is just a dialogue Mass, the kind we call a "missal Mass" where there is no reading of the Scriptures in English. The people make their responses in Latin. But there is no singing. The eight o'clock and nine-thirty Masses are full participation. We like the Gelineau Psalms. They go over very well with our people and they can learn them in two minutes, the antiphon. The schola, of course, is prepared to sing the Psalms. The laymen do all the Scripture reading, and read the commentary. By this time, the people know about forty antiphons and we try to pick out a Psalm that best fits into the meaning of the Mass and that part of the Mass for that day. Our commentaries have been published by Benziger [*That They May Share*] and Father Frederick Mc-Manus of the Catholic University of America, who is president of the North American Liturgical Conference, wrote the introduction to it. The commentary is what the pastor gives to the reader each Sunday. The commentator's task is to lead the people and to keep their attention focused on what the priest is doing during the Mass. We have someone else who is the reader of the Scripture. Now at the High Mass, the people sing the Ordinary of the Mass and the choir sings the Proper and a motet, and sometimes a part of the Ordinary, but never the whole Ordinary. The last Mass of the day is a dialogue Mass with a reader for the Scripture.

McDONALD: You have the children's Mass each day at eleven.

LONGLEY: Yes. And that led to another change in policy. We used to have High Mass every day at which all the children were present. Frankly I was bothered about compelling them to go to Mass. We must take human nature into consideration and I have a tendency to fail to do that. I'm thinking of super-nature all the time and sometimes fail to realize that it's people we're dealing with and that they do get tired and they do get bored. I've got to beat that into myself and use myself as an example, because I'm the first one to get bored and tired and I'd better be careful, lest preaching to others I myself should become a castaway. So in recent years we have come up with a variety for the children. We have a couple of High Masses a week, and we have what we call a "Middle Mass," which is dialogue but has no reading of the Scriptures and no commentary, so that the children learn how to use the missal; we have that once a week. Then, twice a week, we have Mass with commentary and hymns or Gelineau Psalms. That makes up the five school days. And we set these Masses according to the Feast, the nature of the day, and we recognize the greater Feasts with greater solemnity. We have this eleven A.M. Mass all year round, in summer too, and on Sundays it's the Solemn High Mass. Then, in the matter of compulsory attendance, first of all the children attend Mass as a class group every other day. But if they prefer they may go to a certain designated classroom and study during that time instead of going to Mass. We put no pressure on them. There is no persecution of those who choose to sit it out. Relatively few children take advantage of that, but we insist that their rights be protected. It's had a healthy effect on the whole school community.

McDONALD: The Sisters don't subtly, even unconsciously, discriminate against those who choose not to attend Mass?

LONGLEY: The Sisters suggested this plan, God bless them. That leads on to something else. I was in the Army ten years and came out a lieutenant colonel. And, whether I like it or not, that has had an effect. Certainly as a chaplain I had no command. But maybe because I taught leadership and command at the Staff college (but frankly I think it's my own basic personality problem), I have had an awful time being permissive. My attitude as a young pastor was, "Now look, folks, God has appointed me to this place to take care of you and while I'm certainly willing and glad to listen to you, in the last analysis Father knows best." I'm sure that the good Lord's concern for the welfare of His people saw to it that I had my eyes opened and my nose bloodied a few times. Also I had people come across my path who were really wise and helpful. And then I have been helped by my reading. After all, it is the Church, not the priesthood, that is Christ. The priesthood is to serve the Church. If we read history carefully, we'll see that the Pope responds and makes a decision and calls a Council when he is sensitive and aware of a need that is reflected among the people.

Also, somebody recently wrote that never have the people of God, of themselves, been heretical. The people of God have what theologians call the *"sensus communis"* which is not quite common sense in our colloquial language, but a common sensitiveness to what is right and what is truthful and to what is wrong and what is false. In other words, one of the great authenticating media of the Church is the people's reaction to something, how they think about it. That's always been the case. And so I have become increasingly aware that it's important for the pastor to keep his ear to the ground, to learn what the people think and feel.

McDONALD: That could go to an extreme, too, couldn't it? You can't simply acquiesce in everything the faithful might want because at times they may want the wrong things.

LONGLEY: Oh, yes, but that's where the grace of office comes into play. It's the help one receives from the Holy Spirit in doing one's job as a pastor. But the pastor must keep himself sensitive to the needs of the people and then go up to Mount Sinai and meditate over it.

McDONALD: In what other ways do you implement this dominant theme of your parish, this idea of unity and love?

LONGLEY: We have what we call "little parishes" throughout the parish. You know, in this country we have the problem of the huge parish, thousands and thousands of people in these giant parishes and the priests sitting in the rectory, not knowing where to begin or to end their work. So the priests use their time to meet the emergencies—the fallen-away Catholics, the marriages that need to be validated, the sick and the dying to be cared for, the children to be instructed. This is all, of course, priestly work. But it doesn't involve the priest in that day-to-day social life of the parish which is so resonant in the daily celebration of the Mass. We got the idea of the "little parishes" from Father Bernard Meyer's book, *Lend Me Your Hands*. He is a Maryknoll missioner and he explained how in China, where a parish was spread over miles and miles, the mission priest organized what we call here "little parishes." So back in 1956 I called in a very competent layman, Charles Ryan. I told him the problem, gave him Father Meyer's book to read and then we discussed it. We then called two other competent couples in. They lived in other parts of the parish and we discussed this further and we all saw the need of having something between the parish and the home. These three couples were then asked to go out and find other couples and to form a nucleus in each general area of the parish. That has continued. We've had our ups and downs, with as many as sixty registered cells of six or eight couples each. Now it's down to fifty, more or less. But, by cell growth and patience, the thing has kept moving along and it has developed a neighborhood consciousness.

McDONALD: What do these cells do? Are they basically study-club units, or action groups?

LONGLEY: Their mission is sanctification, the translation of the grace of the Sacraments into active, real sanctification of the person, the family and the neighborhood.

McDONALD: How do they program this thing?

LONGLEY: We have a monthly meeting for every couple that is a cell leader. A materials committee and the over-all leader of the group then discuss projects to be studied or worked on for the following month. There is no set program for all the cells, all the "little parishes." We try to be extremely permissive in this matter. Some cells, of course, start out merely as social groups meeting for a good time, but we don't say, "You're all wrong." Rather we try to have the area leader introduce some serious material into their discussions. At first, I had visions of great crusades going on in all the "little parishes," a lot of converts being made and that sort of thing. And a younger, but wise priest, Father Lawrence Murtaugh of Rochester, who has great insight into all of this specialized group movement, said, "Don't worry about that. Their very presence as resonant, vibrant, Catholic Christians, tied together in a charitable, purposeful unit in the neighborhood in the community, will radiate sanctity and prepare the ground for things to come later."

McDONALD: The work of the "little parishes" varies then, from cell to cell. One might be a study and discussion group; one might be an action group.

LONGLEY: Yes, we hope that all of them will come around to the regular technique of Catholic Action cell work and growth, the "See, judge and act" process. We have about 350 couples in the "little parishes" now. That's about 25 per cent of the parish. That's another thing—I thought, at first, that the whole parish could be organized into "little parishes." I thought everybody could be involved. But I made a mistake. It seems to me now that this is a special vocation which some have and which some are trying to see if they have and that it is not, perhaps, intended to involve everybody—I mean this cell membership and work. We try to emphasize in our monthly spiritual homily and direction that we give to the leaders of the "little parishes" that they must not set themselves above their fellow Catholics who are not interested in becoming members of the "little parishes." We say that the leaders of the "little parishes," above all, must observe this oneness in love. St. Paul had to rebuke the Corinthians from time to time because some of them thought they were holier than others. We haven't had very much of that superiority feeling in our parish. Another mistake I made was trying to involve the "little parishes" in fund-raising projects. Some of the people came to us and said, "Father, I thought you wanted us to be a spiritual endeavor, not doorbell-pushers for fund drives." So, I had to retreat on that and I said, "Very well, we'll safeguard your spiritual mission and not call on you as members of 'little parishes' for these drives. But we may call on you as members of the parish." They've been most generous that way.

McDONALD: That raises the question of how you solve your financial problem. You must have a heavy debt in your new parish.

LONGLEY: Oh, we're dreadfully in debt. Way up in the $600,-000's. But we paid off $30,000 since last August and we hope to pay off another $15,000 this month.

McDONALD: Can you run your parish and pay your debt off simply with the contributions you receive each week? Or do you have to have special fund-raising events the year round?

LONGLEY: We have had a fund-raising drive which was not too successful though it did increase the weekly contributions somewhat. Let me put it this way—another mistake I made was that I thought I could do it all and I had to learn the hard way that when I was put together I was not made a wizard in financing. I have a hard time disciplining myself to develop that instinct or know-how that so many priests have. So, it's worked itself out that I've assigned to me an assistant who is a very mature young priest and very able in this area. He supervises the fund raising and takes care of the bookkeeping. We have a volunteer bookkeeper and my assistant supervises the bookkeeper and advises me as to progress and tells me when it's time to put a pitch on for this and for that. So, he's completely in charge of financial administration. It relieves me a great deal.

I regret that it is we priests who must do this kind of work, that a priest has to be used for that work in the present economy of the Church. But because of the problem of lay trusteeism in the Church in this country in the last century, the Church is very sensitive about it. Maybe some day we can realize again what St. Peter said about our not being ordained to wait on tables and so let us get deacons to help us. Maybe we can some day develop a class of dedicated men who can help us, who are better educated and better equipped to go into the forum of finance.

McDONALD: Well, do you have to have bazaars and raffles and things like that to supplement your weekly envelope receipts and to make your mortgage and interest payments?

LONGLEY: We have a minimum. We have one big blow a year, called "St. Richard's Fair." It's a three-day affair and last year it grossed $14,000 and netted about $10,000. But we've kept away from harassing the people with a raffle this week and bingo the next.

McDONALD: The cumulative effect of constant money-raising is bad, I suppose.

LONGLEY: Yes, it is. It's canonizing things that should be cannonaded.

McDONALD: And yet, you have to make your payments.

LONGLEY: Yes, we have to make our payments. But God has provided. It's been rough. In some ways there have been some rather bitter crosses. But who's going to flinch?

McDONALD: What other parish organizations and actitvities do you have?

LONGLEY: It's all in our parish directory. I have a copy here. We have theology institutes, the St. Richard's men's club, the Women's Council, Legion of Mary, credit unions, other specialized groups.

McDONALD: Do you think a parish has any obligations toward the intellectual life of the parishioner? You mentioned a theology institute for the laity.

LONGLEY: I would never want anyone to think I'm saying our educational program is *the* way to solve the problems that might exist in this area. But it is *a* program. The unifying element in our whole educational program is our work in the pulpit, our preaching, because our preaching is based on the Word of God in which we are united. We have an inquiry forum for people who want a refresher course in doctrine or for people who are interested in becoming Catholics. We try to supervise the training in the school by the daily homily at Mass, a "dialogue homily" in which the children at Mass take part in the discussion of the Word of God. The homily for the children is about ten or twelve minutes long. Also our Sunday sermons are carefully outlined and prepared to develop a single theme. Now the theme is union in Christ; we're preparing actually for Liturgical Week.

McDONALD: How long can your Sunday sermons be?

LONGLEY: Ten, fifteen minutes. The Mass does take longer and some people shop for a short Mass elsewhere. Unfortunately they can't all eat the strong meat. The pulpit, then, is the focal point. But we also emphasize the parish library, which is strictly theological—no novels, a small lives-of-the-saints section, but mostly all good contemporary theological works. And then, of course, we have the theological institute and that is a great effort to communicate high-level instruction to the laymen. We consider that a service to the whole community, not just the parish. We invite all in the Minneapolis-St. Paul area to attend these classes. The fee is $5 a semester per course. Each year, we offer two courses. This year the courses are on the Protestant Reformation and ascetical theology. The first semester on ascetical theology was on the theory of it and on spiritual development and formation. The second semester is on translating one's personal spirituality into useful, active, apostolic life. We bring in the Franciscan Fathers from the theological faculty at the Franciscan Conventual Seminary, Assumption Seminary. They do the teaching. There are two one-hour classes each Sunday night with a break between so that both husband and wife can attend one of the classes while the other is at home.

McDONALD: How is your whole parish program being accepted by the people?

LONGLEY: It is having a good effect on many. It seems to disturb others on initial contact. And if we can ask those others to be patient and to sit and listen, oftentimes they come back and say, "I now understand and am 'with it.' "

McDONALD: Do you control, or manage, the education of the children in the school, or do you leave that pretty much up to the Sisters?

LONGLEY: We keep in close rapport with the Sisters. In the teaching of religion we're taking the Scriptural approach, the one favored by the new German Catechism. And then the teachers and the Sisters are always in on these dialogue homilies, or discussions, in church during the eleven o'clock Mass every day and they get the way the wind is blowing. I draw out of the children the direction in which we're moving and the teachers naturally help the children along in that same direction.

McDONALD: What about the interest in religious vocations? Have you noticed any increase in that interest?

LONGLEY: Oh, yes. This year, we have two in the major and four boys in the preparatory seminary, and we have a new novice in the Sisters of St. Joseph. We have another girl going to make her simple profession. There is a growing interest.

McDONALD: Is there a tendency for a parish organization, or

any organization for that matter, to become moribund and dead after it loses its purpose for existence? So often we see organizations that perhaps once had a reason for starting but no longer seem to be serving any useful purpose and yet they just continue along. I suppose you have to keep re-examining these organizations and dropping those that are no longer alive.

LONGLEY: Yes, indeed we do. We had several organizations I felt were not fulfilling their purpose. I did not disband them, but I sort of passed them by. When the members came to me, I said, "You prove to me by your own enthusiasm that you can fulfill a useful purpose in parish life and the organization will survive."

MCDONALD: What is your working day like?

LONGLEY: We delegate as much as we can of all the work involved in running a parish. We simply supervise their work and only when they need help and come to us do we get involved in it. That relieves us of an awful lot of detail work. About my daily schedule, I usually wake up about 5:30 in the morning and I cannot go back to sleep. It's not a fitful nervous situation; I've had enough sleep. So I get up and say Matins and Lauds and Prime and Terce and read my meditation book and have sort of a quiet thinking time. And then I take my bath. One of my war injuries was a broken back and I need a tub bath every day to get all the kinks out of my back. I take my bath, at which time I may read *Jubilee* or *Worship*. I have breakfast around ten to eight, because I celebrate Mass at eleven. After breakfast and until Mass I have paper work, answering letters, that kind of thing. At 10:15 I go to church, say Sext and go into the confessional. Father Kenney and I take turns in the confessional and some days we're both needed, for a half-hour before Mass. After Mass, I make my thanksgiving and stop by the Sister's office to see if she has anything to bring up. After lunch, which Father Kenney and I eat alone, I may nap for ten or fifteen minutes and then I start reading, turn on my FM radio and listen to some good music while I read. There are no phone interruptions; the phone doesn't ring in my study. If a call comes in downstairs that requires a priest, I am informed on the inter-com and then I will answer it.

MCDONALD: What are you reading at the present time?

LONGLEY: Now I'm reading *Counselling a Catholic, Heroic Sanctity, The Rainbow.* I like to read anything by people like Gleason, von Zeller, de Lubac, Danielou, Bouyer.

McDONALD: Do you have time to serve as a spiritual director for individuals?

LONGLEY: God has provided the parish with a wonderful help in my present assistant, Father Kenney, who is sold on the sodality, the real sodality talked about in *Bis Saecolari.* He's organized it on the grade and high school level and is now approaching the adult level. The result is these kids are asking for spiritual direction. For years, we've discussed meditation and the discipline of meditation for the children. Parents are coming in now and they are wondering what's come over their kids. They say, "Our son comes in and turns off the television, turns off his favorite program, and tells us he's going to be in his room in silence for a while, meditating. What's it all about?" That gives us the perfect opening to give a little series of instructions on meditation. So, Father Kenney, with this sodality approach, is furthering this effort at spiritual direction. But we have never hurried giving the Sacrament of Penance. First, we have insisted that it be called the Sacrament of Penance, not "confession." Confession is part of it. And we have, I hope, effectively instructed the faithful in the threefold effect of the Sacrament. Grace is restored when sin is forgiven. The sinner is reconciled to the Church. Third, as the Fathers used to say, there is conversion and renewal because by the grace and direction you get, you are converted over and over again.

McDONALD: Do you have time to give adequate direction in the confessional?

LONGLEY: We insist on it. Every penitent is going to get attention when he gets in. And it doesn't seem to take more time than anyone can manage. I'd say about 90 per cent of the people receive the Sacrament about once a month.

V

Writing

WALTER KERR

WALTER KERR was born in 1913, in Evanston, Illinois. He attended De Paul University for two years, dropped out for a couple of years during the depression, then entered Northwestern University, where he got a B.S. and an M.A. degree in speech. He then went on to teach in the drama department at the Catholic University of America.

In 1950, Kerr became drama critic for *The Commonweal* and in 1951 he was made drama critic of the *New York Herald Tribune*, a position he holds today. He has written and directed *Sing Out, Sweet Land*. With his wife, Jean, he wrote and directed a revue, *Touch and Go*, and a musical, *Goldilocks*. He directed the play *King of Hearts*, written by Jean Kerr and Eleanor Brooke. He is the author of *How Not to Write a Play* and has contributed to *Horizon* several articles on the theater.

Kerr has done a number of adaptations for the Omnibus television program, including *Oedipus Rex*, Molière's *School for Wives*, Christopher Fry's *The Lady's Not for Burning*, and Mary Chase's *Mrs. McThing*. He is now a member and drama consultant of Saudek Associates, an independent television production company.

The interview took place in the Kerr house in Larchmont, New York—the house whose acquisition and features have been so delightfully described by Jean Kerr in *Please Don't Eat the Daisies*. Here, twenty miles from midtown Manhattan via the New York, New Haven and Hartford Railroad, Walter Kerr writes his "Sunday pieces" for the *Herald Tribune* and his special articles and books. He works in a large, first-floor study whose walls are lined, floor to ceiling, with books and recordings. His huge desk faces two large windows yielding a magnificent view of Long Island Sound. The Kerrs have five children, but none of them were in evidence at the time of the interview. Some were in school, others were in the remoter regions of the sprawling home.

MCDONALD: Brooks Atkinson, one of your colleagues, has said that it seems to him the times are big but the plays are small. Do you agree with his estimate of the situation?

KERR: It seems to me that the focus of the common mind may be small. We may be concentrating on some terribly special and terribly isolated ideas. If that is so, I wouldn't be surprised to know that the times are portentous almost as a result of this state of mind. If there is a vast tide sweeping over a people who only want to look into a tiny corner for dust, I would think that the times might in fact sweep over such a people.

MCDONALD: I'm not trying to put all the burden on playwrights by saying they should think big when the generality of people aren't, but . . .

KERR: One might hope that they would. But playwrights, historically, have become big only on those rare occasions when the entire nation is big. It's something I don't even like to think about because it seems to have a great deal to do with nationalism, with an upsurge of nationalism in a community.

MCDONALD: Jingoism?

KERR: Not jingoism, no. Really it's a virtue, I suppose. There have been periods of tremendous confidence when everybody is looking forward and thinking "Honest to God, we've got it licked; we're going to go now." That happened in Greece at a certain time. All of a sudden they just felt that they were full of a new and exciting social and philosophical idea and, wham! they produced—for seventy years only—a vast body of drama. It happened again with Shakespeare when England felt it was on top of things; the playwrights thought big because everybody was thinking big. You get it for a very brief time—about forty years —in France, during the time of Molière and Racine and Corneille. You get an echo of it in our time in Ireland. One of the most important bodies of contemporary drama is the Irish period of about thirty or forty years ago and it happened just exactly at the moment when Ireland disentangled itself, got free and felt she was going to become great and powerful.

McDonald: In our own time, what plays would you put in the category of "great" or even "near great," just among those you've seen in the past ten years as a critic?

Kerr: To me the most interesting playwright, the best playwright, is Tennessee Williams. I see no way around that. I think he's the most genuine artist. I think he has great passion and power, which is a rare thing in our theater.

McDonald: Do you think Williams has fallen into a formula situation now?

Kerr: I wouldn't call it a formula, no, although I am sure he's acquired habits. He's discovered what explosions of passion and violence work best for him, and perhaps he uses them with a little more calculation now than he did before. If I have a worry about him, it's that he might be moving into a narrower vein of exploration, he may be dealing increasingly with the aberration rather than with the somewhat more universal. There's a great difference, I think, between *Summer and Smoke* and *Sweet Bird of Youth*. *Summer and Smoke* is a study of frustration, all right, the story of a girl who cannot adjust herself sexually, or to her need for sex. You may wish to call that a neurosis, but at the same time it's quite a common neurosis; it's a problem that verges on universality. Also, she makes her own mistakes and suffers for them; she's responsible for what she does. She obviously could pull herself together somewhere along the line, but won't. *Sweet Bird of Youth* is very effective theatrically, but by this time we are dealing with neuroses that are more hopelessly crippling, with paralyzing aberrations that move only in a narrower, more restricted channel of human behavior. That's what I am afraid of at the present time with Williams—with *Cat on a Hot Tin Roof*, with *Sweet Bird of Youth,* with *Suddenly Last Summer.* You see, when you become entangled with cannibalism you may have landed in a *cul de sac.* I hope not, because I admire Williams so much.

McDONALD: So far as the American theater goes, though, he is the big hope that you see.

KERR: I think he's the most talented man we have. Another thing you've got to say out of respect for him is that he is intensely productive. He's producing a body of work. He's not a 'playwrote.' He's not a writer who did one smash, and five years later returned with a pale echo of it. He doesn't protect himself. He doesn't hide in the corner wondering if his next play will be as good. Year after year after year there's a Tennessee Williams play. That's very important.

McDONALD: Who else, besides Williams, would you single out for any special commendation?

KERR: There are the obvious playwrights who are always grouped with him. Arthur Miller, unlike Williams, doesn't have a large body of work. I think that that is damaging to him. I wish he had a play every year. There is, of course, William Inge, who has been producing quite regularly, though he works in a softer, less vigorous form and therefore, while he's very good indeed in his form, doesn't achieve the power of Williams and doesn't seem to have the same kind of stature. He, too, tends to become increasingly special in his subject matter. His last play (which was his first failure, by the way) was, again, a play about the Oedipus complex. In moving away from the major concerns of the major part of your audience, a playwright may lose both appeal and importance.

McDONALD: In one of your recent Sunday pieces for the *Herald Tribune,* you touched on that problem of appealing to the major concerns of the major part of your audience, but it was in connection with the clamor of television writers and artists for freedom to handle what they call "adult themes." I think your point was that when they have the freedom, they write on themes which are not really adult.

KERR: I'm intrigued every time I listen to a conversation, say, between television playwrights. Now it's true that they are really under a ridiculous set of taboos. They're at the mercy of what a sponsor is willing to put out money for and therefore they have very little freedom of theme. I'm all for freedom of subject matter and I sympathize with them when they ask: "Why can't we do adult themes?" However, when they start to specify the adult themes they are eager to handle, the list almost always begins and ends with homosexuality and our friend the Oedipus complex. At this point I start thinking: are these adult themes? Each of them strikes me as being essentially a problem of adolescence, however prolonged the adolescence may be. When we finally see such scripts they're invariably written in terms of teenagers. The question I keep asking myself is: why not go into the problems, the sins and the vices that do beset actual adults, those things which affect grown people who, having come to their presumed maturity, still get into trouble? What are their difficulties and struggles?

McDonald: That brings up, it seems to me, that whole problem of evil and the artist's handling of it.

Kerr: I think there ought to be freedom of theme, obviously, in the arts. If something exists in nature and it is the business of the artist in some way to record, illuminate, mirror nature, then he is clearly free to use any of these materials. I know this has occasioned many discussions among moralists and critics. The answer that seems to me most satisfactory is that successful handling of a theme depends upon the degree of elevation or detachment with which it is approached, the degree of objectivity that is brought to it. How true is the portrait, how honest has the writer been? Does the artist cheat or sentimentalize? If he does, he has dealt less than honorably with his theme.

McDonald: Wasn't it Maritain who talked about the "altitude" at which the artist works as being so important? I think he used that term in correspondence with Mauriac in a discussion about the novelist and his relationship with evil. You don't, then, want the artist to connive with evil?

Kerr: Of course not. But he's got to wrestle with it.

McDonald: Some years ago in an interview with Msgr. Martin D'Arcy, S.J., we got on this subject. I suggested that if a thing is good artistically it cannot be bad morally. He said he

would go along with that in general. But he mentioned one particular book, Norman Douglas's *South Wind*, which, he said, was
extraordinarily well done but that underneath it was very wicked.
That raises another question, doesn't it? How can one really tell
whether the artist is conniving with evil? Now, of *Tea and
Sympathy*, I believe you once said that the ending to that was
a "hoked-up" thing.

KERR: The ending to *Tea and Sympathy*, I believe, is senti-
mentalized and somewhat unreal. It doesn't solve the psychological problem clearly. Are we to conclude that the boy's
problem is now resolved because of one experience with an older
woman in which, in effect, she mothered him through? What's
the rest of it? Is he going to have to depend on this same assist-
ance for the rest of his life? Furthermore, did he really need
the help in the first place? If so, what *is* his problem? There is
a great ambiguity in the play as to whether the boy is a homo-
sexual or not.

McDONALD: It's not always easy to make that judgment of
whether an artist has connived with evil.

KERR: It's never easy. But I tend to disagree with the notion
that a thing can be "well done" and still "wicked." I think that
"well done" cannot be confined to the quality of the writing
alone.

McDONALD: That's not the whole thing, then.

KERR: I don't think so. The question goes beyond a man's
style to the integrity of his observation. How truly has he seen
what he is attempting to record? Has he seen *all* of it? If what
he imitates from nature corresponds to what is there, then I say
there can be no conflict. We've seen the action in its comple-
tion, in its fullness. We've seen it with its effects, with its causes,
with its nuances and its ramifications. I don't mean you have to
treat the whole world in one play. But whatever area you've
selected to treat, you must treat thoroughly. In short, how accurate is the playwright's vision or observation?

McDONALD: We've heard this said, that you can portray evil
if you show that it *is* evil, if the characters realize it's evil.

KERR: That sounds as though you must moralize and put up a
big sign saying "This is wicked, don't do it."

McDONALD: Now I can conceive of a play—and you've probably seen ten plays for every one I can conceive of—in which
adultery may be portrayed as very attractive, very desirable, as a
solution to a real problem. And it may not occur to any of the
characters in this particular play that adultery is evil. Yet, could
not that play be "well done," very honest, very accurately observed? Yet the moralist could say: "You're making evil desirable." Is there any way that that can be resolved to the satisfaction of the moralist, the critic and, above all, the artist?

KERR: The only thing I can say is, "What do you believe about
adultery?" Let's take it out of the area of morals for a moment.
You can't really do that, but let's try to do it for a moment.
What do you believe happens psychologically as the result of an
adultery? Do you think that it solves a problem without creating
new ones? Does it perhaps half-solve one problem while opening
up six more? Let's say that a man has a relationship with his
wife, and a whole system of dependent relationships has been
built up, in which some integrity is desirable, in which some
keeping of the obligation or of the agreement is obviously de-
manded. If he commits adultery, he has violated something. I
believe that two people can meet and fall into an act of adultery
and that as of six o'clock tomorrow evening they may both feel
a great deal better for it. However, what happens after that? Is
that the end of it? Or have there been created the beginnings of
emotional and psychological problems that now must also be resolved and which cannot be resolved in a way consistent with the
integrity of the husband-wife relationship and the fulfillment of
those other obligations? What we've really done, I'd say, is
begun a story rather than ended one. We have started a great
complex of interlocking psychological and emotional and intellectual events.

Well, what about it all? What happens next? That's what I
want to know. I don't care whether the action ends tragically
or whether it mirrors a fact of sin. But I do want to be sure that
the event that has been selected for imitation has been shown
us in its actual psychological implications. I want to believe it.
I don't believe it when I see (which I rarely see, by the way), or
when I read (which I often read—I think the novel tends to go

into this more than the theater, really), a story about an average householder who falls into a casual adultery and comes out of it emotionally and psychologically unscarred, a happier man, with his marriage improved and his generous mistress bidding him farewell with: "Yes, go back to your wife, dear; we've had just a wonderful six hours." This jolly sequence of events doesn't correspond to anything I know about human nature. I think it's wishful thinking, as much a daydream as some of Hemingway's heroines.

McDONALD: I think you wrote somewhere that you wished people who are always talking about the "moral effect" of a play on its audience would offer some kind of evidence, some kind of measurement of those effects.

KERR: I think our evidence is inadequate.

McDONALD: That is another reason, I suppose, why even the moralist must be cautious about moralizing in this area.

KERR: What bothers me is that the moralist doesn't seem to know his business as thoroughly as he ought to, or as I think he ought to. I feel there is just too much guesswork going on. We tend to assume that something is going to have a terrible effect on people while we have no actual measurements, not only of the degree to which this particular work affects people, but of the degree to which art in general *can* affect people. I think this whole area needs a great deal of study, whatever the outcome may be.

McDONALD: You said in one of your books that catharsis is an answer to the people who say that a violent play will stimulate an audience to go out and commit acts of violence. Yet in the case of some of Tennessee Williams's works, they seem to exert more of an agitating or troubling effect, rather than a purging effect, at least on me.

KERR: That's quite possible. You were upset and agitated when you left. I think it does sometimes happen with Williams and I think one of his real defects, one of his most characteristic defects, is his inability to complete an action. I think he has great trouble "getting out." To me, it's a flaw even in *Streetcar*, and I think *Streetcar* is one of the best, if not the best, play written for the modern theater. I find it troublesome in *Streetcar* that the girl must be hauled away in a straitjacket. I feel I have not come to the end of her story, that I have ducked it, that I don't know what happened to her, that she slipped from me into insanity. That's not an ending, you see. I feel a little cheated.

McDonald: The cathartic action is probably only to be found in Shakespeare and the Greeks.

Kerr: We have to be careful about always falling back on the Greeks and Shakespeare. Of course, they do illustrate it best. It's easy to say "Look, here it is. The *Oedipus* ends in catharsis. In *Hamlet* there is a purging of emotions." But we can see it closer to home. Any time you follow a group of characters and want something for them and they get it, or they don't get it but you're satisfied, you feel: "Ah, yes, this is just, this is right, this is what I wanted to happen. I'm satisfied now." This, too, is catharsis, on however low a level. It's only, I think, when the psychological action is not really resolved that you come out with a terrible feeling of frustration.

McDonald: As a daily critic, you work under limitations of time and space. Do you feel you can do justice, working under those space and time pressures, to a play?

Kerr: Well, I get an hour at most to write a review, and people are always asking: "How can you make up your mind in that short a time? How can you know?" The answer is perfectly obvious. When you go to see a play, not as a reviewer but as a member of the audience, when do you know? You know while you're sitting in the theater.

McDonald: That's right. Your problem is how to express what you know.

Kerr: Yes, that's a writing problem, not a basic problem of judgment. The difficult thing is to sit down and write about your reaction coherently and, if possible, to explain *why* you were or weren't happy. That's fast work. It's even rougher in the case, say, of a really good play, to try to suggest all of its good qualities in the complexity in which they occur in the play. What I think most daily reviewers are unhappy about is not the need to make a decision, but about what the time pressure does to the quality and completeness of what they have written. They brood about the things they wish they could fix and can't. Sometimes I find after certain plays—the plays of Anouilh come to mind for me, lately—that, when I've got through writing the piece and it's gone downstairs and it's in the paper the next day, I wish I could write four other pieces on the same subject. Not because my initial reaction has changed but because I'd like to be able to go into aspects of the play that I didn't have time to touch. I find that Anouilh's plays rattle around in my head for weeks afterwards. *Waltz of the Toreadors* and *The Fighting Cock* are fascinating in their varying lights and shades and juxtapositions of form.

McDONALD: Is it true that the critics are as powerful as some think they are in closing plays or keeping them open?

KERR: They have a power. Everybody knows that if all the notices are good, there's probably going to be a line at the box-office tomorrow—probably, not absolutely. It helps. It makes a difference. I don't think it makes the major difference. I'm widely disagreed with on this, but there are just too many contrary examples. Take *The World of Suzie Wong*—most of the notices were negative and everywhere it has ever gone it has done business. A year on Broadway in spite of some really bristling reviews. Why? I don't know, except that that title seems to pull people into the box-office; they *think* they want to see it. I feel the strongest single power is a kind of audience hunch; they feel, "I'd kind of like to see that." And you can't talk them out of it. Or, conversely, they feel, "Oh, I don't want to see that," and you can't talk them into it. It happens all the time.

McDONALD: Is there much truth to the assertion that because it costs so much to produce a play, everybody plays it safe, gives it the necessary box-office additives?

KERR: More and more that's the obvious solution. You don't have to do it that way, but it's safe. It's a form of self-protection. . . .

McDONALD: What alternatives exist? Does one have to go off Broadway, or what?

KERR: The alternative is to just go ahead and take a chance on producing a good show, hoping you'll get the proper response. *The Tenth Man* is by a capable writer, Paddy Chayefsky, but he's had only one play on Broadway before. It was directed by Tyrone Guthrie, but he's had flops, like everybody else. He's got a very good name, but he doesn't guarantee anything absolutely. There are no stars. And not even a very attractive title; the title is neither unattractive nor attractive—you don't know what it means. OK, you've got no protection, no big theater parties, no big stars to reassure you. You come in and everybody thinks it's going to be so-so. And it's terribly interesting. It works. That's the alternative. It's a very risky alternative because costs are frightening and you stand a chance of losing $80,000 in three days.

McDONALD: Can a play be good, has a play been good, let us say "interesting," not even necessarily "great," but the people just won't go to it?

KERR: I can think of relatively few such cases. I believe that quality will out. It may not "out" absolutely. There's nothing to say that quality will outrun meretricious popularity. A less good play with bigger stars, a more intriguing title, etc., may run longer. But I believe that quality will be successful to a reasonable degree; it'll not be dismissed, not be lost. And, of course, there are various kinds of quality. One of them is competence. Now there are a lot of competent plays that the reviewer must accept because they're competent; you must give good notices to them because you can't give them bad notices. At the same time, they're never going to stir either the reviewer or the audience. When you ask, does quality out, what kind of quality do you mean? Steady quality or brilliance? And the difference can be seen at the box-office too. There's a show on Broadway now called *Five Finger Exercise* which is interesting-competent, very well made. It doesn't stir you, but it's so well made that as a reviewer you must praise it to a decent degree; you must say this is a good piece of work.

McDONALD: You wrote an article for *Horizon* on theater in the round, and it seemed to me you were pretty sanguine about what would happen if this type of theater were constructed and became more or less standard in this country.

KERR: First of all, "theater in the round" is something of a misnomer.

McDONALD: You were talking about the stage surrounded on three sides by the audience?

KERR: I was talking about what I prefer to call the theater

with a thrust, a stage that juts out into the audience. It doesn't have to be surrounded on four sides. Three is enough, leaving a fourth side for the actors to enter and exit and use as a point of reference.

McDONALD: Where have you see this type of theater?

KERR: The best one, of course, is in Canada, the Shakespearean Theater at Stratford, Ontario. It's the most exciting theater building and the only fresh theatrical experience on this continent. I am sure it's the coming thing. It is better, practically and theoretically, for very definite reasons. We've become used to the so-called proscenium-arch stage, which is a peephole stage. But that isn't the natural stage. The natural stage in Greece was an open space surrounded on at least three sides. The natural stage in England was the Elizabethan stage which, again, was a platform surrounded on three sides. Then, with the introduction of painting into the theater at the time of the Restoration, designers became obsessed with perspective and wanted to mount perspective paintings behind the actors. But to have a painting, you've got to have a frame. So they put a frame around the painting though they still permitted the apron to jut out. For a time the actors worked out on the apron, the platform, and the paintings were at the back, framed. Gradually the apron was pushed in and the frame out, so that the actor was now in the frame, too; he was part of the painting. But this is unnatural, theatrically speaking. What you're dealing with now are the form and boundaries of painting, which are not the form and boundaries of the theater. It changes the nature of the experience. . . .

McDONALD: For both the actors and the audience?

KERR: For both of them. You're detached from the actors. They're in one room, you're in another. You're looking through a frame at a static and two-dimensional activity.

McDONALD: This emphasis in the liturgical movement about getting the altar out of the sanctuary and more into the center of the church, the congregation surrounding it on three sides—that rests on the same principle, I suppose. It gets the worshipers more intimately involved in the liturgical action. It makes them participants rather than just observers.

KERR: Yes, you see, it makes for a different experience. And it's more exciting and more in the nature of theater to have this kind of experience. It becomes a communal enterprise, bigger, more intimate, more emotional.

McDONALD: Just proximity alone, the closeness to the actors, would account for some of this audience involvement with the play. Even the last row would be much closer to the stage than are most of the seats in the conventional theater.

KERR: Yes. The actors seem larger because they're not dominated by something bigger than themselves. They have to play to an arena in which they are the central point of interest and their acting expands. My real interest is in the changed nature of the experience, which is more intense and should logically lead us to write larger plays.

The playwright never creates his theater. He finds a theater in existence and he writes for it. Now, when you've got a proscenium-arch theater and he must write for that, he must write to fit it. He's cramped by the box set. He's got to stay inside of it. He must construct his plays on a modest scale. His emotions cannot be as overwhelming in a living-room box set as they can be in a great, big, open-arena platform. Once the playwright is forced out onto this thrusting apron, he will have to expand in order to hold his audience. That's the nature of this new beast and I think we're going to get better plays as a result of it. The fact that we now seem to want it is interesting. The fact that we're experimenting with it means we want the bigger play and are trying to encourage the playwright to attempt it.

McDONALD: Is this type of theater planned for the Lincoln Center?

KERR: In general, I think so.

McDONALD: Are there any objections to it?

KERR: Oh, there is the usual puzzlement, which is natural because we have no experience of such a stage at this time, or a very limited experience. Lincoln Center will, as I understand it, have a thrusting apron. What compromises are going to go on behind that apron is something I don't know about.

McDONALD: Who decides these things? Is it the usual committee of people who gather the money, distribute it and make the aesthetic decisions?

KERR: No, no, no. First of all, the architect is Eero Saarinen, who is adventurous. They have Jo Mielziner advising them from the theatrical point of view. They have Robert Whitehead, who is an experienced producer and who is pushing all the time for a more radical shape. Elia Kazan will do much of the directing.

McDONALD: Father William Lynch, S.J., in his book on the "image industries," talks about the need for what he calls "creative theologians" who will understand the aesthetic requirements and possibilities of the stage and television and films.

KERR: One of the tragic things is that we don't grab them when they turn up. Every once in a while a young man will come along who cares about the field and is obviously capable of dealing with it, like Father Leonard Callahan, O.P., for instance, but there seems to be no place to put him. There are no departments of aesthetics. It's not profitable for his Order to have him working in a vacuum, so he's given another job and the first thing you know his interest has declined with the passing years. I don't know where Father Callahan is now. When I was at Catholic University, he had just completed his dissertation on a *Theory of Aesthetic*. It was a wonderful beginning, one of the best things I know of in the field. I certainly urged it upon my own students in those days, but I don't know whether it is even available now. There were other men who might possibly have been drawn into such a study, but there was—and is—no place to draw them to, not even at Catholic University. I'm sure that the moment someone founds such a department, or at least a branch of aesthetics in a philosophy department, there'll be no difficulty in collecting the necessary faculty. That's something I devoutly wish would happen.

McDONALD: When you started reviewing for the *Tribune*, I suppose you were suspect on both sides, from both your secular readers and from Catholics. Did you ever get that feeling?

KERR: Oh, sure, you get not only the feeling, you get letters. From the secular side, because Catholicism had been so identified with a negative approach to the arts, I was suspect as a Catholic. I wasn't on the *Tribune* more than three weeks, I think, before there was a letter in the managing editor's hands suggesting that I had disliked a certain play because I was a Catholic. The fact

that every other critic in New York had also disliked it, none of
them Catholics, did not keep the letter from being written.

McDONALD: How about from the Catholic side? Did they
badger you?

KERR: They still do. I had a letter the other day asking, "How
could you have objected to that beautiful, beautiful musical,
The Sound of Music?" I objected to the sentimentality of it.
There wasn't anything wrong with the basic material, only with
the sticky treatment. But this letter ended up: "And do you
really call yourself a Catholic?" The assumption was that because a show is about Catholics, it must be magnificent, and is
therefore not to be criticized. There weren't a bundle of such
letters on either side; I don't want to give you a false impression.
And sometimes both kinds are fun.

J. F. POWERS

J. F. POWERS, the gifted short-story writer, was born in 1917 in
Jacksonville, Illinois. His family moved from Jacksonville to
Rockford to Quincy to Chicago.

His first published story, "He Don't Plant Cotton," appeared
in *Accent*. His stories have also appeared in *The New Yorker*,
The Commonweal, *The Reporter* and elsewhere. Many of them
are concerned with the Catholic clergy or with the American
Negro. Two collections of his stories have been published: *Prince
of Darkness* and *The Presence of Grace*.

Powers lives in St. Cloud, Minnesota, with his wife, Betty
(also a writer—she has published stories in *The New Yorker*),
and their five children—three girls and two boys.

The conversation with Powers took place in a room on the
floor above the Walgreen Drugstore in St. Cloud. The room is
bare, save for an old leather armchair and a low, rectangular table
on which is a black portable typewriter. On two of the un-
painted, unwashed walls are a wide-ranging assortment of newspaper clippings. A single light bulb hangs on a drop-cord from
the center of the ceiling. It is here that Powers has been for the

past few years at work on a novel—a work which has been punctuated by the appearance of several short stories in *The New Yorker*.

McDonald: Where did you go to school?

Powers: I went to Quincy College Academy. Then I went to Wright College in Chicago for a semester and I got a chance to travel, driving a car for a man in the South, so I did that. I was supposed to be his secretary and chauffeur. It turned out that I was a chauffeur. That was in 1936, '37, and I thought my only chance to get into the economic system would be for me to be what the want ads called a "correspondent." But I never wrote any letters for him. He was supposed to get me a job on a house organ for U.S. Steel when I got back to Chicago, but when I came back there was no job. Then I went to Northwestern at night, taking only English courses for a couple of years. I worked on the Historical Records Survey, which was a WPA project. And there, I think, I grew up really. The Writers' Project was on the floor below us and the Artists' Project on the floor above us. I saw people then, at a distance, that I'd heard about. I don't remember seeing Richard Wright, but he was there. Arna Bontemps was there; he's now the librarian at Fisk in Nashville. Nelson Algren was there. And Jack Conroy was there, the white hope of the proletarian novel.

McDonald: When did you get married?

Powers: In 1946. We lived first in Avon, Minnesota, which is near St. John's Abbey. We didn't know then that we should have taken what little money we had and traveled.

McDonald: As a matter of fact, you have traveled in recent years, haven't you?

Powers: Well, I taught at Marquette for two years, 1949 to 1951. We left Marquette in June, 1951, and went to Ireland for a year, then came back to live in St. Cloud for a couple of years. In 1956-57, I taught one semester at the University of Michigan. At that point I was better off economically than I've ever been. I was paid pretty well at Michigan and I'd received a *Kenyon Review* fellowship which gave me $4,000. Then we lost the house in St. Cloud that we were starting to feel was our own, but which really wasn't; we lost it to this parking lot and the teachers' college. I wrote a story about that which was published in *The Reporter* in the fall of 1957. It's one of my better stories. Then we went to Ireland again.

McDONALD: Where did you live there?

POWERS: The first time we lived in Greystones, County Wicklow. The second time we lived again in Greystones for only about six or seven weeks. We ended up in a big old Georgian house, colder than hell, sticking out on a point into the Irish Sea in a town called Dalkey, close to Dublin. It had been the town of Bernard Shaw. We came back to St. Cloud in December, 1958. We're thinking of leaving again. It's a kind of disease. You get in a town like this and you think, my God! what if the boys grow up and become Jaycees? It isn't the worst thing, but it isn't the way you want your children to turn out, that and nothing more. In a place like this, that can become pretty important, that kind of thing. Well, that's putting it obliquely. It would be nice to have kids who are educated. I wasn't myself. I don't feel I was educated, or am educated. Hardly anyone is, by my standards.

McDONALD: Did you find you wrote more while you were in Ireland?

POWERS: No, all I need, and I don't write much in any case, is this kind of privacy. I had an office in Dublin. It was in a little better shape than this, but not a hell of a lot better. It was on the fourth floor, a long walk up. And over the weekends, the cats would use the last few steps for their bathroom. Things like that, and colder than hell.

McDONALD: Does it make any difference to you where you write?

POWERS: No, it doesn't matter. What I would like to have is a social life. I've read so many times that writers aren't supposed to have a social life; they're supposed to be lonely men.

McDONALD: Or else they colonize.

POWERS: Oh, I don't mean a writers' colony—I wouldn't like that. I don't like that kind of thing, wouldn't want it at all.

McDONALD: Don't you think that in some of the larger cities you could find other people you'd enjoy being with? But I sup-suppose you've tried that and found people you don't, in fact, enjoy being with.

POWERS: Well, I've changed a lot. When I lived in Chicago I knew more people. I was a lot more patient than I am now with people. I don't mean I feel I should be entertained. But I just haven't got time, you know, for would-be painters and would-be writers, and it seems to me that most of them are would-be in the city. I keep thinking of a different kind of person—my friend Don Humphrey, who died. He came from Milwaukee originally but had lived in St. Cloud from about 1945. He was a silversmith, a tremendous artist. He had been a painter at first. He could carve wood. But he ended up by making chalices. I bought his first chalice for much less than I should have, but it was his first one and he really didn't know, at the time, that there was gold in the chalice business, which there was, but not for him. He made chalices such as nobody has ever made before in this country, that I have seen.

McDONALD: When did you start writing?

POWERS: About 1942 I started to try to publish. I was in Chicago, working at Brentano's. I remember I stayed home and wrote my first published story. I just called up and said I was sick, which I wasn't. It was the only way you could get any time off. I stayed home and wrote that story. It was "They Don't Plant Cotton," a story about Negro musicians in a joint in Chicago. Actually it was about Baby Dodds, the famous drummer who is now dead. That was published in the winter of '43 in *Accent*. My second published story, also in *Accent*, was "Lions, Harts, Leaping Does," which has been much reprinted.

McDONALD: When did you find time to write while you were at Brentano's?

POWERS: I'd come home at night, go to bed and then get up a nine o'clock and work maybe until one, over a period of time.

McDONALD: Did you model on anybody? Was there anything derivative in your work? Did you have any idols at the time?

POWERS: Oh, yes, but I don't think it was derivative. I bridle a little bit at that. Maybe I am derivative, I don't know.

McDONALD: I mean, did you have some writers whom you were consciously aware of and whom you admired at that time?

POWERS: Yes, there were some I admired very much and still do, like Katherine Anne Porter and Evelyn Waugh. Not Waugh for his short stories, though he's written some good ones.

But as a writer, I admire Waugh very much. Actually my early heroes were writers. I didn't come to them through school. It just happened at the library. That was during the depression and I was supposed to be job-hunting. You had to get that morning *Tribune* when it came out the night before, about seven-thirty or eight, and read the want ads and then get up, by God, and be the first in line for a job the next morning. Well, you could go out for a job, to wipe out vats in a soup factory, and you'd find ten men there ahead of you at seven o'clock in the morning. That was the way it was then. So I started reading in the library. I'd go out in the morning, go downtown to the employment agency and then just go to the Chicago library and sit up in the reading room. I did a hell of a lot of reading. Job-hunting was futile. I finally did get a kind of a job, an expense account selling insurance, cold turkey, you know. I had a little flashlight I'd give you if you were a good prospect and a little ringed notebook if you weren't so good. I'd give the notebooks to almost anybody. The little flashlight, I would hold that. But I made enough on that to buy this typewriter, about 1936 or '37, a German machine, Olympia, and a copy of *Ulysses* which I wanted and couldn't get at the library because there was a long waiting list.

McDONALD: Are you still writing short stories, or are you working only on your novel?

POWERS: I'm writing a novel, but due to my circumstances I write chapters and turn them into short stories and sell them as stories, which they are actually—I'm afraid they're more stories than chapters—to *The New Yorker* and that's how I get by. At present I'm drawing advance money from my publisher. That was another thing I had in the bag when I went to Ireland the last time. I had maybe $15,000, from one thing and another—advance, the *Kenyon Review* fellowship, the money from Michigan. But that isn't a hell of a lot when you've got four or five children and you're traveling with all the trunks we had.

McDONALD: Why did you keep going back to Ireland?

POWERS: I like Ireland. I hate it in some ways when I'm there. I know Ireland. I know it's not Bing Crosby and Barry Fitzgerald and *The Quiet Man*. It's not that. But Dublin is a wonderful place in its second-rate way. I mean, it's not London.

But it's still a place where people lived, you know, people like Swift and . . .

McDONALD: Why did you go there in the first place, though?

POWERS: Well, I suppose Joyce and *Ulysses* had a lot to do with it, and *Dubliners*. And I suppose one goes back to one's roots. My roots, on my father's side, are in Ireland. He didn't come from Ireland but his father did—from Waterford where all the Powerses come from in Ireland. I went to Waterford to see how it looked. It was something. Where does your family come from?

McDONALD: Scotland on my father's side. His people landed in Nova Scotia and worked their way down through Canada to upper Michigan and Wisconsin.

POWERS: Where in Scotland, do you know?

McDONALD: No.

POWERS: Well, if you know, you see, and you go back to that little town, wherever it was, you get a funny feeling, to think that your grandfather or your grandmother walked on this very stone. Which is not enough reason to go, but those are the things that you do, or I did, find worthwhile.

McDONALD: You don't seem to place much stock, or do you, in such intangible things as atmosphere, place or country; that has no effect on you or your writing.

POWERS: No, it doesn't. I don't believe in that. My enemy is indolence. I know it. I've confessed the sin—which isn't recognized in the confessional, by the way. I've heard it said that you really can't do any more than I'm doing. And I'm not going to be one of those writers who turn out a lot of books, and suddenly people wish they weren't being published.

McDONALD: Is writing a novel some kind of goal or challenge you have set for yourself?

POWERS: I like novels. I like to read novels. I'd like to publish a book that would give a bigger piece of the world than I've been able to give in any one short story, although I think that, together, my stories come to something like a novel. And I have these characters in my novel who are in more than one of my stories. Also, I'd like to write a book that would be *read*. I've published two books of short stories and both have had very good sales, for short stories—which isn't saying a hell of a lot.

McDONALD: But you're not deprecating the value or the stature of short stories.

POWERS: Oh, no. I don't see the short story as a preparation for the novel, just as a poem is not a preparation for the short story. They're entirely different. The way some novelists write short stories, yes. I think the short story, in a way, is harder to do than a novel, though it isn't so with me because I just don't seem to have the novelist's touch. For one thing, I don't—despite what I am doing at this moment—I don't run off at the mouth quite enough. The way the sea looked, or how the trolley came down the hill, that kind of thing. The Melville kind of thing, where you give the history of whaling in a novel, or, if you're a modern, you give the history of sexual intercourse. I just don't do that. I'm impatient. I can't even read many of the great novels—so how can I begin to write them?

McDONALD: Who do you think is writing well? You said Waugh but, of course, he isn't writing the type of stuff he was writing when you were twenty years old.

POWERS: Well, he's been getting a bum deal lately. I liked his last novel. Catholics keep looking for another *Brideshead Revisited.*

McDONALD: They shouldn't, I think.

POWERS: I think that was a good book, but it wasn't as good as some of his others. It was wine to their gin, you know; gold to their silver, but I think the work in the silver is better.

McDONALD: What about Greene?

POWERS: I'm not an admirer of Greene. I wouldn't know why. There's something about him, as a writer, I don't like. Joyce Cary is another, not that they have very much in common. I read a thing on Joyce Cary just recently in *The New Yorker* by Anthony West. Very good. It explained to me why I didn't like Joyce Cary.

McDONALD: Is anybody writing anything good these days? There doesn't seem to be very much in the novel.

POWERS: There's no novelist I think of in this way—I wonder what his next book will be like. With the possible exception of Waugh.

McDONALD: How far along is this novel you're working on?

POWERS: I'd hoped to publish it this year. But I'm not going to do it now because you have to allow six months for a book to be set up and I'm not through with it yet. I could very well spend the rest of this year writing it. I just finished, in the last two or three days, a chapter that I'd been working on for about a year. It isn't very good, but it's all right, I think. I get to the point where I can't write at all. I mean my critical acumen fails me and still it's the thing that keeps me from just turning it loose. When I was younger, I could come into a room with something on my mind, such as what the Negro has to go through in this country, and I could write a story about it. I did write "The Trouble" at one sitting. It's not a terribly good story, but it's not a bad story. I don't work like that any more. Now it takes me a month or two to write a story. I think they're better stories. I don't read my early stories. Now and then, at night, I may read part of one, if I find I'm working on something that reminds me of something I've gone through before. I might read it just to help myself. I haven't read "The Trouble" for a long, long time. What I know now would have kept me from writing it when I wrote it.

McDONALD: Yes, it's too bad, I suppose, when one gets these cautionary feelings . . .

POWERS: Yes, in a way, but what about the people that don't get them? What about the old boy that just continues to run off at the mouth? Isn't that awful?

McDONALD: What is your novel about?

POWERS: It's a book about this Religious Order I founded—the Clementine Fathers, the Order of St. Clement. I published a couple of stories in *The New Yorker* about them. It'll be about Father Urban—he's right there on the wall, you can see him. Actually it's a picture of somebody clipped from *This Week* magazine. Then there's Wilf, he's the rector of St. Clement's Hill, near Duesterhaus, Minnesota. And then there's Father John or "Jack" and there's Brother Harold. This postcard is something I've just gotten out lately, from Duesterhaus.. The Order has its own postcards. This one reads, "Flocks feeding at St. Clement's Hill, Duesterhaus." They're wonderful cards. I have another one here, "Herds feeding at St. Clement's Hill, Duesterhaus."

McDONALD: Why Duesterhaus?

POWERS: That was the name of a fellow I knew, means bleak house, or sad house, or sorrowful house, in German. The story is about Father Urban's being sent to this foundation of the Order in Minnesota. He had been a big-time speaker, a poor man's Fulton Sheen. He was suddenly sent up here to this white elephant, not as the rector, but as one of the boys, one of the three priests. That's my story, what he did there, how he tried to put the place on its feet, how he worked as a common work-man—because that was the rector's idea about everything, saving string: the pound-foolish, penny-wise kind of rector. Father Urban is not that kind of man. He's what used to be the Pull-man type, now the type with the attaché case, doing lots of good and instilling a feeling in the young men in the novitiate. Father Urban was trying to develop something special for the Clemen-tines. What it was, he wasn't sure—a kind of opportunism, I would say.

McDONALD: Then you had the idea pretty well worked out.

POWERS: Oh, as an idea, I thought it would be a nice little nut-brown novel, all kinds of irony.

McDONALD: What is your problem? A certain chapter, or . . .

POWERS: Oh, just too much detail. I get into things I prob-ably shouldn't get into—the kind of things the hack writer will never do because it's like burning wood in a woodless area. The hack doesn't waste anything. I knock myself out with these post-cards, for instance. What's the point of that? What's the point of writing letters to people that you might work on three or four hours; just for the hell of it, just to give 'em a laugh. I still do that.

McDONALD: Or give tape-recorded interviews.

POWERS: That doesn't happen very often. I wish I had a tape recorder, though. I often think *that's* what I need. I need to come down here and turn on that thing and talk. I don't mind talking. I work in a kind of fog. I hit through to a vein now and then when I know everything is right. I come in about eleven-thirty and go home about six. And that's usually all I work, except when I'm doing a chapter-story and I have to get it done.

McDONALD: You said once that you're not just going to turn this novel out.

POWERS: That's right. I don't care any more about publishing. I don't mean I'm above pride, but that particular kind of ambition is almost gone out of me. And I haven't reached the top of the heap, like Pope John, either.

MCDONALD: Of course, I suppose you could get into a situation where you'd never turn something loose, in which your critical perceptiveness would be so finely tuned . . .

POWERS: That's right.

MCDONALD: You said once, in an interview for *The Catholic Messenger*, "I believe in a realm of excellence. . . . If you work hard enough and have enough talent to begin with, then some day you'll get there. Once it's art, it will last forever."

POWERS: Yes, that's the way I feel about good work. Not all of mine will last, but some few things will, I think. And, considering what I might have been, it's good enough. It's better than being an All-American. It's better than being a big-league baseball player—things I had thought I might be when I was ten years old.

MCDONALD: In your teaching, at Marquette and Michigan and St. John's, you taught creative writing. Can you teach that? What is the limit to what one can do in a class like that?

POWERS: Well, there is a limit, but I know very well I was helped by a teacher who has since become famous, Bergen Evans at Northwestern.

MCDONALD: In what way? You mean he told you what not to do?

POWERS: He told me where I was bad, where I was callow— and I was callow all over the place. I had the feeling he knew what he was talking about. I did not have the feeling he was somebody being polite, somebody being decent, somebody sending away a defender of his reputation. I think a lot of teachers of creative writing do that. They never do tell the people who should be told off. Those people go away and they're often mouthy types and they celebrate this teacher who, if he is also a professional writer, finds this doesn't hurt him at all. The students become claques for him.

MCDONALD: Art and artistic integrity seem to disappear in that kind of a situation. People are just playing at it.

POWERS: You know that's the way it is. That's my big beef

about the arts in this country. Instead of people reading a book or reading a story or a poem, or listening to music the way they'd eat a hamburger, they approach it piously; they approach it like a bunch of damned atheists in church. The point is the arts do exist. I've said this before. They exist, like God, whether we believe it or not. A good poem, or a good story, has an existence whether you experience it or not. There's a reality there. It's the reality of art. And it eliminates, once you feel that, the whole Chautauqua approach to the arts and the cultural scoutmasters who are always with us.

McDONALD: Does that come from emotionalism when confronted by the arts?

POWERS: It's the *Main Street story*. It's Carol Kennicott somehow getting her husband to go to the concert in the high school auditorium; it's the Five Foot Shelf; it's all the good things that are said about paperbacks. But the whole atmosphere, I say, is fakery. It makes for scoutmasters *and* beatniks, all those second-rate people who have come into some kind of prominence. Well, I don't say there'll ever be a society where phonies will not be possible, but if people had any real feeling for literature, this wouldn't be possible. It's the sort of thing Dali does. Dali *is* an artist, but he takes the people by their ignorance and makes a good deal out of it. Ask anybody to name one artist. Dali. Why? How did he do it?

McDONALD: I suppose integrity is the quality that is so conspicuously lacking in all of this.

POWERS: You know what happens when Broadway or TV people get hold of something good that they feel won't quite come off for their audience. This guy has to be this and she has to be that and we'll use this instead of that, and pretty soon, what have you got? A producer's idea of the great difficulty we're going to have getting this great idea over to *them*. You have got nothing then.

McDONALD: I used to see a good deal of unreality in so many church organizations. They put all their effort and energy into the externals. I mean, on some big program, a tremendous amount of energy and ingenuity is expended in securing the right hall at the right time with just the right sound system, plenty of pre-meeting coverage in the press and on television, all of that, and then the meeting itself will have third- or fourth-rate speakers, but nobody cares because the façade is so pretty.

POWERS: We're dressing it up. There'll be some damned religious movie or other and somebody will say, "Did you see that? It's a cute picture." You know the kind of thing that's said when a young man becomes a priest—"So nice for his mother." The Hollywood approach to religion—which is a refusal to accept Christ on the Cross. Christ out in a pasture with the lambs, yes. But Christ the Loser, in this world, uh-uh. We're Americans. We think it has to come out even in the end. It's got to.

McDONALD: In your short stories, there have been two general themes—more, I know, but two that have been general and recurrent—the race theme and the Catholic clergy theme. Had you had first-hand experience with both of those areas of life?

POWERS: I think I can say, without having been a seminarian and without having been a Negro, I have had first-hand experience. I was brought up downstate in Illinois where the atmosphere was rather Southern. It was a town settled by Southerners. The town was Protestant. The best people were Protestants and you felt that. That, to some extent, made a philosopher out of me. It made me mad. That's why Negroes are philosophical, because of their experience. A good man who's lost his job is never the same about industry.

McDONALD: Certainly your insights into clerical life would almost make one think you'd been around priests all your life.

POWERS: I had two friends that went into the seminary. We were in high school together and even grade school. One became a priest and one didn't. When I started out as a writer, I don't think I had any idea of doing stories about priests. My idea of a story then was such things as I wouldn't touch now with a ten-foot pole.

McDONALD: Violence, you mean?

POWERS: Violence and Cecil B. DeMille themes, the things that interest any young person. And most people stay young mentally. It's the mentality of the comic strip and that was what interested me then. Sinclair Lewis began to take me away from it. He was one of my early gods when I was about eighteen, nineteen. But I knew these seminarians very well, and still know them. I became interested in their life which, to me, seemed very romantic. I didn't want to be a priest at any time. I knew from the time I saw priests talking to old ladies on the sidewalk in front of church that that wasn't for me. That doesn't say much for my understanding of the priesthood. On the other hand, there's an awful lot of *that*—all these young pastors in the suburbs who have to knock down thousands and thousands of dollars in order to build this and that. Well, what does that mean? Shaking hands with some guy, and you can't really tell him what's wrong with him because he's got what you need. I'm sympathetic to the priest. I wouldn't want to have to be the first guy that every other drunk calls. And a priest can't go anywhere unless he disguises himself. If he isn't disguised, right away he's got somebody on him who's not a Catholic but who "certainly thinks Fulton Sheen is doing wonderful work" or somebody else who is not a Catholic but whose daughter married one. The priest is a sitting duck.

McDONALD: Of course, you could have written stories about other types of people; it's the observation and insight that count.

POWERS: I could have, yes. I remember being asked if I couldn't change "The Valiant Woman" story around so that I could sell it to a certain magazine. The main character, a priest, should become a professor. I said no. I might have made the change, but it would have been a different thing then. I think the water of irony, the gin of irony maybe, is purer and higher proof in the life of a priest who is committed to both worlds, you might say.

McDONALD: Do you have any stories coming out this year?

POWERS: There's one called "Wrens and Starlings" and it'll be out in *The New Yorker* on May 21. It's a story about Father Urban up at St. Clement's Hill. *The New Yorker* has another one about Father Urban which I wrote in Ireland last year. That story will appear later.

McDONALD: How many chapters do you have left to do in the novel?

POWERS: I have four. I've got to pull it together and it isn't ready to pull together.

McDONALD: Can you tell, when you start working on a chapter, whether it has possibilities as a short story?

POWERS: I can see it right away. I can just spot it, the way these Italians they bring up here can sex chickens, the way they can tell the males and the females right off. I have that feeling about material. You just know whether a thing is going to come off, or whether you're going to have to pump oil into it somewhere, or blood. I've been accused of knowing that too well, of not giving natural birth, just being too wise that way.

McDONALD: Too facile?

POWERS: Just being too clever. Alfred Kazin reviewed my last book in *The New Republic*, and I wrote and thanked him for it. It was a good review. But he said that, although he was never quite able to figure it, what was going to happen in a story, he still thought I was in danger of being too clever that way. I suppose that's the danger of professionalism.

McDONALD: That's a nice danger to have to worry about.

POWERS: Well, I don't have it *naturally*, see? I work like hell. A thing is never really "in" with me in a story. I like to start a story with an idea of writing something, just one thing. I may drop it later on. I work for an end that I can feel. At Ann Arbor, just before Christmas, I saw in Sears and Roebuck's window this little crib which I later put in a story, "A Couple of Nights Before Christmas," which *The New Yorker* published in 1957 in their Christmas issue. This little thing was going around like this tape recorder, with the animals and shepherds going before the stationary crib. They were on a turntable. I knew then I had something. I figured that was it for me. That was Christmas at Duesterhaus.

McDONALD: Does *The New Yorker* do much tampering with your stories?

POWERS: Well, they have their objections, but they haven't tampered with my stuff. I don't mean it's published as I first write it. Very often they have an objection to this or that aspect of it, or they want me to clarify it, and I will. It always gets better, improves with rewriting. When I put a book of stories together, I don't worry about *The New Yorker* stories at all. I know they make sense and that they are grammatical and that they are clear, as clear as I can be. Some of the others I have to think more about, rewriting on my own.

McDONALD: How long have you been working on your novel?

POWERS: Since 1956. I just don't think it will be that long a
book, that's the trouble. Something should be said about the
distractions of moving, selling all your furniture, as we did, and
moving to Ireland with four children and having a baby there
and then moving back.

McDONALD: If your novel is a longer short story—I'm not saying it is—but if it is, does it have that same tone and spirit as
the short story?

POWERS: I don't think it will be. I really don't think it will
be. That won't be its trouble. I just think there'll be too many
words, you know, too many words that don't quite do it. But
you couldn't just cut *them* because what you'd have left wouldn't
be right then. You see? It should have been done differently, it
should have been a different drink. It should have been a mar-
tini instead of an old-fashioned with a cherry in it.

McDONALD: It can't, then, be a matter of simply abbreviating.

POWERS: That's right. It isn't just cutting here. It's form.
That's the thing, form. That's why I had trouble with this
chapter I finally did finish. I couldn't find the form. Now that'll
mean nothing to most people. There's a way of opening a bottle.
There's a way of climbing a fence. There's a way of getting in
and out of a car that's right, or wrong. There's a way of talking
to high school students. The form has to be right.

McDONALD: Does it bother you if you sit here for six hours
and don't get one page done?

POWERS: It doesn't bother me enough. I'm miserable sometimes, but I'm not the kind of guy who's going to crack up, I
think. I think the work, when I finish with it, will be good
enough. And I know that you can't force it. I know that if I
had to write the rest of the book today or lose my life, I'd probably write it and it'd be a wonderful thing. And anyway I'd be
able to rewrite it. I'm not, as far as I know, going to have to do
that. But just to sit down and because my kids need shoes (they
don't as a matter of fact), get the book finished and get another
one out and somehow end up as somebody mentioned in Earl
Wilson's column—it's not going to work out that way.

McDONALD: It's possible for people to write for purely economic reasons, isn't it, and come up with something that might

possibly be first-rate? You read about Dostoevsky who ground
it out and nevertheless came up with some permanent art. Still
he was writing to pay the butcher and the baker.

POWERS: The only writer I know who has written a lot of
books and who is readable and who has written good books
almost every time is Evelyn Waugh. I could reread any of his
books tonight. I don't feel that way about any other writer. I
could read his *Decline and Fall* every year, and I did for a while,
and laugh out loud every time. I think there's a world of books,
of very good books. Max Beerbohm certainly has entered that
world. And *Alice in Wonderland* is one of those books, and
The Wind in the Willows is one, and Waugh's *Decline and Fall*
and others belong on that little shelf of books that are somehow
"more." Something happens. They're simple. The writing can
be very simple, but it holds on in kind of a funny way. It doesn't
sweat, though sweating was involved, and it doesn't miss. It
doesn't seem to care, to try very hard. It's just devastating. I
haven't written any book, probably won't, that will enter that
world. Something will be wrong. I'll be dull as hell somewhere
along the line.

PHYLLIS McGINLEY

PHYLLIS McGINLEY, acknowledged mistress of light and satirical
verse (*The Love Letters of Phyllis McGinley*) and essayist (*The
Province of the Heart*), has been published in virtually every
literary magazine but is probably best known for her verse in
The New Yorker.

She was born in 1905 in Ontario, Oregon, and brought up on
a ranch in Colorado. Her father, a Catholic, died when she was
thirteen years old. Her mother, an Episcopalian, moved to
Ogden, Utah, her home town, and there provided Phyllis with
a Catholic education for a year or two at the convent of the
Sisters of the Holy Cross. Phyllis entered the University of Utah,
graduated in 1927 and then "came East as fast as I could," which
was in 1929.

Miss McGinley (Mrs. Charles Hayden) lives with her husband and two daughters in Larchmont, a suburb of New York. A few blocks away live their friends, Walter and Jean Kerr.

The interview with Miss McGinley took place in the living-room of her large and comfortable home. Bridie, the Haydens' Irish maid, had just put a pork roast in the oven (two Maryknoll seminarians were expected for dinner that evening). The interview proceeded with only occasional interruptions—for coffee and checking the progress of the roast.

McDonald: When did you start writing verse?

McGinley: I am ashamed to say how long ago it was when I started writing. I began when I was six. I'm one of those people who never wanted to be anything but a poet. It never occurred to me, from the time I started in school, that I would ever want to be anything but a poet. I was sure I would write poetry. And because I was so blissfully ignorant, I went ahead and planned to write poetry. It didn't enter my head that maybe I couldn't write it and make a living from it.

McDonald: Who published your first poem?

McGinley: It was The Catholic World, which was a literary magazine in those days, in 1926, when I was still in college. I also published one in The Commonweal in the days when Michael Williams was editing it.

McDonald: When did The New Yorker begin accepting your poetry?

McGinley: I think I began writing for The New Yorker in 1932.

McDonald: What other magazines have bought and published your verse?

McGinley: Oh, practically everybody . . . America, The American Scholar, The Atlantic Monthly—I can go right through the alphabet. Of course, now I write prose, so I make the rounds of all of them again.

McDonald: Do you have a regular working schedule?

McGinley: No, I'm quite literal about being primarily a housekeeper and wife and suburban matron. It is true that I work only when I can. Now, of course, both of my daughters are at college and I have all the time in the world. The only trouble is that now I have nothing to get away from. I used to write to get away from domesticity. Now it's hard to make yourself write.

McDONALD: I thought that one poem about the daughters was simply wonderful.

McGINLEY: The "Ballade of Lost Objects"—"Where in the world have the children vanished . . . ?"

McDONALD: Yes.

McGINLEY: It's one of my favorites, too. I mean I know which of my poems are good and which are bad. And that's one of the good ones.

McDONALD: Well, I like also the "Gallery of Elders" and your "Saints." They're terse and directly to the point.

McGINLEY: I learned to write short. That's what one does. I used to write long, maybe because editors paid by the line. As everyone does who is going to be a respectable and reprintable writer, I learned to contract and now the more I write, the shorter I get.

McDONALD: I have always thought that one could work by that general rule, that the more economical your style, the better.

McGINLEY: It certainly should be that way in poetry.

McDONALD: Have you read E. B. White's introduction and chapter in Strunk's *Elements of Style?* He keeps hammering at this thing, this terseness and economy of words and elimination of all unnecessary parts.

McGINLEY: It's so true. I'm doing my selected verse now and I've been over about 600 poems so far and I've thrown out at least 250 or 300 of them. I was ruthless, without even a pang. I took everything that was dull or long or trifling and I just threw it out.

McDONALD: Who's going to bring it out?

McGINLEY: Viking, in the fall. It'll be called *Times Three.* I'm trying to keep it to 300 poems. I've written about 700 or 750, perhaps more, which have been published.

McDONALD: When did you start writing prose essays? Or have you always written prose?

McGINLEY: No, I never wanted to write prose. *Good House-*

keeping talked me into it . . . I tried it and wrote two or three or four supposedly humorous essays and they bought them, but they weren't what I wanted to do. Then I began writing fairly serious things. I had some opinions I wanted to express and I expressed them in prose and that turned out to be what I wanted, what I could do.

McDonald: The old adage holds true, then, to be oneself. Young writers, at least in the first few years, are so affected. They write as they think they are expected to write.

McGinley: They're imitating.

McDonald: Yes . . .

McGinley: Well, that's very important. They have to imitate. . . .

McDonald: I don't mean imitation so much, as to write a type of thing or in a way they think is the way writers should be writing. You were writing, as you say, light, humorous essays, but you didn't feel right.

McGinley: It wasn't my field, no.

McDonald: But don't you think that that accounts for the success of any writing, that the writer is doing what . . .

McGinley: What he can do, what's original and in his vein. Yes.

McDonald: Yes, there is a tone that is yours, there is no synthetic quality to it at all.

McGinley: The only thing is, I don't think a young writer *has* any tone of his own. I think he has to start out by imitating what he admires and then by imitation he finally gets his own signature. Jane Austen is the perfect example of that. She started out to imitate the woman who wrote *Evelina*, Fanny Burney, who was very successful with *Evelina*. And Jane's very first book, *The Letters of Lady Susan*, I believe it was—a very interesting, little, light novel—is a real imitation of Fanny Burney. And it was pretty good. It was better than Burney. But it was imitation. Then, after she'd got rid of that, she began to write something bigger than Burney ever dreamed of. But she did it by climbing those stairs up to her own vein.

McDonald: It's almost inevitable, I suppose, the imitation phase.

McGINLEY: I mistrust the wildly original in the very young, I really do. They come to nothing, they come to nothing. The real solid ones work up to a meaning and a tone and a signature of their own.

McDONALD: In *The Elements of Style,* White discusses this whole thing of what is style, that it is the person, his being, and his way of looking and seeing.

McGINLEY: It's like charm, you either have it or you don't, I think. There are so many books that could be interchanged, one with the other. And there's so much poetry that could be interchanged and you would never know who wrote it. It's that signature of your own that counts and I don't see any way of acquiring it except by continual work.

McDONALD: I have a feeling, when I read your "Gallery of Elders," that there is a certain inevitability about the way you wrote them, that there is, in fact, no other way to make your points than the way you've made them.

McGINLEY: Remember, I worked twenty-five years to get where I could do that. Yes, I feel that at this time I probably write light verse quite well, but I've spent a long, long lifetime doing it.

McDONALD: I get that same feeling reading Graham Greene, not that I think he's a great novelist . . .

McGINLEY: I'm not sure that he isn't.

McDONALD: Well, I'm not apologizing for the way I feel about his work, but I wouldn't want to imply that I think he is in the "great" category. But I do admire, again, that terseness and economy of words that mark his style. . . .

McGINLEY: I think that people ought to be judged on their best and not on their worst. And Graham Greene has written one really great novel, *The Power and the Glory*—I think it's a great novel and, after all, what more can you ask than one great novel? Or one great poem even? Look at Wordsworth. Think of the nonsense he wrote, dreadful things. William Cole, in his *Fireside Book of Light Verse,* has included a quotation from Wordsworth, a solemn, serious verse which is terribly funny and which he's included in his anthology of light verse because it *is* so funny. But on the other hand, Wordsworth could write very great things. So we judge him on his best.

McDONALD: You mentioned Jane Austen. Is she one of the people you particularly like?

McGINLEY: I think Jane Austen is one of the three or four great women geniuses of all time. She's written six perfect novels, the best novels in English, I think. You may not always enjoy them the most, but I think they are the most nearly perfect novels ever written. In fact, what Jane Austen did was to destroy the novel of manners. She wrote it so perfectly that nobody else could ever do it again. She annihilated it. Or aren't you a Jane Austen fan?

McDONALD: I am when I am reading her, but it isn't the type of thing . . . well, I don't have the time these days to go back and re-read . . .

McGINLEY: Some people think that Jane Austen and Shakespeare were the two great English geniuses.

McDONALD: I loved her when I had to read her.

McGINLEY: Oh, you had to read her? I didn't, you see. I have an essay in my book [The Province of the Heart] called "The Consolations of Illiteracy," in which I tell the joys of an education in which, if you were never made to read these things, if you escaped from college unscathed by knowledge, then you could come to these things without hostility. I didn't read Jane Austen until twenty years ago and, of course, fell madly in love with her. I don't think she's for young people. Oh, she is, but she's more appreciated, I think, in the dry time because there isn't an ounce of sentiment in her, not one iota of romance. She's quite merciless.

McDONALD: Do you find, when you write poetry, that it comes easier when you have, say, a group like the "Gallery of Elders" or the "Saints?" When you have a framework like that, within which you are working, is it easier to write, or can you toss off . . .

McGINLEY: Oh, I don't toss them off. I spend weeks sometimes writing a poem.

McDONALD: I didn't mean that. I mean is it easier to have a set of things, a category, a framework ahead of time, within which you know you are going to work?

McGINLEY: I've found it easier. You see, the lyric impulse drains away at a certain age. I often think if Keats had lived longer he might not have gone on being a great poet. That strictly lyric type of poet sometimes does not last because the lyric impulse, the passion, leaves after a while. I think I definitely wrote my best poetry about ten years ago. I know I did. I find it easier now to write poetry of ideas than the kind of thing I wrote when my children were just growing up, or than the poetry I wrote during the war. Now I find that I do not *feel* that much any more. I *think* more and I find that this kind of thing, like the "Saints" and so on, is like a prose writer writing biography instead of novels. Your creative passion has dwindled, whereas your knowledge is bigger and that kind of thing then comes easier.

McDONALD: Of course, I'll have to read your earlier stuff now.

McGINLEY: Well, it wasn't very good, it really wasn't.

McDONALD: I mean the stuff you wrote at the height of your lyrical powers.

McGINLEY: Such as they are. Let's don't exaggerate them. I'm not talking about myself as a feminine Keats.

McDONALD: But I can't contrast what I think is great with what you say is greater. I don't know what your earlier things were.

McGINLEY: Let's say I've never written anything "great," but I've written some "good" things. I've done one useful thing—I have helped restore the respectability of light verse as poetry, which really had not been done for a long, long while. It used to be perfectly respectable to write light verse as a type of poetry. Then there grew up this great gulf between society on the one hand and dramatic and lyrical verse on the other. And I do think I helped to bring back a measure of respectability to light verse.

McDONALD: Lewis Gannett has said that your poetry will be read and enjoyed long after the serious, social works of the tired, pale poets has disappeared.

McGINLEY: As a matter of fact, the press on that book [*The Love Letters of Phyllis McGinley*] was marvelous and it was because it was the first really good book I'd done; that is, it was a book in which there were few weak poems.

McDONALD: You're not saying you like these less than your lyrical things, are you?

McGINLEY: No, I like them. I've written hundreds of poems, but I don't think I've written more than a dozen really first-rate ones. I think that "Ballade of Lost Objects" is a really good poem, and to be able to write a ballade, which is an artificial form —now I'm talking about myself objectively here—but to be able to write a ballade with real emotion in it, I believe it's not been done before. It's a very artificial form and usually does not carry anything so heavy as an emotion, but that really did. I think "In Praise of Diversity" is a good didactic poem. Someone said that he had never appreciated Pope until he read it. Then I think "Mid-Century Love Letter" is a good poem. The one called "The Doll House" is a good poem. Those four I would consider good poems. . . .

McDONALD: Two of those have the quality of poignancy, but you get it across without the treacle.

McGINLEY: When I was beginning to write, I wrote seriously. I sold poems to *The Atlantic Monthly* and to some of the serious magazines. That's when I was very young, in my early twenties. And those poems were just about as obscure as obscure poets are now. They were quite personal and quite obscure. It's so easy to write obscurely and it's so very hard to write clearly. I don't mean that all obscure poets are lazy, I don't mean that at all, but I think that many of them are. The way I wrote those which are easy to read is that I worked on them for weeks. It took me a straight month to write "In Praise of Diversity." Whether you like it or not, it's one that I happen to like. It took me a straight month, working every single day, eight and ten and twelve hours a day, and it has only about twenty stanzas, I believe.

McDONALD: Ordinarily, you'd think that working over something like that would make it labored and tortuous. In my own writing, I often feel that even if I had the time to go over and rewrite my journalistic material, it would lose some of its spontaneity.

McGINLEY: That isn't true of poetry. Now there are some geniuses who can do it, but I'm not a genius. Shakespeare never blotted a line, they tell us. I understand that Auden can turn out a poem in a morning, but I happen to think Auden's a genius,

too. By the way, in my study of saints, I've tried to find the one
common denominator of the saints. Do you know what it is?

McDONALD: Humility?

McGINLEY: Humility? Not necessarily, no.

McDONALD: Charity, I suppose.

McGINLEY: Absolute charity. That is the one quality in all
of them. They gave constantly of themselves, their money, everything. They have that only in common.

McDONALD: What about some of those cantankerous people
like St. Jerome?

McGINLEY: Of course, some saints were quite difficult people.
But they all gave of themselves, and that's the only quality I can
find that they have in common. Among the saints, there are as
many personalities as there are human facets to the character.
The most marvelous thing about studying the saints is that there's
always a saint for *you*. There's always one whose characteristics
are yours, except that they've been sublimated. I got interested
in saints because my younger daughter was studying them in
school and brought some books home. I was amused by them.
The first one I did was St. Philip Neri because he amused me so.
He always carried two books around with him—a Bible and a
book of jokes. I thought this would make a verse, so I wrote
about St. Philip Neri. And then I thought, what fun, I think
I'll do some of the others.

McDONALD: Did you sell the first one?

McGINLEY: I couldn't sell them anywhere at first. I did ten
of them. Then *Harper's Bazaar* printed two; the *Atlantic* printed
one or two; and *America* printed the rest.

McDONALD: About that selected verse you're working on.

McGINLEY: I'm dividing it into sections. I had the idea of
dividing it into the present, the 1950's, the 1940's, '30's. . . .
The '40's were a lot of war poems, the whole group at the beginning of the '40's are on the war.

McDONALD: You took that pretty much to heart, the war?

McGINLEY: That was what made me begin to write semi-
seriously. Up to that time I had written chiefly real, honest-to-
goodness light verse; you know, the kind that might appear in
Post Scripts in *The Saturday Evening Post*. But the war shook

me, as it did everyone, and probably by that time I had grown up enough to write something more. . . .

McDONALD: Now that you mention the war, I wonder what you think of Virginia Woolf, who, you know, committed suicide and it was said she had been brooding over the war in Europe.

McGINLEY: You know, I don't agree with Virginia Woolf. I don't mean I don't enjoy her, I do. I very much enjoy her criticism. I deplore her point of view, the idea that a woman is at a disadvantage. I am anti-feminist. Virginia Woolf, in *A Room of One's Own*, felt that women get the short end of the stick, because a woman can never do both things—that is, she has to give up one success or the other. Well, I don't think it's important who writes, as long as writing gets done. I don't think it matters whether a woman does it or a man does it. A woman will do it if she has enough genius. But I don't think women have felt that genius is so important to them. They have another duty. I am very anti-feminist. I think that this feeling sorry for oneself for being a woman is nonsense. Of course, women find life unfair, but who doesn't? Life isn't fair and whoever expected it to be fair is very immature and very badly brought up.

Perhaps it's impossible to be a great writer and not be self-centered. I have a thesis about this, that women are not going to be great geniuses, maybe ever, because they are not sufficiently self-centered. You see, genius—and now I'm talking about real genius, not a talent, not a flair, but real genius—is a way of life. To a genius, the exercising of that gift is the whole biological and spiritual reason of his life. Now that is the antithesis of a woman's make-up and function. To a woman who is a real woman the most important thing in life is her children, her family. As long as women still function as women, I do not think they'll be geniuses because they find that other kind of thing unimportant. It is not by accident that the few women literary geniuses we've had have been either unmarried or childless. There've been none I can think of, except minor ones. Jane Austen, George Sand, George Eliot were either spinsters or childless.

McDONALD: Cyril Connolly says some place in his *Enemies of*

Promise that the pram in the hallway is one of the great enemies of talent, of literary promise.

McGINLEY: Perhaps that is one of the reasons there aren't more Catholic writers.

McDONALD: Harry Sylvester once wrote an article to that effect.

McGINLEY: It's perfectly possible. To the non-believer, it's possible to just slough off marriage or family if it gets in the way of your writing. But if you are a highly moral man, you accept your responsibilities and if those responsibilities interfere with the free exercise of your talent, then you don't freely exercise your talent. Now that is, I suppose, deplorable aesthetically, but in the long run it makes for a better world.

McDONALD: I suppose, in the economy of things, there will always be those who will do what the married man with a family might have done but couldn't do.

McGINLEY: Look at Bach, though. How many children did he have? Twenty? It has only been recently that the heel as hero has become a part of our folklore. The legend of the rake as writer is quite new. There have been rakes as writers, don't misunderstand me, but they were not built up as heroes. On television the other night I saw the dramatization of Somerset Maugham's *The Moon and Sixpence* and I was appalled. The satire in that book was drained out of it and here was Laurence Olivier playing for all he was worth the saga of the Absolute Cad, the Absolute Heel as Hero. That wasn't really implicit in the novel. That's a romantic notion that's taken hold of this generation, that talent is its own excuse. Our great men were supposed to be moral men at one time. If they weren't, it might have been forgiven them on the grounds that they were talented. But nobody expected people to go out and behave like heels out of a sense of duty. Now they're *supposed* to behave that way. . . . I think back to Thomas More, who was a saint and a writer, and to Chaucer, who, so far as I know, was highly moral. But then I always admired More because he was a hero to his son-in-law and it isn't everybody who can be that.

Could we stop this for a moment for a cup of coffee?

(*Miss McGinley went to the kitchen and returned with coffee.*)

McGINLEY: I don't know where this is heading. Is it only about me, or about my ideas?

McDONALD: It's about you and whatever you're interested in.

McGINLEY: Well, one of the things I am interested in is Catholic education. I think it needs an enormous amount of revision. I've thought this out very carefully—I think there are far too many Catholic colleges in America. In fact, I am against complete Catholic education, the way the bishops were back in the 1800's in this country. You know, this whole thing could have gone a different way. The Catholics might have gone exclusively into the public schools, as Bishop Ireland wanted it.

McDONALD: You've done some research in this matter then.

McGINLEY: I've read widely in it because I feel very strongly about it. I feel that that is at the bottom of this wall between Catholics and Protestants, a wall that should not be there, you see. The non-Catholic's fear and hatred of the Catholic Church would have been largely dissipated by this time if Catholics had entered more strongly into community affairs and into the public school system. Bishop Ireland was one of the leaders who did not want separate Catholic schools. He said that the Catholics, a new immigrant group, should be assimilated into the American community. Unfortunately this came up right at the time when Liberalism was harming the Church abroad and the Pope thought that "Americanism" was harming it here in this country and that gave the big impetus to the people who wanted separate Catholic schools.

McDONALD: What do you mean when you say you are "against complete Catholic education"? Do you mean completely separate?

McGINLEY: I mean I am against running the child from kindergarten through college in completely separate Catholic schools. I am afraid such Catholics never will form a part of the real America and we will still have Catholics and Protestants staring at each other over the fence and not really speaking to each other or understanding each other. I can understand why Protestants fear the mass weight of this kind of education. Of course, it *is* education for morals and Catholic children have to have morality somewhere along the line. But never to meet on equal terms with Protestants and Jews is to me rather sad.

McDONALD: When do you think Catholics should get their Catholic-school education?

McGINLEY: I wish every young Catholic person could be in a really first-rate Catholic high school. That is when the child is most impressionable and the brightest. I think there should be marvelous Catholic high schools, so good that public high schools couldn't compete with them. Let children go the first four or six grades to the public school. Of course, there are lots of reasons why changing over to the Catholic school at the seventh grade would be difficult, but that is when the young need good, sound, intellectual and theological training—between the sixth grade and the end of high school.

Then I think it's a pity that there are so many underprivileged Catholic colleges, so much duplication by Orders, each with its small college. What there ought to be, it seems to me, are four or five Catholic universities in America so good that people would be clamoring to get into them and it would be a privilege and a prize to be able to work in them. They'd be towers of learning in America, instead of what we have now, spreading ourselves so thin.

McDONALD: I think it's true that we don't have enough scholars of distinction in any one discipline that we can stock every one of our Catholic college and universities with them.

McGINLEY: There isn't that much money either. Catholics haven't yet learned to leave their money—or their fortunes—to Catholic colleges.

McDONALD: Dr. George Shuster has been talking about the importance of discovering and encouraging a child's intellectual gifts when he is in high school.

McGINLEY: I know Dr. Shuster is on my side in this. Now my girls went to Catholic parochial school and Catholic high school, but we have very good Catholic schools here. Then they went to secular colleges. I felt that they had had enough Catholic education. They felt—and I did, too—that they should no longer be separated from their non-Catholic friends. It seemed to me that if, after twelve or thirteen years of Catholic education (and the last four years very heavily imbued with philosophy, theology, etc., because the nuns at Sacred Heart gave courses in philosophy and theology in the high school), if they couldn't remain good Catholics after that, they're pretty weak girls. Actually, it has worked out exactly as I thought it would. Their Catholicism has been enhanced. I would say that they are more devout now than they were when they left home.

McDONALD: I'm convinced we have entirely too many Catholic organizations which tend to constantly pull Catholics away from non-Catholics in their community. You know, for every secular organization, we seem to think we need its Catholic counterpart—Catholic Historians, Catholic Sociologists, Catholic All-American football teams, Catholic Stamp Collectors . . .

McGINLEY: I am so against that. It's so foolish. A Protestant friend of mine in Connecticut told me the other day that there has been a very good, strong Boy Scout troop in their village for a good many years when, all of a sudden, the Catholic children were pulled out of the troop and a Catholic Boy Scout troop was started. Well, the whole purpose of the Boy Scouts is defeated by that. It's supposed to mingle boys of all races and creeds. What have we to be afraid of? That's what bothers me—this Catholic xenophobia.

Moreover I think there are many Protestant virtues we might adopt and one of them is a sense of civic responsibility. You can hardly get Catholics to work on any community committee; they aren't trained for it. I think that that is a big flaw in Catholic education, this lack of civic responsibility. Don't you think Catholics sometimes forget the Reformation has been over with for nearly 400 years and that we don't have to fight those battles all over again?

McDONALD: Actually an awful lot of re-examination seems to be going on, on both sides. The Lutherans in Germany are re-examining some of the things they abandoned, and we are hearing about Catholic scholars re-assessing the Reformation and some of its proximate causes.

McGINLEY: The Lutherans are very close; the points of difference are becoming fewer and the points of sameness are increasing. What I think accounts for Catholic separatism in America to a great extent is the very large influx of Irish immigrants at one fairly limited period of time when they had to be held together nationally by their Faith. Their priests came along with them to this country and did a marvelous job. They came with the people like faithful shepherds to save them from the perverse influences of the new urban civilization, and from the effects of an industrial society on an agrarian people. They had to hold on very tight. Also, we all know the Irish are prone to Jansenism. That came over from Douay to Maynooth.

Of course, I'm talking from one side only. I realize there are a half-dozen sides. Truth is a prism, not a plane. But I do think this one side has been neglected. What cheers me is that there seems to be a new leavening, a thrusting out of new ideas among more and more American Catholics.

J. L. O'SULLIVAN

J. L. O'SULLIVAN, dean of the College of Journalism at Marquette University, is recognized as one of the outstanding journalism teachers in the United States, respected alike by teachers and practitioners of the art of journalism in both the secular and religious fields.

Dean O'Sullivan was born in Hutchinson, Kansas, April 28, 1894, and studied journalism at Marquette, graduating in 1914. He worked on *The Milwaukee Sentinel* from 1912 to 1915 and then worked for the United Press in Milwaukee, Indianapolis, Chicago, New York and Kansas City.

In 1924, Dean O'Sullivan returned to Marquette as a professor of journalism and manager of the Marquette University Press. In 1928, he was appointed dean of the College of Journalism. In 1931, he organized the Catholic School Press Association, which is designed to help students and teachers of journalism in Catholic high schools and colleges throughout the country.

In 1941, Dean O'Sullivan served as president of the American Association of the Schools and Departments of Journalism and for fourteen years he served as a member of the board of directors of the Catholic Press Association. He helped organize the Milwaukee Catholic Interracial Council, of which he is an executive member, and he is a member of the President's Committee on Employment of the Physically Handicapped and the Governor's Commission on Human Rights.

The interview with Dean O'Sullivan took place in his office in Copus Hall on the Marquette campus.

McDONALD: Do you think today's journalists are better qualified for the work than they were forty or forty-five years ago when you were just starting out?

O'SULLIVAN: I think the ones coming out of journalism schools are better educated and more competent. They know more about what they're doing. They are more reliable and conscientious. And they are more disillusioned because they don't get the opportunity that they used to have for writing and for personal development in the field. More of the stuff is stereotyped and syndicated today; even much of the editorial page matter is syndicated. While papers are devoting more and more space to news, because many of them have to fill in around the advertising and features, still only a few papers are allowing their staffs to develop themselves and their material.

McDONALD: Is this increased syndication altogether bad, or is it a thing with mixed effects?

O'SULLIVAN: Well, papers have lost a lot of their individuality. You get on a plane in New York and read the New York paper; you get to Cleveland and the Cleveland paper has much of the same stuff; and the Detroit paper has much of the same content. As you go across the country, the papers are much alike.

McDONALD: I don't know what the motivation for that kind of journalism is, but it's easier to get out a paper that way.

O'SULLIVAN: And it's much cheaper. Today in many of the smaller daily papers they have the teletypesetter machine. The copy is edited on the other end of the wire and all the local telegraph editor has to do is clip the tape and write the headlines. He can't do much editing of the copy. Some papers, of course, allow individuals to develop their individuality.

McDONALD: Almost invariably those are your better papers, too, aren't they?

O'SULLIVAN: Yes, of course. Papers have become very much a production problem today and the mechanization has limited the amount of individuality allowed in the paper.

McDONALD: Do you think there will ever be a solution to the problem of how to get depth and interpretation into your reporting when everything in the modern press is geared to high-speed gathering and reporting of the news?

O'SULLIVAN: Only a small amount of the paper is developed on the spur of the moment, before edition time. When the reporters and editors show up at the office today, much of the paper is set and ready to go, some sections may even have been printed by that time. Now that type of material can certainly be developed so that there will be reporting in depth. I think that if the papers will devote their space to that type of reporting rather than to the crossword puzzles, the comics and the bridge scores, they will have all the time they need. I don't think it's a question of time. I think that, first, it's a question of expense. You have to hire men who are competent to do that kind of reporting and writing. You can't generalize about papers, but the great majority of them don't retain the men on the staff to the point where they will develop a competence to do that kind of work. Neither the pay nor the challenge and opportunity has been adequate to hold them on the staff.

McDONALD: In other words, the thing hinges pretty much on a publisher's desire. If he wants to put out a fairly comprehensive and deep paper he will do so.

O'SULLIVAN: There are other circumstances, too. For instance, the trend of journalism away from the professional has a lot to do with it. Many people today desire to be professional people.

McDONALD: Did journalism lose its professional status, or maybe it never had that status.

O'SULLIVAN: It was tending toward the professional at one time. But when the American Newspaper Guild decided to go CIO and is now even considering tying up with the mechanical and other unions in the paper and becoming one big union in the newspaper field, this is a swing completely away from the idea of a professional organization. When the Guild was organized, there were a lot of us who had hoped it would be a professional group. But they were bitterly opposed by the publishers and they are still opposed by the publishers. The Guild suffered a great deal. About the only way they could accomplish an improvement of conditions for editorial workers was by associating with other unions. The only way a professional society could have developed would have been for the publishers and editorial workers to co-operate, to work together for the improvement of the profession of journalism itself. But they tended to split and today very few of the publishers will have anything more to do with the Guild than they have to.

McDonald: I suppose it is almost inevitable for newspapers to reflect a purely business mentality.

O'Sullivan: The business people are in charge of many of the newspapers. They are people who came up from the business office and the advertising office. Many of them are now the publishers. As a result, they look on the papers as largely business enterprises. The idea of the great public responsibility of a newspaper because of the work it does, the fact that a newspaper deals with ideas and knowledge—these are not the main themes of many newspaper publishers. Their main concern is with the circulation and with the advertising revenue, with the cost of production of the paper, with the profit of the paper.

McDonald: They have to be concerned with those things, but there seems to be an almost exclusive concern with them.

O'Sullivan: It was always a concern to them, but at one time the editor was the dominant person. On a few papers today a far-sighted publisher, who recognizes the true nature of a newspaper, will let the editorial people have the freedom to operate. Another thing, and this is important, such a publisher will supply the editorial department with an adequate budget so that they can pay the editorial worker almost as much as what the advertising man or the printer gets.

McDonald: Speaking of the awareness of public responsibility, to what extent have the publishers and editors reconciled themselves to the findings of the Freedom of the Press Commission report in 1947? That was the Hutchins commission report on the press which emphasized the social responsibility of the newspaper and at the time there was about 100 per cent opposition from editors and publishers to the commission's findings on the press's performance.

O'Sullivan: It's still about 100 per cent opposition to it. One of the commission's findings, one of its main contentions, was that the press is the only social agency in this country that is not subjected to criticism. The press criticizes education, it criticizes government, social welfare agencies, it criticizes practically every other field, but it seldom criticizes itself. And in criticizing others, the press doesn't demonstrate much humility in the way it criticizes. You see editorial writers write and you hear them talk and you realize there's very little humility in them. They feel they are competent to judge everything. The great majority of newspapers have only one editorial writer and he writes on everything from art to atomic fallout, setting himself up as an expert in every field. Now humility is not a pagan virtue. It's not mentioned by the ancient pagan writers. Aristotle and Plato didn't recognize humility, and perhaps this lack of humility in the press is one of the developments of the rather pagan age in which we live.

McDONALD: Wasn't another contention of the Freedom of the Press Commission that the press did not recognize its own nature as a vital social instrument for the common good of our society?

O'SULLIVAN: The newspapers recognize themselves as a public agency where it is to their advantage to do so. They don't realize they are a public agency to any great extent when it comes to judging the effects of what they print.

McDONALD: Occasionally you hear someone say that improvement in American journalism cannot come from the journalism schools because the schools are teaching a strictly technical or vocational kind of journalism. Now, in fact, that is not true of many schools of journalism, including Marquette. It seems to me that such critics are judging journalism education on the basis of a very limited experience of that education. Perhaps they saw such education in one or two journalism colleges and feel that a purely technical education is universally true of all journalism teaching in this country. It certainly isn't true here at Marquette.

O'SULLIVAN: A number of journalism schools today require a liberal arts background and I don't think Marquette, in requiring that background, is with the minority of journalism schools. I think journalism schools have developed well in the last twenty-five or thirty years and that they will be even better. I think they would be better if the publishers would co-operate with them and support and help them instead of criticizing and attacking them all the time. The journalism schools which are not giving their students a good education and which are, instead, giving them only a technical education are trying to produce the kind of em-

ployee a publisher wants, someone who can go out and fit right
into the publisher's paper. Within the last year one head of a
school of journalism lost his job because he wasn't supplying the
type of hired help the publishers in his state wanted. He was
trying to see that his students first of all got a good education in
both journalism and liberal arts.

McDONALD: To what extent should a journalism student take
liberal arts courses in college? Is there an optimum ratio of
liberal arts to journalistic studies?

O'SULLIVAN: It runs about 75-25, 75 per cent liberal arts and
25 per cent journalism courses. But that liberal arts can go
several ways, too, you see. If a school permits the student to get
his liberal arts education by taking Sociology I, History I, English
I, Psychology I—all the beginning courses—he isn't going to get
much of an education. A lot depends upon the type of journalism courses offered also. Many of the journalism courses at Marquette and elsewhere are purely extensions of liberal arts courses
—Public Opinion, Government and the Press, The Press and
Society, Editorial Writing, Ethics of Journalism.

McDONALD: You mean there is always the danger of "voca-
tionalizing" the journalism curriculum?

O'SULLIVAN: That's right. If you offer, for instance, six courses
in photography, four courses in typography and two or three
courses in editing, then your journalism education becomes purely
technical. A reporting course can be very much liberal arts in
nature. In the ancient liberal arts program, you had oratory,
composition, rhetoric and poetry. Today you can't reach very
many people by oratory or by writing poetry. But you can reach
them through the media of mass communications. Certainly
learning how to reach people using modern methods is as much
a liberal arts discipline today as it was in the medieval days.

McDONALD: One hears these days that the age of written communication is coming to an end, that audio and visual media will
soon take over the whole field of communications. Robert
Hutchins commented recently that even the Great Books have
been put on long-playing records so we can be spared the trouble
of reading them. Do you think written communication is on
the way out?

O'SULLIVAN: I think people are always going to have to read.

You cannot study a thing just by hearing it or by seeing it flash on a screen. I don't think the average person is alert enough or keen enough to grasp material that way.

McDONALD: Maybe he won't want to grasp it, though. Maybe something so easy and effortless as looking at a television screen will unfit him for studious work.

O'SULLIVAN: Well, I certainly haven't given up the hope that people will always want to learn, that there will always be a natural desire for truth. I certainly can't conceive of any civilization lasting very long if the people don't read and study.

McDONALD: The secular press seems to be trying, consciously or not, to combat the commercial threat of television by imitating television, by trying to make the papers more visual, by printing more pictures and less reporting.

O'SULLIVAN: Some are trying to meet the competition by being more entertaining. Television has it on them, and will always have it on them, as far as entertainment is concerned. I think the way to beat the other fellow is to do the opposite of what he is doing.

McDONALD: To do what you can do and nobody else can do?

O'SULLIVAN: That's right. Newspapers can publish complete, comprehensive, intelligent articles that will give readers information on which they can reach conclusions. I don't think that television can do that half as well. What do you remember, for instance, about an Ed Murrow program that you saw a year or two ago? Can you remember its material content? It may have seemed to be strong meat to you at the time you saw and heard it. It may have seemed very important. But you don't remember anything about it now.

McDONALD: A couple of years ago, the Fund for the Republic sponsored several television discussion programs on the press, with Louis Lyons, Murrow, Eric Sevareid, and Martin Agronsky all discussing the press. It is significant, I think, that the sponsors of the program felt it necessary to publish these discussions, which more or less proves your last point—that if a thing is important and worth studying it has to be put into some kind of form which will make its study possible.

O'SULLIVAN: You can refer to that material when you want to know something about the subject discussed. Ten years from now, you may be studying something and will remember that Sevareid had said something about it at Harvard. But if what he said hasn't been printed, you're sunk. The knowledge and history of a society are accumulated in printing.

McDONALD: You have seen some of the great, legendary figures in American journalism in your time, haven't you?

O'SULLIVAN: Yes, I have seen some. Paul Mallon who wrote a Washington column; and Ring Lardner, I used to see him frequently. And then writing in the same building that I was in were Franklin P. Adams and Walter Lippmann. They were working for the old *New York World* then.

McDONALD: Does it seem to you that the writers in those days got a bigger kick out of writing then than they do now?

O'SULLIVAN: Writing had a tremendous attraction for them. That attraction has been lost, to some extent, because there is little professional appeal and also because opportunity to develop their talents is limited.

McDONALD: Although conditions might be tough in various fields of journalism, that seems to be only part of the problem. The other part is the man himself, how much drive and determination and competence he has.

O'SULLIVAN: Not only that. It's also how worried he is about earning a weekly salary, how willing he is to take a chance. The one thing today that differs much from the period when I started working is the pressure on individuals to keep up with their neighbors. There were more people willing to take a chance forty years ago. People would quit a job, without having another, and go some place they liked better. I know one very good reporter who quit his job one day because he was asked to do something he didn't think he should do. He went home and told his wife and his wife got a job herself to help support the family. Today he's one of the top reporters in the country.

McDONALD: Has the art of teaching journalism changed much in the thirty-five years or so you have been here?

O'SULLIVAN: You're always changing. No competent teacher does in any one year exactly as he did the year before. You're always learning and that is one of the marvelous things about teaching. Another thing, you adapt your teaching to each class. No two classes are the same in intellectual ability, competence or any other way. The first thing a teacher has to learn is what his students are capable of doing and then give them enough so that they will always be stretching to achieve their full capabilities.

McDONALD: Have there been any changes in curriculum in these last three decades?

O'SULLIVAN: We have learned more of the principles of journalism which we can teach. There have been more theory courses developed, and many of the things regarding mass communications are new. Everything in journalism is not cut and dried; it hasn't all been decided. In fact, there's much in journalism that is still unknown. Few know exactly what the objectives of newspapers and journalism education are. We don't have all the answers and we've been pioneering in it now for fifty years at the College of Journalism here. Some people who criticize journalism and education for journalism may learn some of this some day, too. A couple of weeks ago, this Professor Parkinson who wrote *Parkinson's Law* spoke at the meeting of the American Society of Newspaper Editors and he spent half his time screaming about journalism schools, finding fault with them because, he said, students should be getting a liberal arts education. Sitting in front of him were twenty or twenty-five deans of journalism schools who are responsible for their students' getting a better liberal arts education than are the liberal arts students at their universities. Parkinson doesn't know anything about journalism education. He thinks that a student in a journalism school spends four years studying proofreading and typography.

McDONALD: We've said nothing about Catholic journalism and the Catholic press in this country, and I am wondering what percentage of Marquette's journalism graduates go into Catholic journalism.

O'SULLIVAN: I think a little less than 5 per cent. The last time we made a study on it, we had about 1,000 graduates and I think about 74 of them had gone to work in Catholic journalism. Not all of them are still in Catholic journalism, but that many had gone into it at one time.

McDONALD: What do you think about the opportunity for the journalist in the Catholic press today?

O'SULLIVAN: Certainly the Catholic press has bigger publications, much more substantial publications now than fifty years ago. The papers are commercially more successful. There were very few commercially successful Catholic publications of any kind fifty years ago. Many of the Catholic papers then were privately owned; the laity published most of them. Today, ownership is by the diocese and the bishop is in the position of publisher. I don't think the position of editor of a Catholic paper carries with it today the distinction it used to have fifty years ago. The editor of a Catholic paper then was really a distinguished person; he was pointed out on the street as an important man in the community. I am thinking of men like Humphrey Desmond of Milwaukee, Father Phelan of the old *Western Watchman*, Father Hecker of *The Catholic World*. These men were given great recognition by the community. Now generally a priest is appointed editor by his bishop. Actually most editors of Catholic papers stay in that position only a short time and they move on. And they're glad to move on because they aren't given the recognition they deserve.

A study was made a few years ago and it showed that few of the priest-editors of Catholic newspapers had been advanced to the rank of Monsignor. And many of them were loaded down with other duties. They are pastors assigned to a parish, they are chaplains for a home for the aged, they direct the Catholic Charities. I know one editor who has six jobs like that and he wasn't able to devote more than an hour or two a week to the paper. That shows what was thought of the paper by his bishop. It was thought he could edit a paper in his spare time, with both hands busy on something else. I know of an editor of one of the great Catholic diocesan papers of this country who was appointed as pastor to a rather ordinary parish. The lead on the story said that Father so-and-so had been "promoted" to be pastor of this parish. Well, I suppose the work of a pastor is the work that a priest wants to do and that's what he expected to do when he entered the seminary. In that sense, it might be a promotion. But the idea that it is a distinction, greater than being the editor of the paper, is rather alarming.

McDONALD: The Catholic press's performance in general seems

to me to have improved in the last ten years, even on the editorial side. There seems to be more awareness now of the idea that a paper has an obligation to be of maximum usefulness to its readers.

O'SULLIVAN: I think the editors were concerned ten years ago with circulation and advertising, that kind of thing. However, even today, if you attend a convention of the Catholic Press Association, you will still find little attention paid to the content of papers and much more attention paid to advertising, promotion and other aspects of the business side.

McDONALD: How many Catholic papers do you see every week?

O'SULLIVAN: Thirty or forty.

McDONALD: Do you have any observation, any general comment, to make on the performance of the Catholic press? Any striking strengths or weaknesses that you see?

O'SULLIVAN: I'd say the main deficiency is one of vitality, the spark that makes you look for the paper every week, the material that is solid and substantial. The Catholic press carries out its teaching function well and has improved in some other areas so that it is effective.

McDONALD: But the treatment of the news is superficial?

O'SULLIVAN: It's that mechanical, stereotyped process again. You have to get out a paper this week so this goes in and that goes in and this goes in this column and then the other half of the page is for this, etc. I think that's why the paper isn't read more. Of course, some papers do better than others, but many lack spark and individuality. Readers want continuity of content also; they want to know they can get from the paper something each week that they need. I have urged some Catholic papers to feature a Catholic family each week, and to write about it in very human terms. For instance, Dorothy Day, when she started, did that kind of writing very well. Even today, when I pick up *The Catholic Worker*, I read through it in the hope that there will be something about Dorothy and her daughter, Tamar. I'm very interested in that family, though I have never met Dorothy's daughter. But her writing about it got me interested.

McDONALD: In talking with other people not connected with

the Catholic press, people who are experts in their own line, whether it be sociology, education, writing, whatever, the most usual complaint I hear about the Catholic press is that it never treats anything with sufficient depth, that it never gives major problems major attention.

O'Sullivan: One of the most enlightening and instructive talks I've listened to in a long time was Senator Kennedy's talk on politics and religion at the American Society of Newspaper Editors convention a few weeks ago in Washington. Few Catholic papers even mentioned that he had given the talk. I tried to get one man to print it in his Catholic paper and he wouldn't touch it.

McDonald: I did see it in *The Catholic Reporter* of Kansas City.

Do you have any last, parting observation on the press—Catholic or secular?

O'Sullivan: Just this, I think we are not going to have a good press in this country without good schools of journalism, and if we don't have a good press, then our society, as we know it, is going to end. When the people don't know, they don't care. People accept their ideas from symbols, and if they are uninformed they may accept the symbol of the swastika or the hammer and sickle as well as any other. The press must support schools of journalism, and I'm not talking about financial support. I am talking about moral support. Every time I go to a meeting of editors and publishers, I go with the expectation that I will hear somebody criticize schools of journalism.

McDonald: It seems to me that the publishers must first have the desire to produce better papers; unless they have that desire, the papers are not going to be better.

O'Sullivan: If they had just half as much desire to produce a better paper as they have to make money, that would be enough. The first thing the newspapers have to do is make a decision as to what news they want to cover. When they make that decision on the basis of material the reader needs to know, they can quit devoting time, energy and space to much of the other content they're now carrying. Recently an ape died in the Chicago zoo. All of the Chicago papers devoted pages to the news. Each of the papers must have assigned several reporters to spend full time on the reporting and writing about the event for a period of several days. Banner headlines were carried on page one over the stories of the death, disposition of the body and the possible successors. Many pictures were printed and the total space of news and pictures undoubtedly equaled, if it didn't exceed, the number of column-inches that would have been given to the death of the city's leading citizen. When the newspapers make the right decision as to what their readers really need to have, they can concentrate on that kind of news and they can develop people competent enough to report that news. And they will have to pay those people adequate salaries to keep them on the staff. You know, the American readers never asked for comic strips. The newspapers started comic strips and educated readers to read them. The people didn't say, "We want crossword puzzles." The people don't say, "We want features about apes." Unless we have a press that will inform the people, give them the information necessary for them to have, we cannot exist as a society. Our whole principle of government is based on the people having the information that they need.

JAMES O'GARA

JAMES O'GARA is in his ninth year as managing editor of *The Commonweal*, a weekly journal of opinion edited and published in New York by Catholic laymen. He was born in Chicago in 1918 and is married and has two children. He attended Catholic parochial and high school, majored in philosophy while working for his Bachelor's degree at Loyola University in Chicago, then got a Master's degree in sociology at Loyola.

Before the war, for a little over a year, he was an associate editor of the Chicago *Catholic Worker* and assistant director of St. Joseph House of Hospitality. He was in the Army from October, 1941, to September, 1945, serving in the infantry in the southwest Pacific.

After the war he was co-founder in 1946 of *Today*, the national Catholic student magazine, serving as editor until 1949. After leaving *Today* he was managing editor of *The Voice of St. Jude*, published by the Claretian Missionary Fathers, and served for two years as lecturer in sociology for the Institute of Social and Industrial Relations at Loyola. In February, 1952, O'Gara became managing editor of *The Commonweal*, and from 1953 to 1957 also served as lecturer in sociology for the School of Education at Fordham University. He has contributed to many publications, including *The Catholic Mind, America, The Sign, Jubilee,* the *Catholic Digest.*

The interview with Mr. O'Gara took place in his office at *The Commonweal*

McDONALD: Have you ever defined the purpose of *The Commonweal?*

O'GARA: It's probably easier to describe the magazine in what it does than to try to give any kind of an academic statement of its purpose. *The Commonweal* is a weekly journal of opinion edited by Catholic laymen. It is concerned with the temporal order, with the political, social and cultural issues which are the layman's particular province. In this area the layman's general role, as I see it, is to be a bridge between the Church and the temporal order, to apply Christian principles to particular problems of the day. And this is the area in which *The Commonweal* operates. As a lay-edited magazine, it has a particular advantage in that it clearly does not speak for the Church. The editors try time after time to make quite clear that we are speaking as journalists who happen to be Catholics.

McDONALD: The fact that you must, as you say, try to make that distinction clear "time after time" suggests a problem or an ambiguity here.

O'GARA: I don't know whether it so much suggests an ambiguity as that it suggests something about the nature of the Church in America and something of the way in which people outside the Church view the Church.

McDONALD: Do you think this problem is peculiarly American?

O'GARA: I think *The Commonweal* is understood much more readily in Europe than it is in America.

McDONALD: Because there is in Europe a tradition of lay-edited periodicals?

O'GARA: Yes. And because intellectuals in Europe are perhaps more used to the idea of Catholics, as Catholics, grappling with temporal issues, involving themselves but not even pretending to involve the Church.

McDONALD: Why is it that we have this problem in America? Why do people continue to confuse a lay Catholic magazine with an "officially Catholic" or a denominationally Catholic magazine or newspaper?

O'GARA: Because of our past immigrant status, I would say, there has been in this country a traditional reliance by lay Catholics on their clergy. The clergy did supply leadership in many areas outside of the purely religious, and they supplied it in a way that was necessary. Now lay people are achieving higher social and educational status, and they are taking a more prominent position. But the tradition that tends to identify any views publicly expressed by a Catholic as somehow being an official Catholic position is still with us.

McDONALD: Does Maritain's distinction in his book, *True Humanism*, hold here, the distinction between publications which are Catholic "by denomination" and those which, like yours, are Catholic "by inspiration"?

O'GARA: I don't know if the distinction would apply entirely to us. In any case, I myself am not overly fond of trying to fit existing situations into abstract categories. Maritain's concept is an interesting one and I think the concept is valid. I think, though, that we at *The Commonweal* have to face the fact that our situation, for various historical reasons, *is* slightly ambiguous. The magazine is often called "Catholic" and there are very good reasons why it is quite accurate to call it "Catholic." All the editors are Catholic. We endeavor to bring Catholic principles to bear on specific problems in the temporal order. A very large percentage of our contributors are Catholics. In these senses, then, it is correct to speak of the magazine as "Catholic." But this does not mean what many people think it means. For one, it does not mean *The Commonweal* is an "official" Catholic publication, such as a diocesan newspaper owned and published by a bishop would be. But this distinction between the official and the non-official publication is not the whole thing, either. An editor of an "officially Catholic" newspaper can take positions on temporal issues of the day, and his prudential decisions on these matters would have no more official standing than they would have in a non-official Catholic publication.

So the essence of the question does not depend upon where one's views are published but rather on the nature of the thing under discussion. On issues which involve prudential, practical judgments, Catholics are free to disagree. In no way can one say there is an "official Catholic" position on such issues. I would, however, add a P.S. It seems to me that on these questions a Catholic journalist has a serious obligation to endeavor to bring his thinking into conformity with the basic principles of Catholicism and in particular with the social teaching of the Church, as enunciated, for example, by the modern Popes in their encyclicals and Christmas peace messages. Freedom of Catholics to disagree should not be interpreted to mean they can arbitrarily take any position they like on subjects, say, like the United Nations. There is a very serious obligation in conscience on the part of Catholic journalists to study Papal statements and principles in this area. I'm all in favor of free discussion. I don't believe, at all, in beating people over the head with Papal encyclicals. There is a wide area of Catholic freedom in which to disagree on prudential issues and people should be extremely careful not to suggest that someone is not a good Catholic just because he takes this or that position on a practical, prudential question. With all this said, though, it is a striking fact that many Catholic editors, some of them well known in the Catholic press, show practically no acquaintance with what I would consider to be quite basic Catholic principles. Week in and week out, they consistently take positions that are exactly opposite to the spirit of Papal directives and encyclicals on everything from labor to the United Nations.

McDONALD: How would you distinguish "Catholic principles" from what non-Catholics would think of as "sectarian dogmas" or "doctrines"? Catholic principles, it seems to me, are valid not only for Catholics. The late Pius XII, for instance, delivered two major addresses on the need for world political organizations and world law, a juridical world order. In one sense, what he was saying was in the area of "Catholic principles." But as he himself said on both occasions, the need and desire for world order and world law corresponds to a "natural" longing in man. He rooted this fundamentally in the natural law. So these are "Catholic principles" in the sense that the Pope expressed them, but they do not originate or terminate among Catholics, do they?

O'GARA: I would agree with your point. I used the term "Catholic principles" in a general sort of way to distinguish from Catholic dogma. I'm not talking about things that a Catholic learns from Revelation, but rather of things that derive from what Catholics would call the "natural law."

McDONALD: When you and your fellow editors sit down to write editorials in *The Commonweal*, do you habitually and consciously try to write them in such a way that readers will not make the mistake of thinking your position is the Church's "official position"?

O'GARA: We do that habitually and consciously and every other way you'd care to think of an adverb for. We are extremely sensitive on the subject. We think this is one of the bad mistakes Catholic journalists easily make—trying to lean on authority and to canonize one's prudential opinions by calling in the Pope. It is true that the general direction of, say, Catholic social thought tends toward international organization, an international juridical order, free migration of peoples, etc., but the steps from these general principles to particular legislation are numerous and one can accept the general Catholic principle and still feel that this or that particular piece of legislation, or this or that particular organization, does not, in fact, meet the necessary requirements for one's support. One must avoid what might be called the "party-line mentality."

McDONALD: And yet, you have what you said earlier, a certain body of Catholic thought and tradition and teaching on such things as world juridical order.

O'GARA: There is, indeed.

McDonald: It isn't a "line," but what would you call it?

O'Gara: Practically speaking, I would say that the burden of proof in a specific case involving such questions would be on the Catholic who says that a particular piece of legislation or a particular organization does not square with Catholic principles. The spirit of Catholic social thought is strongly in favor of international organizations and an international rule of law. We all know that no organization or law in the concrete political order is ever perfect, and it seems to me this fact would put the burden of proof on the Catholic who is opposed to the specific, concrete thing. I don't think a search for perfection is justification for rejecting such organizations as the United Nations.

McDonald: When *The Commonweal* came out in 1952 with an endorsement of the candidacy of Adlai Stevenson for the Presidency, several Republican Catholic friends of mine were upset. Again, this ambiguity seemed to be present. They seemed to think that *The Commonweal* was a religious organ that had no business taking a stand on a political election campaign. The magazine's decision did not bother me. I mean I didn't see any particular incongruity.

O'Gara: We at the magazine have discussed that thing many times since, and there is, I think, a considerable amount to be said against our endorsing any candidate, precisely because of the danger that people might misunderstand what our endorsemen meant. Actually, we didn't intend to endorse anybody as the 1952 campaign approached. Editorially we favored the nomination by the Republican Party of General Eisenhower over Senator Taft. We felt that Senator Taft's traditional isolationist position would imperil the free world's defense against Communism, while Eisenhower stood for a united Europe, a strong Europe, American troops in Europe and the like. Once Eisenhower was nominated, we intended to make no further endorsements. However, as Eisenhower's campaign wore on, he seemed to be making a very determined effort to pick up the Taft supporters. His speeches took an increasingly isolationist turn. He put very heavy stress on defense cutting and budget cutting. If we made a mistake it is quite possible that it consisted in taking his campaign oratory too seriously. But at the time we became increasingly concerned that the election of Eisenhower would represent a victory for traditional isolationist Republican sentiment which, in turn, would mean American withdrawal in Europe and, we felt, the turning over of a large part of the world to Communist forces. We finally felt that honesty almost compelled us to state frankly our preference for Stevenson, so that nobody would have any feeling that in our editorials we were in fact favoring Stevenson week after week while lacking the courage to say so frankly. But our endorsement was not, of course, a question of party affiliation but one of principle.

McDONALD: How do you determine policy on *The Commonweal?* Do you have regular policy-making meetings?

O'GARA: We have a good tradition on this. *The Commonweal* is, I think, one of the few magazines still publishing in this country in which all the editors play a vital day-by-day, almost hour-by-hour role in determining policy. All the editors write editorials every week. As a matter of fact, I recently figured up that in the eight years I have been with the magazine, I have written well over a quarter of a million words of editorials. At our editorial conference we determine what we are interested in writing about, what should be covered and, in a very quick, not detailed way, we make sure we're in agreement on our position on the particular issues.

McDONALD: If there is disagreement between editors, how is that resolved?

O'GARA: It begins with discussion. One tries to persuade the others, or three try to persuade one. However, the right of the editors to protect their names is always quite clear. No unsigned editorial can appear in *The Commonweal* to which I take exception, or to which any one of the editors takes exception. If an editor doesn't agree with the point, that editorial cannot appear as if it represented his opinion. It can appear, as has been done in the past, as a signed editorial, but it cannot appear as if it represented all our views. So when a reader sees unsigned editorials in the magazine, as he does every week, he does not know which editor wrote a particular editorial but he knows it represents the views of all the editors.

McDONALD: How many editors do you have besides yourself as managing editor and Edward Skillin, the editor?

O'GARA: James Finn is an associate editor and Richard Horchler is an associate editor. We also have John Brubaker, who is the advertising manager, our drama critic, Richard Hayes, and our film critic, Philip T. Hartung. We have our correspondents in Great Britain, Paris and Rome. Then we have the girls in the clerical end; their number varies with the season, but it averages out to about ten girls.

McDONALD: Is finance a constant problem with *The Commonweal?*

O'GARA: If there were a stronger word than "constant," I wish you'd use it. I should say, though, that friends who are in the magazine business are always surprised that we do as well as we do. We come within $15,000 or $20,000 a year of being self-supporting.

McDONALD: How do you meet this deficit, then? Where do you get your money? You don't have to name names if you don't want to.

O'GARA: Well, there's no secret. I wish there *were* some big angel whose name I would have to conceal. Last year was a typical operation. We had a committee that formed a group called "Commonweal Associates," friends throughout the country who are sympathetic with the point of view of the magazine. The Associates contribute $100 each for one type of membership, $50 for another. There are no privileges connected with the membership, just the satisfaction that they are supporting something in which they believe. It was a very successful thing.

McDONALD: How many subscribers do you have?

O'GARA: About 23,000. We fluctuate between 21,000 and 25,000. In this, I think we pretty much match the general subscription pattern of the journal of opinion, whether Catholic or not.

McDONALD: Can anything be done, that hasn't been done, to increase circulation? It seems to me that in a country with more than 40,000,000 Catholics there must be more than 23,000 sympathetic with *The Commonweal's* point of view.

O'GARA: I'm inclined to think that the circulation ceiling for the magazine at this point in history would be about twice what it is now, say about 50,000. Why don't we have it? Well, for a variety of reasons. For one thing, we do not have the capital to do much promotion. To mail a reasonably decent promotion piece to 20,000 people first class could cost about $2,000, and 20,000 is a small mailing. We should mail to 100,000, 150,000, 200,000. Also the editors are too busy. If you compare the number of editors we have with the number on any comparable magazine, I think you'll see that our editors work very hard and have little time to devote to promotional activities. Really good promotion people come high and we can't afford to hire a high-powered promotion man. We used to run an ad two or three times a year in *The New York Times Book Review* and that was extremely effective, but also extremely expensive.

On this subject of *The Commonweal's* circulation, Milton Mayer once said something that I thought was very wise. He said the magazine is in a sense creating its own readership, for it is a quite specialized publication. It's certainly not a popular magazine. It was never intended to be. It's not a mass-circulation magazine. We often publish things nobody else would publish because we think they're valuable. We're creating our own readership in the sense that the intellectual level of the whole country as well as of the Catholics is rising, so that more and more people have a taste for the tougher type of magazine and thus we'll have more and more readers. Our future is, in a sense, dependent upon the general cultural level of the American Catholic community.

McDONALD: What do you do about finding the type of manuscripts you want? What are you looking for in your manuscripts, more the concrete than the abstract type of thing? Are you more interested in articles dealing with actual, specific problems and situations rather than with the theoretical or intellectual things?

O'GARA: Again, that's a question that is framed in rather rigid categories and is therefore hard to answer. It is highly abstract and, I think, poses an either-or situation which does not really exist.

McDONALD: I just had the feeling that *The Commonweal* is more interested in the specific than in the theoretical, in other words that you want articles on things that are going and real rather than the ought-to-be type of thing, or the idealistic type of thing.

O'GARA: I don't think I would agree. Actually, the editors have almost a weakness for the abstract. At least the highly theoretical and abstract article is most likely to find a home in *The Commonweal*. But we don't tend to judge in these categories. I would say we're simply interested in what we consider to be good thinking, good writing, good reporting on almost any subject. We conceive the Catholic spirit to be one which welcomes that which is good.

McDONALD: But you are a journal of opinion.

O'GARA: That's just a handy descriptive type of phrase. Actually in the magazine it says that *The Commonweal* is a weekly review of public affairs, literature and the arts. These are our primary concerns. That description covers a range so wide that almost anything can be and has been fitted into it.

McDONALD: Do you tend to give readers what you think they should be interested in as literate people and as informed and responsible citizens?

O'GARA: Again, I think I would give a bit of an individualistic answer. *The Commonweal* is one of the few magazines still left where we don't concern ourselves too much about reader reaction.

McDONALD: What appeals to you, then, you publish.

O'GARA: That's what it comes down to, personal journalism in the old tradition. We judge an article as we see it and if we think it's interesting and worthwhile, or even if we think it is just worthwhile, we'll publish it. In a few cases there might be not more than 500 people who care about this or that particular article but nobody else would publish it for those 500 people. If we think it's important we publish it.

McDONALD: I'm inclined to agree that the idea of trying to publish a magazine in which every article would appeal to every reader is journalistically and intellectually unwise.

O'GARA: It is quite possible, I think, for the elements of popular mass culture to corrupt the publishing world unless we're careful. All kinds of magazines, too many probably, publish for what is considered to be the man in the street, the mass taste.

There are plenty of those magazines. *The Commonweal* is not intended to be a popular magazine, it is intended for rather well-educated people who are seriously interested in the world and in the relationship between their religious beliefs and the world. This is where we operate. Popularization is all right, but it's not our business.

McDONALD: You don't think you have to articulate in every editorial this relationship of religious beliefs to the world.

O'GARA: No, I'd say it's rather implicit. The editors, and I think most of the readers of *The Commonweal*, are interested in achieving a conformity between their lives as citizens and their religious beliefs. Our editorial positions represent our effort to do this.

McDONALD: To what extent do you seek manuscripts and specify what you want?

O'GARA: We get very many manuscripts in the mail, unsolicited, and they are all read. Most of them are not for us. But every manuscript is read by at least two editors. This is a time-consuming process, but it makes sure that no one editor's hasty opinion will reject something that might be worth considering. If there's any hope for an article, everybody reads it. If there's still a question, everybody reads it again. Every once in a while some unsolicited contributor turns out to be a very good, useful, long-time contributor to the magazine. Also we solicit manuscripts. The editors have an idea conference once a week. Ideas for articles are put forward and we think of somebody who might be interested in writing about the ideas that have struck us.

McDONALD: Do you frequently publish articles with which the editors violently disagree? I mean articles presenting viewpoints with which you disagree?

O'GARA: It's not as frequent as we might like because there is a tendency with this magazine, as with any other, for people who are sympathetic to our general point of view to send us articles. But there is still room for a lot of disagreement within that general point of view, and we publish articles more or less regularly by some long-time contributors who disagree with us quite strenuously on some point or other. Our standards here are quite simple: competence and responsibility. An article can be completely in disagreement with what we think on a particular issue, but so long as it's well argued and responsibly done, we will publish it.

McDONALD: Do you have a kind of pool of contributing writers from which you draw?

O'GARA: Yes, but we are constantly looking for new people, as I think any magazine of quality is. It's hard for small-circulation magazines to pay enough to keep people for a long time and writing, say, every other week or so. We have many people who write for us three or four times a year because they like the magazine and its viewpoint. That means such a man will write an article and get $50 or $60, whereas his usual fee in other magazines would be from $300 to $1000. This is a labor of love that nobody can expect every week.

McDONALD: People like Evelyn Waugh and François Mauriac have written for The Commonweal, haven't they, though they could command much larger fees elsewhere?

O'GARA: Yes. Waugh, for example, very kindly gave us first publication rights to his Love Among the Ruins before it was published anywhere else, for a very nominal fee which he then gave to charity. Gestures like that, of course, represent a great contribution to the magazine, as good or better than any cash contribution.

McDONALD: The occasional articles by people like Bishop John Wright or Bishop Robert Dwyer have been helpful, too, I would think.

O'GARA: That is one of the interesting things about The Commonweal—it has always attracted many distinguished Catholic thinkers and writers. And, although it is a magazine edited by laymen, a surprisingly high percentage of the contributors are drawn from the clergy and some of the hierarchy.

McDONALD: Getting away from the magazine for a moment, are you, in general, optimistic or pessimistic about the future of either the Catholic community or the general community in the generation ahead?

O'GARA: I'd be hard pressed to decide whether my views should be called optimistic or pessimistic. But there are problems. On the one hand we have the increasingly obvious fact that our cul-

ture is becoming secularized, that the Judaeo-Christian traditions
are being drained out of it. People still behave in a civilized or
moral fashion, although many of them have ceased to hold the
principles on which this morality is based. Society can continue
to operate on that basis for a while, but for how long? I think
we are exhausting our capital of inherited religious values. That
is one problem. In addition, I think Catholics need to think a
great deal more about what it means to live in a society like our
own. It seems to me we have to face the realities of the world in
which we live. Things are changing, our whole style of life has
undergone a transformation, traditional values are being challenged and in some cases abandoned. I do not think the Catholic
response to all this has yet been adequate.

McDONALD: What do you mean when you say we must face
up to present-day realities, the world as it is? Are you thinking,
for instance, about the pluralistic nature of our society?

O'GARA: Pluralism is becoming an overworked word, perhaps,
but I think it is obvious that many Catholic journalists and
spokesmen still tend to express themselves in unrealistic terms.
What they have to say has little relevance to the world in which
we actually live. Catholics, for example, often don't seem to
understand that we represent a minority in a nation of 180,000,-
000 people—a strong minority, but a minority—and that in the
normal political process of persuasion and pressure and the back-
and-forth movement, it is not always possible to do exactly what
Catholics would like to do or see done. We have to learn how
to live in this kind of society, how to present our views effectively
and also how to behave, if you want, when we lose a decision.

McDONALD: You're not suggesting, though, that if we become
the majority, we would smash the opposition, as some people
think we might be tempted to do?

O'GARA: Not at all. The concept of the majority in purely
numerical terms is not too meaningful in this context. I think
one is talking in terms of the total culture and the content of the
culture, not so much in terms of counting noses. It would be
foolish to say that this would be the same America if 98 per cent
of the people were Methodists. I presume such an America
would be Prohibitionist and whatever other things one associates

with Methodism. It would be equally foolish to say that if America were 98 per cent Catholic, the culture wouldn't be different; I would suppose such a culture would reflect Catholic values. What I would insist, however, is that these Catholic values are not anti-human values. I don't think people are really afraid of Catholic values. I think perhaps they are more afraid of some of the Catholics who claim to be speaking for Catholic values and who actually, so far as I can see, are not. Instead, such Catholics seem intent on presenting an image of the Church as a huge, monolithic power structure intent on picketing and boycotting and censoring. That is a behavior pattern peculiar to a minority status; I do not see how behaving this way helps the Church in the long run, and in a democratic society it seems to me the wrong way to mold public opinion and influence legislation.

McDONALD: But you would say that secularism is the big problem that you see as an observer of the contemporary scene.

O'GARA: Yes, and it's a dual problem—for the Western world in general and for the Catholic community in particular. I don't think Catholics have given enough thought to the problem of how to challenge secularization within a culture such as ours. It is an inescapable fact of modern history that Catholics have absented themselves from many areas where the crucial decisions have been and are being made. Catholics withdrew because many modern political ideas, ideas about freedom and liberty, had become associated with people who were in many cases genuinely anti-clerical, genuinely opposed to the Church. So there has been a tendency among Catholics to identify the ideas themselves with their anti-religious authors and to be absent when great ideas were being born and great institutions were being formed. Somehow we must reverse this process.

McDONALD: In the problematic scheme of things, where do you place the whole Church-and-State issue?

O'GARA: All of us, in my opinion, are going to have to face problems more squarely and think about the underlying issues more deeply than is the general rule so far. The issue is complex, of course, and I can't do more than touch on it here. I wish more Catholics writing on the subject reflected America's historical tradition and the unique nature of the American society. I think many Catholic writers fail on this score. On its side, the non-Catholic community doesn't seem to realize at all how many of the most-quoted Catholic statements on the subject represent European reactions to specific European situations. In fact, although it sounds naturalistic to say it, most Americans don't seem to appreciate the extent to which the United States is unique. After all, this country is less than 200 years old. The Church has lived for 2,000 years with every kind of government one can imagine—from monarchies to dictatorships to republics. I do think Catholics need to do more thinking on Church-and-State questions. But most of the Church-and-State quotes that are used so often against the Church in this country come from a European context and reflect history that most Americans do not know much about. We Americans have very little sense of history, but any American who imagines that the prophets of the Enlightenment in France were seeking there the kind of separation of Church and State that we have in America is laboring under a delusion. The separation the Enlightenment spokesmen had in mind was simply the capture of the Church by the State, a debasement of the Church. To that, of course, the Church could never agree, in any country, and it would be nonsense to expect her to. But that is not a reflection of the American experience, which was historically unique. On the other side of the coin, I think it is fair to say that very many European Catholics have only the most primitive conception of what the American political system is, how it operates, and why it took the form it did. They show a profound ignorance of how well the Church has fared under the American system. As I see it, then, this is a two-way problem. Non-Catholic Americans need to develop a sense of history on the subject so they will not take Catholic statements made in a specific historic context in Europe and think they can be simply interpreted as a condemnation of the American system. We Catholics, on the other hand, have a serious obligation to see if we are not often parroting European sentiments that have become textbook clichés, even though they have little or no relevance to the American situation.

McDONALD: Do you think we ought to sort out the things in

Catholicism which are merely accidental in this area of Church-and-State relations, I mean things that are accidental in history according to geography (Europe) or time (the medieval period)?

O'GARA: I would hesitate to disagree with you, but I would also hesitate to try to say what is essential to Catholicism in a particular Church-and-State relationship, and I don't know just who would make such an attempt. All I'm saying is that history is long and that the Church already has a lot of history behind her.

McDONALD: Well, I didn't mean more than what might appear. I mean that Maritain, for example, talks about the moment in history when the monarchs and the bishops were frequently the same people and they were the same people for very good historical and political reasons, the exigencies of the moment. In other words, there was a theocratic situation existing at a certain time in history, but that doesn't mean the welfare of the Church depends upon any kind of a return to that particular Church-and-State relationship.

O'GARA: It certainly doesn't and the point is a good illustration of the fact that discussing Church-State problems does involve some understanding of history. The bishop often was the temporal ruler in order to prevent chaos. That wasn't an ideal and I think today everybody would agree it wasn't ideal. Quite the contrary—one of the great benefits brought to political thought by Christianity was its stress on the distinction between Church and State. That should be emphasized more. As far as practical Church-State issues in the United States are concerned, I wish more people were aware that the bishops of the United States have in fact spoken authoritatively on the subject. In 1948 Archbishop John T. McNicholas, speaking as chairman of the administrative board of the National Catholic Welfare Conference, on behalf of all the Catholic bishops reaffirmed the traditional American Catholic position, stating solemnly that Catholics in the United States support the Constitution absolutely, including the First Amendment, and that we are not in any way seeking a union of Church and State. I don't know how it can be made any more clear than that. All of us need to understand that on particular applications and interpretations of the First

Amendment—say, on issues like school buses, transportation of parochial school students, and the like—there can be two or three or four different positions, all perfectly respectable from a constitutional viewpoint. Adversaries in such issues should see them for what they are—differences of opinion and constitutional interpretation, not the opening shots in a great civil war. Here it would help immeasurably if each side would really listen to what responsible spokesmen on the other side are saying. And this seems to me a good way to close—with the hope that in the near future we may begin talking *to* rather than *at* each other on these and a multitude of other questions.

VI

Learning

MONSIGNOR JOHN TRACY ELLIS

MONSIGNOR JOHN TRACY ELLIS, professor of church history at the Catholic University of America, Washington, has written eight works in church history, but is best known for the paper, "American Catholics and Intellectual Life," which he gave in 1955 at the annual meeting of the Catholic Commission on Intellectual and Cultural Affairs.

That paper, since published in book form, touched off a wave of self-analysis and soul-searching inside the American Catholic community that has not subsided yet. It offered evidence attesting to the general lack of intellectual vitality and influence of American Catholics and outlined the historical and contemporary causes of their meager scholarship and scholarly achievements.

Monsignor Ellis was born in 1905 in Seneca, Illinois. He attended St. Viator College and the Catholic University of America and also did some postgraduate work at the University of Chicago and Harvard. He was ordained in 1938. He taught history at St. Viator, the College of St. Teresa, and has been a member of the Department of History at the Catholic University of America since 1935.

His books include *Cardinal Consalvi and Anglo-Papal Relations, 1814-1824, The Formative Years of the Catholic University of America*, and a biography of James Cardinal Gibbons. He is at present working on a general history of the Catholic Church in the United States.

The interview with Monsignor Ellis took place in his large, neat study in Caldwell Hall on the university campus.

McDONALD: Have you had any reason to revise any of your estimates or conclusions since you gave your paper on Catholics and the intellectual life?

ELLIS: Certainly not substantially. If I were to sit down and write it again there would be no substantial difference. There'd be a few ancillary differences. I think I would have allowed a little bit more time to elapse before expecting Catholics to show outstanding scholarly achievement. But, offhand, I can't think of anything else I would change. The major points I would not change at all. I don't want to appear arrogant and smug about it, but truly, I don't think those who have set out to refute it have really done so.

McDONALD: I haven't seen too many adverse comments. By this time, I imagine you're pretty philosophical about criticism and attacks anyway.

ELLIS: Yes, and I have a rather bad ulcer which I've had for thirty years. I have a tougher skin than I thought I had; this hasn't upset me in the least.

McDONALD: Was that paper something you had been . . .

ELLIS: Ruminating?

McDONALD: Ruminating and thinking about during the twenty-five years you had been teaching here?

ELLIS: Very much so. When Father William Rooney of the Catholic Commission for Intellectual and Cultural Affairs asked me to give a paper, I said I'd be willing, yes, "provided you are willing to take some rather strong criticism." He said, "You may speak as you please." "Very well," I said, "I've been thinking about this for a long time." And I started the writing of it with the thought that here was my chance to say what I have been thinking. So I simply did it.

McDONALD: That certainly was a milestone in the history of the Church in this country.

ELLIS: I must say it caused far more reaction than I had anticipated, and I mean that in all sincerity.

McDonald: When we published the text of that in *The Catholic Messenger* at Davenport, we sold 2,500 extra copies of the paper; we got requests from every part of the country for that article.

Ellis: It wasn't long after it appeared in *Thought* and in your paper, in the fall of 1955, perhaps a month later, that I fully realized that I had merely said what literally hundreds of our people had been thinking.

McDonald: There was a terrific response at the beginning. What interests me is whether, after all that initial soul-searching and self-scrutiny, much reform is being carried through. Are some of the situations you described in your paper being corrected?

Ellis: I wouldn't wish to pose as knowing everything that's being done, nor would I want to attribute what is being done to that essay. I think improvement was on the way, regardless of my essay, but perhaps the essay hastened it. But I'll give you an example now of some progress. A week ago, Georgetown University had an "authors' reception" to honor twenty-six professors who had published books in 1959. That would be one little indication of the changed attitude on the part of many of our people. A decade or two ago an "authors' reception" of that kind would, I believe, have been almost unheard of in Catholic circles. We're beginning to show appreciation for intellectual achievement.

McDonald: That was one of the things I recall your emphasizing in your paper, a general indifference on the part of American Catholics so far as intellectual accomplishments are concerned.

Ellis: The attitude we have toward intellectual excellence is quite important. I don't think there is yet anywhere near the number of dedicated people in Catholic higher education that there should be. I don't mean to say that they are lazy. But too many are merely routine and run-of-the-mill people. They do their teaching in a conscientious manner. But there are not enough who are so in love with learning that it becomes a kind of passion with them.

McDonald: Might part of the reason for this lie in the fact that we know our ultimate citizenship lies beyond the city of man, and so it is difficult to get aroused about scholarship?

ELLIS: I think that has a very definite part to play.

McDONALD: Is there a paradox working here? Is there a contradiction between complete dedication to scholarship and the intellectual life on the one hand, and ultimate concern for our eternal citizenship on the other?

ELLIS: There is no contradiction. There might be in the minds of a few people. Unfortunately, here is what I think has happened: too few ecclesiastical superiors have let it be known by those under them that this sort of thing, excellent scholarship, was particularly desirable. Many of them have laid great emphasis on the dangers of intellectual pride, but they have failed to mention the dangers of intellectual sloth which, to me, is just as much of a moral defect and just as much of a sin as pride. After all, it's morally wrong to discourage a man of gift and ability. Our Lord said if you've got a talent, it should be used.

McDONALD: There are other ways to encourage humility than by denying a man the opportunity to use and exercise his intellectual talents.

ELLIS: Of course there are. I don't think there's any doubt about it that one of the things that's held us back is the attitude that we have the truth, so what's the use to bestir ourselves? One would like to ask them: "What in the name of God are you doing with the truth you have?"

McDONALD: Is the climate in our seminaries one of defensiveness, or apologetics? You mention in your paper that one of the bad effects of anti-Catholic bigotry in this country, historically, is its encouraging of a predominantly apologetic rather than an apostolic attitude on the part of Catholics. Is there some of that still in our Catholic seminary training?

ELLIS: Again, I wouldn't want to pose as an authority on our seminary training. But I do certainly think that it is improving. Here is an indication of what I mean, which was a slight experience I had at the annual meeting of the National Catholic Educational Association in Atlantic City a year ago. I attended a session on major and minor seminaries. There were about 200 priests present, no laity. The principal point of the speaker's paper was the importance of accreditation of the seminaries by the secular accrediting agencies in this country. Two or three or

four got up and spoke about having had their seminaries ac-
credited by these agencies, and how much benefit they had
derived from it. Three or four more rose to ask questions of
these men, how they would go about getting such accreditation,
etc. I didn't hear so much as the faintest objection to the idea
itself. Now that could not have happened twenty years ago. At
that time the secular agencies would have been denounced, and
the attitude would have been: "What have we to learn from
them?" Today, not even a whisper of criticism. In fact, they
seemed eager to find out how to go about it. Now, when we've
got to the point where the seminary professors are eager for
secular accrediting agencies to come in and evaluate them, we
have made progress.

McDONALD: Immigration was certainly a factor that bulked
large in the history of American Catholic intellectual life the last
two or three generations. But has that pretty well spent itself
now, so that we can no longer excuse present shortcomings because of our immigrant past?

ELLIS: We certainly cannot, even though we still have with us
some vestiges of that immigrant status.

McDONALD: You said in your paper that one of the serious
defects in American Catholic higher education is the duplication
of effort, the multiplication of colleges, and especially the thin-
ning out of our slender resources on the graduate-school level. Is
that still true today?

ELLIS: It's pathetically true. There is scarcely a major city in
the land, except in the South and certain portions of the West,
wherein examples of this wasteful duplication cannot be found—
including our own city. And the closer look you take at some of
these institutions—and the record of their work—the more does
the fact stand out, and the more deplorable does it appear in the
light of their relative impoverishment in adequate library facilities, up-to-date science laboratories, faculty members with first-
class training and academic stature, and, needless to say, over-all
endowment. It is difficult to escape the conclusion that this situation indicates little, if any, long-range planning, to say nothing
of an understanding of what is implied by a commitment to

education at the college level, and even less, of course, at the level of the graduate school.

McDONALD: We don't have that many resources to permit duplication of these offerings.

ELLIS: Of course we don't. But we go on playing that we do. And what is at the bottom of a lot of this, I am afraid, is institutional pride.

McDONALD: You said in your paper that financial insolvency may drive some of the schools to drop some of these duplicated offerings.

ELLIS: Yes, I said that five years ago and I have not changed my mind. The threat of bankruptcy is one of the few things that can do it, unless there should be a disposition on the part, let's say, of ten or twelve of the leaders of Catholic education in this country, representing as many elements as possible, to do something drastic to remedy the situation. For example, the Jesuit Fathers, the secular clergy and laity, the Benedictines, the Holy Cross Fathers and others—all ought to come together and form a national planning board. They would meet with terrific opposition at first. But if they had the persistence to see it through, prestige would gradually be gained and in the end everyone would benefit.

McDONALD: Has anything been tried like that?

ELLIS: No, not that I know of. One of the things that saddens me about our own institutions is to see us fail to take action like the four in western Massachusetts: the University of Massachusetts, Amherst, Mount Holyoke and Smith, combining, as they have, to make certain courses mutually available to students of their institutions. They are all within ten to fifteen miles of each other. If one school is strong in economics, say, or in art, the others send their economics or art students there for classes and credit is given. But I know of nothing of this kind among the Catholic colleges. It would be salutary if representatives of the Catholic institutions could be assembled and told what they're really doing, and that this sort of thing is holding back our progress.

McDONALD: Has this ever been discussed at an NCEA meeting?

ELLIS: Let me cite you the only example I know. I went out to St. Louis, at the invitation of the College and University Department of the NCEA in April, 1956, to take part in a discussion of my paper, that is, the year after I had given it. I gave the talk to an audience of between 300 and 400, mostly Catholic college presidents and deans. What better body could you get? Following the paper, the question period started and gave promise of being genuinely worthwhile. But after several questions, the presiding officer said it was time for a committee report of some kind and that the discussion must be closed. Frankly, I was deeply disappointed. They had just reached the point where something substantial was being said and the whole discussion was abruptly terminated.

McDONALD: Perhaps one of these NCEA meetings should be devoted to just this problem.

ELLIS: If I had any voice—I have none, but if I had anything to say about the College and University Department of NCEA —I would schedule a session on The Evils of Duplication, just that and no more. And I'd like to see the initiative come from the laymen; not because I don't think priests belong in the hurly-burly of debate, that isn't the point. But I would like to see the laymen more articulate, playing more of a deciding role in all these things.

McDONALD: George Shuster and others have been talking lately about laymen not having enough policy-making voice in Catholic colleges and universities.

ELLIS: That's true. He's right. However, again, I see very definite improvement. In the Catholic college and university world of this country, the departments I know best are those of history. More and more, the laymen are coming to the fore. For example, Father Thomas McAvoy has just resigned at the University of Notre Dame after almost twenty years as head of the department, and Marshall Smelser has come in. At Loyola in Chicago, Paul Lietz, a layman, has been head for some years. A few years ago, Donald R. Penn, who got his doctorate at the University of Wisconsin, went in as head of the Department of History at Georgetown.

McDONALD: Some people, and I'm sure you've heard and read

this, too, have been advocating dropping the first six grades of our school system in order to concentrate more of our resources on the high school and college level.

ELLIS: I'm not so sure that that is what must give, if give there must be. But I am afraid that we missed the boat, all of us, when we did not follow our Canadian neighbors in some such arrangement as that of St. Michael's College at the University of Toronto. I was there last October and spent a most interesting weekend. St. Michael's has no financial burden to bear for chemistry, physics and biology laboratories. The St. Michael's students take those subjects at the University of Toronto, while they take their philosophy, history and theology at St. Michael's.

MCDONALD: And those science subjects are the most expensive ones from the standpoint of the school's budget.

ELLIS: That's right, and the Canadian plan is all so wonderfully co-operative. St. Michael's is a corporate college of the University, and there are three other colleges: one is Anglican, one is Non-Conformist and one is secular. The same pattern exists at the Universities of Western Ontario and Saskatchewan. Oh, what that plan would have saved us in money if we had been able to do that here!

MCDONALD: That whole idea would be anathema to the traditionalists among us, I suppose.

ELLIS: To the traditionalists, perhaps, but not to the growing number of more progressive minds in our ranks. In this respect I would hazard a guess that the traditionalists are going to be so badly outnumbered in a relatively short time that they will not carry much weight at all. It's coming so fast with our educated people. For instance, there was a man in here last week who was attending the White House Conference on Youth. He was a Californian, quite distressed about our own inability to appear to better advantage before our fellow citizens on the question of relations of Church and State. One of the things that bothered him were certain propositions in the Syllabus of Errors. As I said to several priest friends the next night, "We have come upon a new day when the laymen are discussing Pius IX and the Syllabus of Errors. Thank God!"

MCDONALD: You have said that you are by nature rather impatient. Are you optimistic or pessimistic about the future of the Church in this country?

ELLIS: I'm not at all pessimistic.

McDONALD: Do you think things are getting better?

ELLIS: Oh, yes.

McDONALD: I mean both internally and externally, the condition inside Catholicism and Catholic-Protestant relations outside.

ELLIS: I do. Let me threw the ball back to you. It's your kind, the laity, who must take the lead. I'm not pessimistic. I think in every way we're improving our position *vis-à-vis* our non-Catholic neighbors. If Senator Kennedy should be nominated at Los Angeles, I think we are in for a considerable amount of unpleasantness between July and November. But I don't think it will be a repetition of 1928. In that sense I think we've made definite progress. Politicians are realistic people, you know. I suppose there are no more realistic people in all the world than politicians, and when they read that more than 40 million Americans are now Catholics, they are not inclined to let their prejudices get completely out of control. A hundred years ago, in the years just before the Civil War, the Catholics were a small, despised and insignificant minority. They could spur us around, and the Know-Nothings did. But we have nothing like that any more. That day is gone. It's up to ourselves now to act our part.

McDONALD: It would be unfortunate if we were to conclude from our numerical strength that we could become arrogant and pushing.

ELLIS: Yes, it would be bad, very bad indeed. One of the things that I think the present situation dictates for the good of the Republic and the Church, is that we make it very clear that we have no attachment to union of Church and State, that we believe in religious toleration as a universal principle for the whole world, not only for us, but for the whole world.

McDONALD: What do you think accounts for the lingering suspicion with which non-Catholics regard Catholics in this country? Nobody could have spoken out any more plainly than Archbishop McNicholas did in 1948 against any idea of union of Church and State and in support of our democratic society as we have it in this country. Yet there is still suspicion about us over this Church-and-State relationship. I realize that bigotry dies hard. But are we doing something to keep the flames of bigotry alive? Is there anything in our behavior or in our actions that would make us suspect?

ELLIS: There are a few things in our behavior, yes, that do contribute to this suspicion. One thing, I believe, is the way some of our spokesmen go about putting Catholic doctrines before the public. Like birth control, or the censorship of films. There is no question about our having the right—and the duty—to enunciate our doctrine; nobody questions that. But I do think we owe it to the Church and to ourselves that it be made clear that these are our views for our people, and for any other Americans who may care to be guided by them, but that we're not attempting to cram them down the throats of those who do not share our beliefs.

McDONALD: You are now working on a new history of the Church in this country?

ELLIS: I have a leave of absence to do this. It was originally to be a one-volume work. Now, by the look of things, it's going to be at least two large volumes. I am well over 300 pages and am not yet to the English colonial missions.

McDONALD: When you work on a book that is elaborate and definitive, do you have enough resources in the Washington area here? Or do you have to go outside it?

ELLIS: Oh, yes, on a general work of this nature, I have what I need here. You see, this isn't anything that requires original research, that is, research in the sense of going to archives. What I have had for a number of years are a series of four or five large, black notebooks; they're over there in my desk. They include 750 pages of single-spaced typed notes for my courses in the history of the American Church.

McDONALD: Is that more or less the basis from which you are working?

ELLIS: That's right. So it isn't a question of doing original research. I do have to check things, of course, and I'm finding some very revealing things in checking, errors in other authors (and I'm sure I have errors in my own)—such things, for instance, as certain quotations cited as of a certain page. You go to that page and it's not there at all. But as far as resources are concerned, I can come reasonably close to doing my work right here in my own room. And then I accumulate a lot of little things to look up and I go either to the Mullen Library right here across the campus or, if they are not there, I go to the Library of Congress.

McDonald: Has there ever been a good history of the Church in the United States?

Ellis: It's been 75 years since John Gilmary Shea wrote his story *in extenso,* in four volumes. And that only came to 1866. Nobody since has attempted anything at all like an extensive history of the Church.

REV. ROBERT J. HENLE, S.J.

Father Robert Henle, S.J., is dean of the graduate school of St. Louis University, a position he has held since March, 1950. He was born in Muscatine, Iowa, September 12, 1909, entered the Society of Jesus in 1927 and was ordained in 1940. He received his Ph.D. in philosophy from the University of Toronto in 1954. He has been a teacher of philosophy at St. Louis University since 1943.

Father Henle has written innumerable articles, papers and books on philosophy, education and the theory of learning. In addition he is a member of many learned societies, both Catholic and secular. He is recognized as one of the ablest administrators and keenest minds in Catholic higher education.

The interview with Father Henle was recorded in the library of *The Catholic Messenger* newspaper, Davenport, Iowa, in August, 1959.

McDonald: Does your work as dean of the graduate school allow you to do some teaching also?

Henle: Yes, I manage to teach at least one course a semester. I regularly teach the history of modern philosophy on the undergraduate level. And I have a course which I created a couple of years ago for the benefit of graduate students who have had no philosophy at all. We were concerned that so many graduate students have no philosophical background, no "general" views at all, and acquire at the University only a high degree of specialization, often very technical. I try to bring them up against the problems created by the humanities and science, philosophy and science, theology and science, which are, I think, the basic problem of our modern culture. I try to give them some notions as to how disciplines differ, how certitudes vary in different disciplines, and how different methodologies have their own peculiar strengths and weaknesses.

McDONALD: You think keeping your hand in teaching is important, then.

HENLE: Oh, yes. And I've also kept up my work with some of the national associations, including those that are out of the strictly administrative line. I've worked with the Philosophy of Education Society, for example. I'm the only Thomist and the only priest that's ever been its national president, which I was three years ago.

McDONALD: That is a secular society?

HENLE: Yes. It started in 1940 as a small discussion group in New York and Pittsburgh. It now has 400 members and is, more or less, the organization for the philosophy-of-education people. I would say about 90 per cent of its membership is Deweyite. I started working with them about thirteen years ago and there was considerable opposition then to having Catholics as active members. I have found this a very rewarding association and I think, over the years, we have been able to reduce the distance between our two ghettos.

McDONALD: Is there any truth to this statement that John Dewey has been betrayed in some respects by today's Deweyites? Is it true that some of his modern disciples have taken some of Dewey's principles and perhaps some of his intuitions and from these have erected an educational philosophy or system that Dewey himself might disavow if he were living today?

HENLE: I would certainly say that if you take Dewey fully and completely he is much better than most of his followers; certainly the extreme wing of the progressive movement represents a different kind of thing, really, and if they represent themselves as Deweyites, I would say they are falsifying. Actually this extreme group got much more from Rousseau and from the Romantic tradition and from some schools of psychiatry than they did from John Dewey. As a matter of fact, Dewey himself repudiated some of those extremes.

We forget sometimes that Dewey was raised in a New England atmosphere and that he was reacting against an extreme kind of German Hegelianism. His strictures on a lot of things have to be read in the light of that. So that his stricture, for example, against authoritarianism is only intelligible in many cases if you remember that he is talking about a very strict kind of strait-laced Protestantism. Also when he attacks, as he did constantly, *a priori* philosophizing, he was really talking about Hegel. I think all his life Dewey identified Plato and Hegel and the great Christian tradition; he treated them as if they were one tradition, all sharing the same great flaw. One of the great weaknesses in John Dewey, as in Kant, was his lack of sound knowledge of general history as well as of history of philosophy.

McDonald: Do you think there are elements in Dewey's thought that lent themselves to extremist interpretations?

Henle: Yes, but you must remember that by 1910 he was pretty well developed in his philosophy, and that's a long time ago. The family structure and the classroom structure of 1910 are much different from what they were in 1940 or 1950 in this country.

McDonald: Did he himself believe, with Rousseau, in the natural goodness of man, that if you let a child alone he will perfect himself?

Henle: I think Dewey believed in the natural goodness of man all right, but not in a natural goodness simply left to itself. He would insist, I think, that the teacher has to run some of this thing, that students have to have guidance, there have to be goals.

McDonald: To what extent have our Catholic schools adopted or accepted some of the bad features of Deweyism, extreme permissiveness in the classroom, democracy with a capital "D" in the classroom, learning-by-doing?

HENLE: That is a difficult question because it's historical. About all I can do is give impressions or opinions. I'm not too worried about excessive Deweyite influence on Catholic teachers. I think there's a self-corrective element in Catholic education and in our tradition. I think some of this "Deweyism" has been good for our school system, some of this "permissiveness" and "doing." After all, "learning-by-doing" is not exclusively a Dewey idea. We've often been too theoretical and too bookish, so that some of this, I think, is good for us.

McDONALD: You say there is a self-corrective tendency in Catholic education?

HENLE: Yes. And, of course, as in any large group of people who are theorizing and studying, you will always get a blend of positions. There is a lot of room in Catholic education and in the Catholic philosophy of education for a variety of opinions. We have some fundamental principles, but these do not dictate down to the last iota how you are going to run a school system. The extreme Dewey positions, where they exist in our system, are being softened; they're being softened in both the Catholic and the non-Catholic schools. I would say that the straight, dogmatic Deweyite of ten years ago no longer exists, or at least that he is very rare.

McDONALD: Perhaps he has just gone into hiding for awhile.

HENLE: No, there have been certain significant developments in educational philosophy in this country. The ethical problem has upset a great many educators. Dewey thought that good people working together by democratic processes would come up with good moral principles and conduct. I think that if you were dealing with people who came out of New England in Dewey's time, that might have been true. If you take any handful of kids out of good Protestant homes and put them together and let them discuss, they're going to come up with fairly decent moral principles. But I think when the Deweyites were faced with things like the Nazi impact on youth, the Russian experience, the business of existentialism, they began to realize that "democratic processes and discussion" weren't enough. A man at one of these meetings six years ago, an old man who must have been 75 or more, got up and said he had been indoctrinated

as a Deweyite in college, that he had fought for Deweyism for
35 or 40 years and that now he was repudiating it because of
what he said it was doing to the morals of school children. A
lot of them feel this way. I think there's a great void in the
philosophy of education in the United States right now and that
people are re-grouping and re-thinking their positions. This
creates a tremendous opportunity for Catholic thinkers.

McDONALD: Are they doing much about it?

HENLE: Far less than we ought to. I don't like to overwork a
word, but I don't think we've got far enough outside the ghetto
yet. We're not really thrusting out into the other intellectual
groups as we ought to.

McDONALD: A few years ago, your own university, the philosophy department of it, sponsored a seminar with non-Catholic
philosophers. You invited people like Eliseo Vivas and Sidney
Hook and others to come in and discuss philosophical problems
with your own people. Do you think the seminar was worthwhile?

HENLE: It was excellent.

McDONALD: Why?

HENLE: Well, to take it just from our own standpoint: Here
was an opportunity for our own professors and graduate students
to sit down with some really intelligent non-Catholic philosophers, people who had been up to then just names in a book,
to sit down with them and see how they think and talk, how
they work.

McDONALD: Did it make for more respect for the Vivases and
the Hooks? Did it make for respect on both sides?

HENLE: It made for respect on both sides. People began to
see how a man like Hook thinks; what, for example, is missing in
his insights.

McDONALD: Did they see any of his sincerity?

HENLE: Yes, yes. And they began to see and respect non-
Catholic philosophers as people struggling with real problems and
people you can get through to in discussions. The seminar lasted
five days and it was pretty intense. Each morning we had a
Thomist philosopher and a non-Thomist give a major paper, talking to the same point. Then there was a quizzing of both speak-

ers and discussion from the floor. In the afternoon we broke up into discussion groups.

McDONALD: What were some of the discernible effects of this seminar on the people who were not Catholics?

HENLE: Well, Hook was taken aback several times. He was astonished to learn that Catholics could discuss things and differ radically on philosophical points, argue about them, and still be Catholics. He was astonished to find nuns who could carry on philosophical discussions. We had some nuns there, very bright nuns with Ph.D.'s in philosophy, teachers of philosophy. Hook said he had always thought that the only thing nuns did was nurse people and take care of orphans. We had a little trouble convincing him that we did not maintain every word in a Papal encyclical was a *de fide* definition. He had always assumed that everything in an encyclical was dogma. The whole thing made quite an impression on him, so much so that he canceled his plane reservation and stayed until the end. He had planned to leave after the first day or two. I have heard since that he has invited a number of Thomists to speak to his classes at New York University.

McDONALD: Do you think Hook saw a little more clearly the real relationship in the Church between authority and freedom?

HENLE: I think so. But we're just not doing enough of this kind of discussion.

McDONALD: Archbishop Karl Alter has said more Catholic professors should be teaching in non-Catholic schools. Would there be any opposition in those schools to Catholics on the faculty?

HENLE: In some cases, Catholics would be in a difficult position, yes. It might not be simply because they were Catholics, but more because of the "politics" in higher education. There isn't anything like the academic freedom we think there is in higher education; it is full of politics. But I think Catholics are in a position now where anything we do that is intelligent, sincere, straightforward will be welcome.

McDONALD: Are we doing as much as we should?

HENLE: Probably not. We haven't enough qualified people yet, and of those we have, not enough of them are doing this.

McDONALD: Perhaps Catholic universities could make it a little easier, perhaps they could do more to encourage their scholars to enter more of the secular organizations by paying their membership dues, freeing them to attend their meetings, write papers for their publications, that sort of thing.

HENLE: One of the problems is that we've got parallel Catholic organizations along with the secular learned organizations. What often happens is that a dean will say to a professor: "OK, you can go to one meeting this year; I'll pay your way." If the professor selects the Catholic meeting, it means he won't get to the other, the secular meeting.

McDONALD: Father Paul Henry, the Belgian Jesuit theologian who visits this country every year or so as a visiting lecturer, once told me how shocked he was a few years ago when he attended a meeting of the American Philosophical Association in Detroit. The Catholic Philosophical Association had met a day or two earlier, but only five or six Catholic philosophers stayed for the American Philosophical meeting. He thought that was terrible.

HENLE: It is bad. Of course, you want competent people at those secular meetings. You wouldn't want just anybody walking in there and trying to treat the secular scholars as if they were an eighth-grade class. This is always a danger. On the other hand, a dean should know which people to send to which meetings; he should be able to select the most competent Catholics on his staff to attend those meetings.

McDONALD: What accounts for our lack of engagement in these societies and organizations? Are we timid, overcautious, especially compared to European Catholic philosophers and theologians? Or is it because we think we're self-sufficient, that we don't need to mix with the others, that we can't learn anything from them?

HENLE: I think all of those things are present. First of all, we're traditionally more separated from non-Catholics than we would be in France where the intellectuals are pushed together. I think some of our people are complacent—they say: "Why listen to error?" or "These people are not sincere" or "They're not intelligent or well-trained." I think, also, there may be some timidity, some fear on our part that these people are going to look too good against us. There's also a lack of money and a lack of planning. And there is also a haunting memory of "not-being-wanted" in this Protestant culture.

McDonald: The purpose of Catholic participation in these discussions should not be to score debating points.

Henle: Oh, no, not that. That would be the worst approach you could make. We must attend and take an active part, sincerely and simply. I find one difficulty with Catholics who attend these meetings is that they tend to become a separate group within the meeting. You'll see five priests sitting in a knot and four nuns sitting in another knot. When lunch comes, the four nuns take lunch together and the five priests take their lunch together. Then they go home and complain that they don't meet anybody at those meetings. And often the Catholics do not attend the business meetings. But this is where you convince people you're really interested in the welfare of the organization, and where you can contribute some real help in the development of the organization. I've sat through every business meeting of every conference I've attended, and some of those business meetings are the longest sessions I've ever been in, from seven at night until two in the morning. But I feel I owe this to the organization and my fellow members.

McDonald: Didn't you attempt five or six years ago to start what I believe was called a course in Christian wisdom on the graduate school level, in which liturgy, among other disciplines, would be taught? Did that ever come to fruition?

Henle: It never worked out. We were trying to develop for the lay Catholic what a superb theology program would do for the clerical scholar. I think we failed mainly because we couldn't get an adequate staff and we couldn't get adequate students. We weren't ready for it.

McDonald: Simply labeling your religion courses "theology" doesn't solve anything here.

Henle: No. Some schools call their courses Theology I and Theology II but it's still the same old Religion I and Religion II that was taught years ago. I think the consensus of religion teachers in our colleges and universities is that we haven't got a good series of texts yet. And we haven't yet solved the problem of what college religion (or theology) should be. And you're constantly being undermined by shifts in the high school. You don't know what the high schools are going to do.

McDonald: What's wrong with college religion, the teaching of it? Is it too formalistic, not realistic enough?

Henle: First of all, there is a clash of viewpoints regarding objectives. Some people take the pastoral attitude and view the religion course as an instrument for the encouragement of daily Communicants and good Christians. Others say religion in a college should be taught in a strictly rational way; that the emphasis and tone should be intellectual and that the question of moral effect is secondary.

McDonald: Is there any objection to going deeper and actually teaching theology to lay students?

Henle: The question is what do you mean by "deeper"? By "deeper" one man may mean making a retreat, which may not involve any great additional intellectual depth, but might mean a depth of personalization. Another man might mean by "deeper," studying theology, reading the Acts of the Councils, the original documents of the Church the way you read St. Thomas or Shakespeare. Then you've got the question of approach. Should you emphasize Scripture? Should the emphasis be on the life of Christ? Should it be the historical approach? Another great difficulty is that the Catholic students, if they have had eight years in a Catholic grade school and four years in a Catholic high school, come to the college religion class thinking they know all there is to know about religion. And so there's a psychological block in the learning process.

McDonald: Perhaps one of the solutions is to put some of your very best university teachers in the religion department.

Henle: And have them teach religion from the freshman year, yes. I've always said I don't care which approach you take— whether you teach them the liturgy of the Mass, or the history of the early Church, or the life of Christ. To me this is not the important thing. The important thing is that religion suddenly becomes to the college student a great intellectual experience and challenge. But as long as the student thinks his religion class is just more of the same thing he's heard for twelve years, or that it's the same old Baltimore Catechism with bigger words, you're in trouble.

McDONALD: Robert Hutchins once told a group of Catholic educators that our Catholic colleges and universities have been making a great mistake in the development of their curriculum. His view was that they should stick to what has made the Catholic intellectual tradition great down through the centuries—in other words, the humanities, literature, philosophy, history—and not be scattering our energies and resources by putting up professional and vocational schools, such as law and medical and dental schools, business colleges and all the rest. Would you agree with that? Is it the duty of the Catholic school to take in boys because they want to be businessmen or lawyers or dentists? Is the good we're doing proportionate to the amount of money and energy that has to be expended?

HENLE: That is a tough question. I think you have to answer it in every case within a very concrete situation. If you were to ask me, for example, whether certain Catholic institutions should now start a medical school, I would say unequivocally they shouldn't. But if you were to ask whether it is a good thing that there be some Catholic medical schools, I would say yes.

McDONALD: If you already have a medical school, then it would not be wise to drop it.

HENLE: That's right. But, again, if the best that could be done was to operate a third-rate medical school, I would say we should drop it. The medical school at St. Louis is doing some very important research. I'd say that is important to the Church.

McDONALD: You mean it has an apologetic value.

HENLE: Just this week there was an article in *Time* about a scientist doing some important research and the item relates that he is a graduate of Loyola of Baltimore and got his doctorate at Catholic University. I think this is important, that these things happen. There's no way of arguing with a man who says Catholics can't produce scientists except to say, "There they are."

McDONALD: Is there any other value besides this apologetic value?

HENLE: Well, I think it's also important to keep people who are engaged in scientific work in an atmosphere in which there are philosophical and theological interests. It is very important for graduate students in, say, chemistry or accounting to be in a center of learning where the relevance of theology and ethics is frequently a matter of high-level discussion and more often still in the general background of teaching and discussion. Also it helps Catholics and non-Catholics alike to keep their biochemistry or mathematics in balance, keeps them from finally drying up into biochemistry until there is nothing they can see or think except that.

McDONALD: Can you say a boy has had a "Catholic education" if he has attended, say, a business or engineering school at a Catholic university and has had only what they call "survey courses" in such things as religion, philosophy, literature? If such a student graduates and is morally, politically and philosophically naïve, can he be considered to have received a Catholic education as it is traditionally understood?

HENLE: Engineer education has shifted a good deal in the last ten years. The demand within the engineering profession for a more solid set of humanities on the undergraduate level has grown very strong. Our engineers are not getting "surveys" any longer; they're getting very solid courses.

McDONALD: Do they have to take, say, twelve to fifteen hours of philosophy?

HENLE: They take twelve. The liberal arts boys take eighteen. We've increased the humanities with the support of the engineering people. More and more practicing engineers are getting into the administration of large companies and they find they must be able to write and read and talk and that they need a broad, general background of ideas. Engineering is one of the disciplines I would hold to very strongly. If it is important to Catholic education to have contact with the best brains and the most intelligent people and if engineering schools are today drawing off a great amount of the talent in American society, then it is quite important that Catholic schools educate some of these engineers.

McDONALD: The engineer's is a specialized talent, of course.

HENLE: Yes, but if you take the freshman class in engineering and the freshman class in liberal arts, the average IQ of the engineering student is higher. I have said—in a moment of enthusiasm, to be sure, in one of our meetings—that if it came to a choice, I'd keep engineering and drop the arts school. About fifteen Jesuits went after me. I said: "Wait a minute. I'm not dropping the arts school. I'm merely trying to emphasize how important I think engineering has become in modern life. I just feel that St. Ignatius would take one look at our society and say, 'By all means, let's educate engineers.' "

McDONALD: I had heard that engineers were now coming more and more into administrative and executive positions in industry. Is this the rule rather than the exception now?

HENLE: The history of engineering firms in St. Louis illustrates this very well. Just within my association with the University, many engineering firms have grown from modest undertakings into very large companies. In all of these it has been found that management should more and more draw its people from engineering. We have helped in this by opening two evening degree programs which have become very big. One leads to a degree as a Master of Business Administration and the other as a Master of Science in Engineering. Many engineers take both programs. They have had their bachelor's degrees in engineering and are already at work with local companies. Nobody can do this in less than six semesters, three years. Some of them go four or five or six years. Another thing, this program has brought into the university a large number of non-Catholics, with good effect, I think, throughout the city.

McDONALD: Are those master's courses completely technical?

HENLE: They're heavily scientific. Our theory of engineering education at the University is that we must train the engineer in something basic because three years from now he's going to be doing something different from what engineers are doing today. Engineering work is shifting all the time. There are courses, naturally, that have to do with design and that sort of thing, but more and more we are insisting on depth in mathematics, more knowledge of physics, chemistry.

To come back to your earlier question, I think it's quite important that you get the bright boy coming out of high school and that as he goes through your engineering school he is educated within a Christian context and is given some solid work in the humanities, particularly if he is going to end up as the director of a company or of a section in the Federal government, a research section, say, or as a professor in a university.

McDONALD: I agree with you. My only question is whether he is in fact getting some of this solid training in the humanities along the way.

HENLE: He is getting some, perhaps not as much as we would want. And it probably varies from place to place. A lot of those taking this master's program in engineering take my theory of knowledge course too, or one in English or history. These graduate engineers feel a great need for courses like these.

McDONALD: Do you think that operating these non-liberal arts programs could have a depreciating effect on your liberal arts program? Is there a danger that the technical and scientific programs might drain off too much of the University's resources?

HENLE: I don't think so. It's hard to determine that kind of thing. But if you were to take just the money aspect of it, suppose we cut out all these non-liberal arts programs, how much support would we get for a liberal arts program? This is awfully hard to say, but I think we'd lose a lot, because we are getting considerable help from McDonnell Aircraft, Emerson Electric, Monsanto. One reason is that we've been sending class after class of engineers into those St. Louis companies.

What frightens me a little bit is that so many little Catholic colleges around the country are trying to give master's degrees and trying, too quickly, to become universities. This, I think, will spread the total Catholic money and total Catholic talent too thinly. This could be serious.

McDONALD: Jacques Barzun, among others, has talked a lot about the ritualism of university "advancement," particularly the acquisition and symbolism of the Ph.D. He paints a rather bleak picture of the young scholar caught up in this system and in a process which seems to have little relevance to genuine scholarship. Is there much of that ritualism in the Catholic university and if so how does one get rid of it?

HENLE: That's very complicated. Nothing differs so much from school to school as the graduate program. Graduate schools are really unique institutions. I'd want to say, "Which one of my Ph.D.'s are you talking about?"

McDONALD: Some specialization is necessary, of course, but doesn't that militate against the broad, general education a Ph.D. should have? He should really be a master of many things.

HENLE: That's right. I gave a talk on this, the basic difficulties with the American Ph.D. program, a year or two ago at the National Catholic Educational Association meeting. I'm a traditionalist on this, but I don't believe in turning the Ph.D. program inside out and orientating the whole thing toward teaching. I think that would be a serious mistake.

McDONALD: You distinguish between teaching and research and . . .

HENLE: Yes. I believe that research on this level is essential. But it should be research. I think the difficulty is that the word research has become a catch-all. In many schools what passes for research is . . .

McDONALD: Fussiness?

HENLE: Yes. Or it's helping some other fellow do something. Say I'm a professor or microbiology and I've got a big project going. This is my life project. I've spent ten years on it and here's a little point I want investigated and cleared up. Along comes a graduate student and I say, "Fine, here's your dissertation. Investigate this point for me." I lay it all out for him. I know what I want and I tell him what to do. Instead of my evaluating the student, seeing what his interests are, what his background is and what would be best for him, I turn him into a technician for my own selfish purposes.

McDONALD: Is that a usual occurrence?

HENLE: I wouldn't use the word usual. It happens often enough, though, to make you worry.

McDONALD: What would be the greatest disability of the young student who wants to go on into graduate work at your university? Is there one single area in which many of them are weak?

HENLE: The failure to have control of language is common. In the last five years, we've had the problem of people coming into graduate school with no control over any language, even

English. If you say a man does not need control of language, that takes a whole dimension of scholarship out of his life.

McDonald: Would you say that after Latin, German is important, or . . .

Henle: It depends on your field. We're doing a complete re-study of language requirements in our school with a view to setting up a pattern of languages for each field. Traditionally, German and French have been most important. But right now in meteorology Russian is the most important foreign language of all. The Russians are publishing meteorological data and studies like mad. The Soviet Union has something like twelve Arctic weather stations. We've got one. They're all publishing daily bulletins. In economics we put Russian on a par with German; we'll take either one for graduate work.

McDonald: Do you think the bright students should begin learning a foreign language before they enter high school?

Henle: In two years, I'd say you're going to see that happening everywhere. It's already happening in some areas. I've seen some excellent textbooks that start language in the third grade. This would grow faster except that because of our past negligence we don't have enough competent language teachers.

McDonald: Where does Greek fit in?

Henle: The classical language people require some Greek of all their students. In philosophy, we require Latin, German and French. James Collins, you see, won't do a German philosopher except in German, or a French philosopher except in French. And all the medieval philosophers are in Latin. We don't really care, then, whether students actually pass the language test in graduate school. If they're taking Kant from Collins, by the end of the semester they will either have flunked out or they will be able to read German. If your department really uses the languages, then the language requirement will take care of itself.

McDonald: We still hear occasional arguments about whether philosophy should be taught systematically or historically.

Henle: It's still pretty much a systematic and formal method that's used in Catholic schools. We have history courses, but the general approach is systematic. I think undergraduate philosophy should be taught in a systematic fashion, but based on a problem method. You haven't time to teach all the philosophy through the historical method. Secondly, the student doesn't have the background. I think what happens at a lot of non-Catholic schools is that they give a rapid survey of philosophical thinkers—thirty-five pages of Plato, fifteen pages of Aristotle, eight of St. Thomas. What can a student get out of that kind of thing? I think very strongly that in the undergraduate school, you should have an organization of your principal philosophical problems. In metaphysics, for example, you should teach the substantive philosophical positions.

But I also think that at some point they should have history. Father William Wade teaches a senior course in that and it's pretty much a confrontation of everything they've had—modern positions, atheism, pragmatism. He forces them to re-think everything they've learned in college. He'll give as strong an argument as he can for pragmatism and let them try to answer it.

McDONALD: I've heard about that course. It would be a fairly strong medicinal treatment.

HENLE: But you see you can only do that if the students have already had a pretty good training, systematic training, in philosophy.

McDONALD: It gives them a real rather than merely a notional assent.

HENLE: Right. Father Wade doesn't give you any proofs for the existence of God, for example. He gives you reasons why you can't prove it. And then he just keeps arguing and arguing until the students themselves bring it out.

McDONALD: The Socratic method?

HENLE: Yes, a directed Socratic method, with people who have already had some background.

McDONALD: Is there ever any trouble with students or their parents? Are they ever upset because Father Wade disturbs the students and refuses to give them the answers to the problems he raises?

HENLE: Occasionally we have some trouble, not with parents or students but with other faculty members. They are concerned because the student is upset. Maybe sometimes a student really is upset, but I think if he is going to be upset by this, he ought to be upset under those circumstances, not when he gets out and is unable to handle it at all.

McDONALD: I was reading the other day that the teacher-student ratio at Harvard is something like one to eight. I suppose such a ratio would be unheard of in our Catholic schools with overworked professors, large classes and the like.

HENLE: That's part of our lack of showing in this country. You take a priest, let's say, who goes to Toronto and gets his doctorate in philosophy. He comes back home, all excited about philosophy. He want to teach and to write and to study and to think. He gets back and they give him twelve hours of teaching and Saturday afternoons he hears Confessions and he goes out to a parish quite a distance from the college to say Mass on Sundays. During the summer he gives spiritual retreats. Also he's got convert instructions to give. He's got no secretarial help. Now here's a layman who comes out of the same thing. He has a doctorate and he goes over to Yale to teach. In a year or so, he's got a teaching load of six hours a week. Maybe he's got a graduate assistant. In three or four years he's got a part-time secretary. He becomes head of the department and he's got two secretaries, full professorship, a couple of graduate assistants. If you add up ten years of the first man's life and ten years of the second man's life, the second man will have published six times the amount of material the first man has published. An uninformed observer might simply conclude there's something wrong with the first man because he hasn't published much of anything.

McDONALD: I think a man like Monsignor John Tracy Ellis would say, This is true, but let's correct it.

HENLE: Oh, sure, so do I. I say, by all means, let's correct it.

McDONALD: Perhaps more respect for learning by people who control pursestrings might help.

HENLE: Precisely. Selling it to the public, that sort of thing. But here's one thing that's happening—it's happened in my own time. The people that are becoming rectors and Provincials and prefects of studies of Religious Orders are those who know from personal experience what's wrong with this. This is going to make a great deal of difference in the next generation.

SISTER MARY EMIL, I.H.M.

SISTER MARY EMIL, I.H.M., has been a member of the Sisters, Serv
ants of the Immaculate Heart of Mary since 1937. She is an
associate professor of philosophy at her Order's Marygrove College, Detroit.

For the past three years, Sister Mary Emil has been on a leave
of absence from Marygrove College and has been serving as
executive secretary of the Sister Formation Conference, an organization which was established in 1954 for the purpose of
developing the spiritual, intellectual and professional formation
of American Sisters engaged in teaching, hospital and social work.

The Sister Formation movement, which has been described as
one of the most significant developments in the history of Catholic education in the United States, involves the pre-service and
in-service training of 164,000 Sisters. It has held a series of re-
gional and national meetings and its proceedings have been
published in four successive volumes by the Fordham University
Press. The Conference publishes a quarterly *Bulletin*, edited by
Sister Ritamary, C.H.M., of Ottumwa Heights College, Iowa,
who also has edited the proceedings.

To Sister Mary Emil has gone a great and deserved share of
the credit for guiding the Sister Formation movement through its
first years. In September, 1960, Sister Mary Emil turned over
her post as executive secretary to Sister Annette Walters, C.S.J.,
of the College of St. Catherine, St. Paul. She has returned to work
assigned by her own Religious Order but will continue to serve
on the National Sister Formation Committee.

This interview was held in Sister Mary Emil's office at the
National Catholic Educational Association, Washington, D.C.

McDONALD: You said in the introduction to one of the volumes of the Sister Formation Conference proceedings that there
were three major difficulties faced by Sisterhoods: time needed
to complete degree courses; resources to pay for the cost of teacher
preparation; and a generalized understanding of the needs and
problems in the formation of teaching Sisters. Have any or all

of these three difficulties eased since the advent of the Sister Formation movement eight years ago? I suspect that the difficulty of securing adequate financial resources would still be a formidable one.

SISTER MARY EMIL: Yes, it is still formidable, although there has been an improvement. It never was the greatest difficulty, however. In Sister Formation we do not worry too much about our ability to do anything once we get sufficiently convinced that we ought to do it. That doesn't mean that the Sisters have great resources. But, somehow or other, ways will be found; they were found in the past. The task ahead is not as great as the task that faced the pioneer Sisters. I like to recall the spirit of the Sisters who set up schools literally in the middle of forests, and educated themselves in the early days. They sometimes learned high school subjects the week before they taught them in the classroom. Many of these self-taught nuns were real scholars. Almost every Religious community still has some of these Sisters; most of them are golden and diamond jubilarians by now and in the infirmaries. But their students passed, when admission to college or normal school was by examination, and we will be hard pressed to match the devotion they exhibited or the loyalty they inspired.

McDONALD: You're insisting, then, on historical perspective so far as problems and difficulties and improvements are concerned.

SISTER MARY EMIL: Yes, and I think one of our problems today is to realize that the perspective itself must change so quickly. Between 1946 and 1956, for instance, the number of states that required a bachelor's degree for teachers went up from 16 to 37. Within the next two or three years, all but two or three of the states will have the degree requirement for beginning teachers. This is extraordinary progress. If there *is* a lag in general understanding of the need for more advanced training of teachers, it is understandable that it should exist and we need to be patient with it.

McDONALD: What was the condition before Sister Formation, so far as pre-service training of Sisters is concerned? I think you mentioned on one occasion that 118 Religious communities had no educational facilities of their own and no easy or economical access to such facilities.

SISTER MARY EMIL: I wouldn't like to make too sharp a comparison of conditions before and after Sister Formation. One of the largest communities in the country had put in a plan of degree training for its Sisters a year or two before Sister Formation really got under way. And whether or not Sister Formation had come on the scene there would have been greatly stepped-up pressure from state and voluntary accrediting agencies. Improvement in teacher training was inevitable.

McDONALD: What was the need, then, for the Sister Formation movement?

SISTER MARY EMIL: The movement and the Conference, which are two things, introduced a certain element of urgency into the picture. More importantly, they brought about a very effective kind of collaboration, first of all in the realm of ideas and then in the exchange of facilities and teachers.

McDONALD: There hadn't been too much co-ordination of ideas up until that time?

SISTER MARY EMIL: I think that's true. There had been beginnings, however. Teacher education had been talked about off and on for years at National Catholic Educational Association meetings. The publication in 1940 of Sister Bertrande Meyer's book, *The Education of Our Sisters*, was a landmark. And Sister Madeleva's paper, "The Education of Sister Lucy," was given four years before the start of Sister Formation and it is still being quoted. Our work would never have come into being if it hadn't been for the advice of the Holy Father in his famous address to teaching Sisters in September, 1951. That was the allocution we meant to apply to ourselves at the NCEA convention in the spring of 1952 in Kansas City.

McDONALD: Can you make any comparison at all between conditions before and after the start of Sister Formation? There was an immediate and spontaneous response to the idea of Sister Formation when it was proposed. So there must have been some prior conditions to account for that response.

SISTER MARY EMIL: The Holy Father's advice to the teaching Sisters fell on such responsive ears in the United States because there was widespread uneasiness among the higher Superiors themselves. There were multiplied pressures of all kinds being put on teaching Sisters. The Superiors felt that Sisters were being asked to undertake a very complex apostolate without sufficient preparation. It wasn't that the Sisters didn't get the preparation eventually, but that preparation was sometimes spread over a period of two decades of summer school classes. And the spiritual preparation, the instruction and the training in asceticism, likewise had to be acquired by the Sisters in too short a time. The Superiors generally felt that this wasn't a solid enough foundation for the Sisters in active works. People looking on Sister Formation from the outside tend to think of it simply as a movement to lengthen the education of Sister teachers. The program is also a lengthening and deepening of the spiritual formation. We haven't said as much about this in public because, for one thing, it concerns us more personally, but it is a major objective.

McDONALD: When you say that Sister Formation attempts to "lengthen" spiritual training, what had been the length of the spiritual training period?

SISTER MARY EMIL: Because of the great demand for teaching Sisters, with schools being built all over the country, the Religious communities thought that the best service they could render the Church would be given by sending Sisters out at the end of their novitiate. In some communities, this occurred at the end of a one-year novitiate, in others, it was at the end of a two-year period. The communities were not opposed to longer intellectual or spiritual formation; that would have been absurd, and the Superiors would not have entertained such an idea. But this was their way of meeting a need of the Church in a loyal way.

McDONALD: As an emergency measure.

SISTER MARY EMIL: Yes, and, of course, the emergency turned out to have no discernible end, either then or now.

McDONALD: It seems to me that Sister Formation is not an easy thing either to write or speak about because it inevitably implies a comparison, with a danger of over-sharpening the contrast, betwen Sister-training before and after Sister Formation.

SISTER MARY EMIL: That is true. I wouldn't want to be a party to giving the impression that our Sisters of yesterday were not properly formed. I can say that we ourselves have more than one directional worry about the Sister Formation movement. And not the least of these is an anxiety about how we can make sure that these stepped-up training programs of today and tomorrow will produce a Sister who is as good a Religious and as dedicated a teacher or social worker as the Sisters we have always known in this country. American Sisters have been simple, humble, sacrificial, ascetical, enthusiastic, hard-working Religious. Now we're going to get them much more concerned about professional and intellectual advancement. This concern can't be a matter of self development in a selfish sense; that would be contrary to the Religious ideal.

McDONALD: I suppose that would be a danger present in any self-development program, any self-improvement program, the danger of undue self regard or self interest.

SISTER MARY EMIL: Yes, although in the case of the Religious, the deviation would be more serious. It would be unrealistic to say that this danger will not exist. There can be no intrinsic incompatibility, surely, between the ideas of "Sister" and "intellectual" or "Sister" and "scholar"—but the intellectualism and the scholarship will have to be caught up in a *community* endeavor and assume a communitarian character.

McDONALD: That is where the spiritual training comes in and the integration of the spiritual with the intellectual, doesn't it?

SISTER MARY EMIL: Yes. The intellectual development must be apostolically oriented, objectively; it must be apostolically motivated, subjectively. What is involved, then, is the whole problem of the apostolic formation of Sisters. Apostolic formation, we are finding, is an elusive concept. There is no one, of course, who would maintain for a moment that we should *not* form apostles. But it is another thing again to devise a recipe for it. There are few English works on the theology of the apostolate, and even those are just beginning to appear.

McDONALD: Historically, has the integration of the intellectual and the spiritual been worked out successfully in the past?

SISTER MARY EMIL: There are precedents for it in the Religious Orders of men, of course. This is complicated, however, by the fact that the training of the Religious men is usually also clerical training. All of these Orders, moreover, devote a much longer time to the training of their members than we will be able to set aside in the foreseeable future. We are very pleased now to have a five-year and, in some cases, a six-year period in which to form a good Religious and a scholar and to try to unite the ideals of the scholar and the Religious in that of the apostle. But five years is still a very short time.

McDONALD: To come back for a moment to that problem of self development and the danger of selfishness entering in. Does this also involve a problem of the danger of pride?

SISTER MARY EMIL: My fear is not of pride, exactly. Do you remember what Mother Janet Stewart said about the warnings against intellectual pride having been written for men? And selfishness is a strong word too. I would not wish to overemphasize this point of fearfulness. Certainly whatever fear we have is not one which should keep us from forging ahead and improving ourselves; it is a fear which should induce us to watch our motives and make very sure that the forging and striving is *really* for the common good.

Let me put this in another way. The ideal of the Sister-intellectual, if understood properly, is quite acceptable and desirable. The idea of the Sister-career-woman is something else again. In the years ahead of us every Sister, whether she be teacher, nurse or social worker, will have to labor at her profession. I would say that she should work at it with even greater intensity than should the lay woman who has taken it up as a career. Nevertheless there is something repugnant about the notion of Sisters with careers. To me "career" connotes a carving of a little niche for one's self, of achieving for the sake of achievement or for monetary reward, fame or reputation. All of these goals are and should be foreign to our Religious state and consecration. But we do not automatically insure ourselves against this type of self-oriented striving just by making some pious statement of intention. To insure the Sisters against it, really, should be one of the main objectives of the Sister Formation movement.

McDONALD: Aren't young women who go into the Sisterhood, even given this grand and glorious five-year collegiate and spiritual training, still giving up a great deal, making a considerable sacrifice? It seems to me they already have a good spirit of unselfishness or they wouldn't be entering the Religious life in the first place. And the Religious communities are getting these young women who are headed in the right direction from the beginning.

SISTER MARY EMIL: The grace of vocation has already given them a wonderful start. That is true.

McDONALD: You're merely saying that this spirit can be lost or diminished, some of that vision and that heroism can be vitiated unless it is specifically guarded against in the formation period.

SISTER MARY EMIL: This heroism of the postulant when she gives up the world is still an undifferentiated kind of thing. Certainly it is not to be disparaged; it involves some of the greatest sacrifices a person can make. But there can be in it strong elements of rather unreflective enthusiasm. This is one of the real challenges of Religious life—to bring it about that the generosity of the postulant will remain for a lifetime, but that it will be based, increasingly, on more solid principles and on a better understanding of what the Sister is giving up. If this initial heroism is not channeled along apostolic lines, I think there is great danger that it can be lost. In that case, if the determination remains and the apostolic motivation is absent, you will have a career-woman in the convent. This is why it should be a prime purpose of the Sister Formation program to aim at apostolic formation. I see this as being done through both the college curriculum and the program of instructions given by the mistresses at every stage in the Sister's training.

McDONALD: You say that the unique and major contribution of Sister Formation has been its efforts at integrating the spiritual with the intellectual, rather than getting the idea of bachelor's degree requirements to become an accepted thing?

SISTER MARY EMIL: We have tried to win acceptance for the goal of the bachelor's degree, of course, but this objective is not peculiar to Sister Formation.

McDONALD: You would say that you speeded up the degree idea, however, wouldn't you?

SISTER MARY EMIL: The idea was speeded up all right, but the formation programs were not. The contribution about which we are happiest is the lengthening of the period of spiritual training and the organization of juniorates.

McDONALD: What, precisely, are juniorates?

SISTER MARY EMIL: "Juniorate" is a word which can stand either for a period of formation or for an established formation center. Some of the communities call them "scholasticates." A congregation of Sisters can be said to have a juniorate in the sense called for by the Sacred Congregation of Religious when it keeps the young Sisters in a special house or department of a convent set aside for this purpose for a period of full-time study and spiritual training for two or three years after the novitiate.

There is some variation in this from Order to Order. The most common pattern is one in which the Sister spends a first year as a postulant, two years as a novice, and two more as a junior. Some communities have one-year novitiates; others have three-year juniorates.

McDONALD: And all the while the Sister is in these various phases she's also taking her college work?

SISTER MARY EMIL: This is perhaps what is distinctive about the Sister Formation programs of the United States by comparison with those in Europe. We like to stretch out the college work through the whole training period. In this sense, of course, Sister Formation should eventually work out a distinctive type of higher education on the American Catholic scene. A college curriculum administered within the total context of a Sister Formation program is one which addresses itself to a distinct student sub-culture and with a distinct all-over purpose, and the collegiate program as a whole is bound, eventually, to reflect these differences. So—if you ask me about contributions already made, I would say that the organization of juniorates and the lengthening of the spiritual formation program are the most important actual accomplishments. If we look to the future, I would say that the emergence of Sister Formation programs as new and high forms of college education is a development to watch and pray for. And to tie this up with what we were discussing earlier, I should say that the effecting of an apostolic fusion of the spiritual with the intellectual-professional training is the highest Sister Formation goal of all, and the one which it is most vital for us to work toward.

McDONALD: Are you planning to have a series of conferences just on that problem?

SISTER MARY EMIL: That is an excellent idea. I think we

should pursue it. The goal we envision would catch up the full potential of the Sister in the entire movement for social reconstruction which the modern Popes have tried to initiate.

McDONALD: In one of the papers you gave at a Sister Formation meeting, you hit that social question rather hard.

SISTER MARY EMIL: Your own writings do the same. I have been observing for a long time that the same people tend to favor certain movements in the Church: Catholic Action—the Catholic intellectual movement—the Catholic social movement—the liturgical movement—the movement for Christian art and music. They have the same proponents and the same opponents. I like to think that Sister Formation is one of these movements, and I have found in the past that I can assume, *a priori*, that a priest or a layman who is known to be a leader in any of these fields will be sympathetic toward Sister Formation as soon as he knows anything at all about it. I must say, however, that in spite of this friendly co-operation from all the leaders, it seems to me that there is an astonishing failure to realize and to activate the potential of the 97,000 teaching Sisters in each of these fields. A man from Mars, for instance, might read through hundreds of pages of the last three or four years' debate on Catholic intellectualism without ever discovering that there were teaching Sisters or that Catholic education in our country has almost been built on their services. It is like that with Catholic Action. You seldom hear of the Sisters' role in Catholic Action or in the training of lay apostles. I think it could be argued that the failure to exploit the Sisters' potential in this area may be one of the causes, at least, for the slow growth of Catholic Action in the United States.

McDONALD: What do you see the Sisters' role to be?

SISTER MARY EMIL: I see the Sister as the person who trains the lay apostles. I do not see her actually doing the work of the lay apostolate, of course. But it is hard to see how we can harness the resources of our tremendous Catholic educational system to this movement which all the modern Popes have pleaded for, unless we equip our Sisters to exercise a leadership role in Catholic Action.

McDONALD: You would include Catholic Action as part of the Sister Formation program?

SISTER MARY EMIL: Yes. I think of Catholic Action as having a mystique, a rationale, and a technique. The mystique derives from such doctrines as those of the Mystical Body, and the Indwelling of the Holy Spirit, and from what we can work out about the social practice of the virtues and the social implications of the liturgy. The technique—to jump to the third point —derives from the specialized Catholic Action movements which have achieved success so far—like Legion of Mary, Young Christian Workers, Christian Family Movement, and many others. It is unified only in the sense that certain common elements can be pointed out—small-group organization, milieu specialization, see-judge-act procedure, and similar features. It may not remain the same, but it has been tremendously successful until now. Now the Sister's basic spiritual formation can very easily confront her with the mystique of Catholic Action, and she can be given a tremendous and spiritually based enthusiasm for this work. The technique is something which she can learn from a little reading or from the watching of a little role-playing. But the whole area in between, which I have called the rationale of Catholic Action—this cannot be learned so easily. The "why" and the "how" of Catholic Action can be assimilated quickly, but the "what" of Catholic Action, the specific goals of social reconstruction at a given time and place in history—this cannot be conveyed except by a long and systematic effort. If we can ever work that out and thus release the Sisters' potential for the formation of lay leaders, the graduates of a Catholic school system such as we have in the United States would really make the better world for which Pius XII and our present Holy Father have called.

McDONALD: How can the rationale be effectively communicated?

SISTER MARY EMIL: I am not sure that I can answer that question. This is not yet in the realm of achievement in present Sister Formation programs. I think I can tell you *what* we need to do, however. Our Sisters need to be given a comprehensive and scientific grasp of the whole Papal program for social reconstruction, international and national. I am thinking of the Papal program, now, not as a collection of general principles and specific little suggestions which could be covered on 45 mimeographed pages, but as a plan for whose implementation the understanding of social philosophy and the knowledge of many social sciences is required.

McDonald: Is anything being done along this line in any of the Religious communities?

Sister Mary Emil: Some beginnings have been made. It is not hard to sell the ideal of a curriculum which would accomplish all this, but it is next to impossible to induce the colleges to make the curricular sacrifices and adjustments necessary to put it into operation. To give you a simple example—there are few who would argue today that every teacher should not know the fundamental principles of political science, of economics, and of sociology, or who would deny that all teachers should be acquainted with the problems and cultures of other peoples. But when it comes to inserting a substantial block of such study into the Sisters' college program, we run into obstacles centering about credit hours, upper and lower division work, major programs, and the simple unavailability of enough Sister college professors in the social science areas. The doctoral programs in Catholic universities for some of the areas we would like to see taught—international ethics being one—do not even exist.

McDonald: What about that curriculum study which the Ford Foundation sponsored for you several years ago?

Sister Mary Emil: That was the Everett curriculum. It has been adopted by a number of communities. Many more have taken over certain features of the plan. In a few years we will be able to evaluate the results. We never thought of it, of course, as a uniform curriculum for all communities, but rather as a sample of how the college curriculum might be used by a Religious community in order to realize some of the objectives we have been talking about this afternoon. I think that this particular plan would supply the rationale for Catholic Action—the understanding of the goals of Catholic social action, and the knowledge of the empirical facts which must be mastered before we can begin to move toward these goals.

McDonald: Do you see a Sister who had been given the ideal kind of college courses you describe as then ready to go out to train lay apostles?

SISTER MARY EMIL: No. The college courses will supply majors for the prudential syllogisms—not minors. The young Sister who has been given the vision of the whole Papal plan, who has mastered her social philosophy and her social science, will still have to see a connection between all of this and her fourth-grade class whose worst social problems might be fighting on the playground or squirting of water fountains into waxed corridors. There is an element of insight here which no one can ever give you, of course, but the Sister college teachers can be of tremendous help in showing the student-Sisters how it is all related —what they have learned in the formation program, and what they must see to be done in the little milieu in which they will be sent to specialize. We would hope, however, that eventually we can turn out a Sister who is able to address herself to any of the problems of our day and who will know the direction, at least, in which she can begin to look for the answers—a Sister who would be passionately concerned with finding the answers and with educating children who will share this concern, even if it means constant and great sacrifice for themselves.

McDONALD: Then you see social justice, the thirst for it, as intimately bound up with intellectual and educational objectives?

SISTER MARY EMIL: Yes. I was impressed with a statement I read recently, by a professor in one of the Protestant colleges. The ultimate test of the effectiveness of a college program, he said, was whether it turned out graduates who were more compassionate and more unified in their thinking than they had been before entering college. I think our Catholic colleges have attempted, at least, to produce graduates who had some kind kind of unitary terminological and conceptual framework within which they could fit what they had learned and which they could use to interpret the thought and life around them. But I doubt very much that our Catholic college graduates are more compassionate than those of other institutions. This should at least be a special objective for the Sister Formation programs— informed compassion.

McDONALD: I was interested in what you said about the need for discipline in the social sciences, too, that it isn't just enough to know what ought to be done in a general vague way. So many today want to take a short cut, I think; they want to by-pass, if possible, the hard, tough work of learning, in some kind of scientific, systematic way, the truths of the relevant disciplines.

SISTER MARY EMIL: There are no short cuts. Even our elementary teachers are called on to teach social studies, and if they do it well, it will be with relevance to a constantly changing contemporary scene. But the news does not occur in the order of a textbook. It has its own unpredictable order—and all you can say about that, for sure, is that unless you know some of your facts and principles "cold," you will be answering the children's questions two weeks after they ask them. Even to interpret the little items in the sixth grader's current events paper, a Sister ought to know some economics, some politics, some sociology, some social and physical geography, possibly even some anthropology. And she must know all of these things in connection with the social philosophy and teaching of the Church. This is a big order.

McDONALD: Is the average Sister's daily schedule so demanding that it is almost impossible for her to "keep up" with current investigations and events in her own and related fields? I mean are there too many domestic chores around either the convent or the school, too many non-intellectual demands made on the Sister? Does she have the time to read and reflect?

SISTER MARY EMIL: Not enough. But I think once we see the goals clearly enough we will take the necessary steps to reach them. There are some fixed elements in a Sister's life, though, which neither can nor should be changed. There is no sympathy among American Sisters, for example, for the idea of cutting down on our prayer life. This is what keeps us going. We would be giving up our character as Religious if we did that.

McDONALD: Certain household tasks can be reduced, though, and such things as grading papers or monitoring the playground during recess periods.

SISTER MARY EMIL: Yes, some sub-professional duties can be done by others. No matter how much we cut in those areas, however, the amount of effort the Sister will still be required to put forth will be heroic. And this call to continued heroism is something which the Sister Formation planners will need to take into account.

McDONALD: Has the number of Religious vocations among young women increased since the advent of the Sister Formation movement? One of the things that seemed inevitable was that with improved training and formation of the teaching Sisters, more and more young women would be attracted to the Religious life because they would be receiving, constantly, favorable and appealing impressions of that life through the Sisters they knew in the classroom.

SISTER MARY EMIL: We can't demonstrate that increase statistically, it's still too early. But the data I pick up just casually all over the country indicate there is a great improvement. That *is* inevitable. If we can realize the goal of the Sister who is cultured and competent and compassionate and if all of this is caught up in an apostolic ideal which American girls can see to be very important and necessary, an increase in vocations will take place.

McDONALD: I know that you favor college education for Sisters taught by Sisters, rather than having Sisters attend college with women who are not Sisters.

SISTER MARY EMIL: It would take more time than you have for us to cover this subject. You can come at this problem from many sides by asking: What is best for the Sister spiritually? Which arrangement will ensure her the best teachers? What arrangement will make possible improved or experimental curriculum? What arrangement is best suited to an integration of intellectual and spiritual elements in the formation program? How best can we prepare the Sister for intellectual and apostolic leadership? I won't answer any of these, but I would like to point out that they should be answered before we make up our minds. Let me approach it from just one side—which may be of interest to your readers. What will best equip the Sister to *serve* the non-Sisters, lay patients, lay students, lay clients, to whom she will minister for a lifetime? We are aiming, in our formation programs, to make teachers, nurses and social workers, but we are also aiming to produce what someone has recently described as more-than-teachers, more-than-nurses, more-than-social workers. This plus-factor is something which you as a parent expect when you send your child to a Sisters' school. Both clergy and laity become disturbed, and rightly so, when they do not find the plus-factor, and get only a professional where they expected a Religious professional.

What they forget, sometimes, is that a plus-factor in our lives must be matched by a plus-factor in our training. This plus-factor cannot be something merely superimposed, something essentially divorced from the intellectual and professional life. If it is to be vital, it must be integrated with it.

McDONALD: Well, can that plus-factor in a Sister's training be given best in separate classes for Sisters or in mixed ones?

SISTER MARY EMIL: Now we are all agreed that it is desirable first to seclude the Sisters for a while and then to have them mix with lay women and lay men—in that order. Nobody—absolutely nobody who has an intelligent opinion about it—would suggest, I am sure, that canonical novices should be mixed with lay men. And at the other extreme, I can think of no responsible planner in Sister Formation who wants separate graduate schools for Religious women. The issue, then, comes down to: How much seclusion at the undergraduate level? Some favor less; I personally would favor more. It is a problem for each community to work out, really, and the kind of college which the community operates will have much to do with the solution.

We need to form Sisters for the future who, for the sake of Catholic education, their schools, and their Orders, will achieve academically, will publish, will be elected to office, will win prizes, will get honorary degrees. And all these things, too, must involve no sacrifice of humility, simplicity or seclusion from the world—for these are integral to Religious life. This will not be an easy combination. It must be practiced—individually and socially, and you must give us time to do it.